FAMOUS LEADERS

OF

INDUSTRY

Fourth Series

YOUNG MEN WHO HAVE SUCCEEDED

By

HARRY IRVING SHUMWAY

Author of

"Albert, The Soldier King" "Lawrence, The Arabian Knight" Etc.

Illustrated From Photographs

L. C. PAGE & COMPANY

PUBLISHERS :-: BOSTON

FOREWORD

ONCE it would have been easy to write an introduction to a collection of success stories. There were so many examples of fine industrial accomplishment in this land of unlimited opportunity. They were to be observed on every hand, even in the town or city wherein one lived. And there was no critic who could say that such things were not so.

But during the last few years changes have come which make us pause. Old men shake their heads in deep doubt, middle-aged men are little less thoughtful, and young men wonder if all the golden fruit has not been picked. Is America done? Is the opportunity to become a top performer in industry completely lacking? When young men have found it difficult to get placed in business, it would seem that such pessimism might be well founded.

I am going to point to one man in this book, perhaps the greatest optimist of them all, and see if his work cannot tell us something to give us confidence. That man is Roger W. Babson and his story you will find in these pages. In his work he lays great stress on Newton's Law of Action and Reaction. He shows how the graph of business goes up and down through the years. And he tells us, using this law, that a sharp decline usually means a corresponding rise, a slow decline a corresponding upswing. In plain words, whatever goes down, comes up again.

That is a common sense view of looking at it. A period of depression, spreading over six or seven years, seems unbearably long while we are in it. But viewed from a distant perspective, say a hundred years from now, it will seem but a "slight hesitation" in the march of progress.

There is no man wise enough to tell us exactly what we want to know. If there were, he would be President of the World, elected for life! In the absence of any such oracle our greatest asset is hope.

I like to think of a certain Princeton football team whenever the future seems to have too many dark clouds in it. This team had no star players, no outstanding players of any kind. It knew one goal from another, however, and could get around the field. They were most emphatically the under-dog in a yearly classic, slated to meet a great team of players. Nobody considered they had even an outside chance.

This Princeton team dug up a slogan from somewhere, not to mention a frame of mind. It kept saying to itself, "A team that *won't* be beaten, *can't* be beaten!" And that team of mediocre individual athletes went out on the field on the day in question and most artistically rubbed the snooty noses of their foe in the mud! It *wouldn't* be beaten, and it *wasn't* beaten!

That particular spirit has dominated all the men who are included in this book. They wouldn't be beaten and they couldn't be beaten. All of them had their vicissitudes, their black moments when they could have quit. But they preferred to go on and fight it out. In one of these stories which you will read, another slogan is mentioned. It is so good that it can be repeated. An old Irishman, who had met adversity and triumphed over it many times, explained his policy thus: "When they throw you down—just spit on yer hands and take another grip o' the pick!" Unlovely perhaps, but a very good slogan in any sort of endeavor.

The majority of the men whose stories follow, had to get jobs in their youth. A job is not a berth or a shelf in living wherein one can stop. A job is just a chance, a chance to show what you can do. Most of these men took the first job offered, which in itself might have been the lowliest of occupations, then proceeded to build it up into something better. That chance might have been nothing more than selling newspapers or running errands. But you may depend upon it, all of them put both feet on it, worked hard and, while doing so, reached for the next best thing.

Opportunity is not dead. While things grow in the ground, while people want products of labor and service, while people merely engage in living—there will be no lack of opportunity. It cannot be otherwise. Those who deny progress should consider Galileo in that unfortunate hour when he was tried by his inquisitors. He was told to deny what he had learned, that the earth moved in an orbit, or suffer death. He made the denial—to live —but under his breath he muttered, "But it *does* move!" And so it does, the earth and all its inhabitants.

We are told by many that "the United States will never be the same again." Well put. It won't. In 1800 it wasn't the same United States that we knew in 1775. And in

1865 it was not the same as it had been before. In 1900
it was vastly different from what it had been thirty years
before. And it has not been the same since the World
War. If we insisted on sameness we'd still be fighting
Indians and living by candle-light at night.

The United States will not be the same old place that
our fathers knew. The frontiers are gone; every last one
of them bowled over. That is true, shall we say geograph-
ically. But how about those other frontiers of science,
art and all endeavor? There is no saturation point in
those frontiers. Indeed, there are plenty of places to go.
Perhaps more than ever before.

Of late we have come to consider our prime essential—
a job. We must have jobs. Young men can't get them
and are unhappy. It may sound like a rash statement,
but a job can be one of the worst things one can acquire.
A much more important thing is to be able *to do something well!*

The depression showed many million job holders that
merely having a job was not enough. Jobs could be lost
and, unhappily, at a time when there were none to be had.
But the man *who could do something well*—the expert—
did not suffer nearly so much. The business houses and
factories could dispense with those who merely held jobs,
but they could not get along without men who knew how
to do something well.

To be expert at something lifts a man out of the ranks.
He is a bit of iron to the business-magnet. Such a talent
actually puts the limelight on him. Jobs have to be
hunted—but industry hunts men who know how to do

something well. This is true even in the countries run by 'isms'; and much more true of our own.

If you would like to know when the United States will really be devoid of opportunity, here is the answer: When the people don't want automobiles, when they loathe entertainment of any kind, when they hate good things to eat, when they don't like nice clothes, when they abhor vacations, when they don't like to live in comfortable houses, when they don't want to read books or go to the movies, when, in short, "they don't want notin' and don't want to go no place"—then this country will be in a predicament indeed. But all signs point to the contrary.

I think if you questioned any of these men whose stories you are about to read, they would tell you that they were extremely grateful to have had the great good fortune to live in a land like ours. I think, too, that they would say they envied you in starting out on your own career. They would like to do it all over again themselves. Which proves it is the adventure and the battle that count—not the dollars.

This is an age of many opinions and much advice. It is no wonder that young men are bewildered as well as disheartened. The virtues of our fathers are now considered by many as out of date. Perhaps the most dampening statement made in recent years is that rugged individualism is not to be desired or admired. There is actually *more* need today to be both rugged and individual. It was good once; it will be good always.

Lastly, massed thinking is ruinous. Opinions get around. "Nobody wants anybody"—"eight millions are out of work"—"there's no chance nowadays"—and such opinions that float around like epidemics. If I may be allowed to give any advice it is this: It is only *one* opportunity that you as an individual want. Ignore the figures of men out of work; you are not six million men or eight million men. You are only *one* man and you need only *one* opportunity.

That opportunity or the result of it, rests entirely on your ability to do something well—with all your heart and interest. It was so in the year 1 A. D. It will be so in any other year A. D. There is no other way.

CONTENTS

CONTENTS

LIST OF ILLUSTRATIONS

xiii

ROGER W. BABSON

WHO PUT THE BREATH OF LIFE INTO
STATISTICS

ROGER W. BABSON

FAMOUS LEADERS OF INDUSTRY

ROGER W. BABSON

WHO PUT THE BREATH OF LIFE INTO STATISTICS

IF Roger W. Babson had lived in the Dark Ages he would have had a good chance of being hanged or burned at the stake. He would have been considered a soothsayer, a magician, and, consequently suffered the same fate that all such extraordinary persons met. Consider him. He could read the signs (not stars, but figures), he could make city buildings spring up in a quiet residential town (almost like a magician makes a tree grow out of a silk hat), and he could actually tell the future by making charts and translating them. Such abilities undoubtedly would have made him a most suspicious character in those skeptical days of long ago.

But we live in an enlightened age, an age when extraordinary persons are not feared but appreciated. None of his first customers ever considered he was in league with the devil; they knew where he got his figures and he explained how he made his prognostications. It looked a little like magic, but it was good, sensible magic. What he did, from a veritable, shoe-string start, is one of America's

3

great romances in business. It is so remarkable, so full of interesting adventures, that it will be impossible to get it into a single chapter in this book. That in itself would be magic.

A more unlikely place for a statistician to be born in than the town of Gloucester, Massachusetts, would be hard to find. The call of the sea has rung in every Gloucester boy's ears since time immemorial. The greatest of adventures beckoned from the tall masts that fringed the town. Yet Roger Babson never bothered his head about this immense, fascinating life that was right under his nose.

He was born July 6, 1875, the son of a local merchant, Nathaniel Babson. His ancestors were sturdy New Englanders; merchants, sea captains, ministers and soldiers. The Babson family was not the wealthiest in town, nor were they poor. Mr. Babson's father was a canny merchant, quite successful. But young Roger was brought up as any boy of a middle class family, not pampered in any way.

At first he was sent to a private school, where he proved a little too much for the gentle lady who ran it. The next school was a little more competent to deal with him; by his own admission he got forty-seven lickings in one year. He kept no chart of such annual movements, but it must have been a peak year. Later he settled down and became a fairly good student.

In the off-hours of his elementary school days, he was not only a member of a gang, but the leader of it. However, the worst acts of the gang consisted of making a lot of noise and fighting with other gangs. In short, he lived a normal American boy's life. In the language of the day, Gloucesterites probably alluded to him as being "full of the Old Ned."

During the summer vacations and off days during the school year he worked at odd jobs; jobs which, at first, he dug up himself. They did not always meet with his family's approval, although they admired his spirit. One of his early ventures in business was that of carrying buckets of water for a Chinaman who ran a laundry. There was no running water, so it had to be drawn from a pump and toted. The compensation was five buckets for a cent. Hard work—but a cent was a cent. Later he had a go at selling papers, and still later another water-carrying venture on a larger scale, with circus elephants instead of Chinamen as the consumers. Finally he went to work on his grandfather's farm, hoeing vegetables, at twenty-five cents a day. This was much better pay, but it was also much harder work.

Roger's grandfather had a milk route and the driver of the wagon sold vegetables in season. One day Roger begged for a chance to do this, when the driver was away sick. This was his first venture at selling—and his vegetable hoeing days were over, at least on anybody else's farm. The next year he planted his own garden, worked like a Trojan, got good crops and managed to sell out. At this time he was nothing but a mere boy, but in spite of his youth he did very well at both raising produce and selling it. As he grew older he learned a little bit about electricity and blossomed out as a youthful contractor, installing electric doorbells and the like. He bought his own stock from the wholesale houses and did all the work.

In one of his high school vacations he took in the World's Fair at Chicago and worked at the job of collecting nickels from the phonograph machines which were then all the rage. He went alone—but nobody succeeded in selling him any gold bricks or Lake Michigan! One year he got a job in his home town at keeping books for a concern that sold spars for ships. This gave him an insight into real business; he not only worked on the books but went out collecting bills, and this is one of the most illuminating courses in the study of business, as anyone knows who ever tried it.

Graduated from the Gloucester High School, he entered the famous Massachusetts Institute of Technology. It was not the college he would have selected himself as he was not technically inclined, but his father insisted on it and it was Tech or nothing. He took the course in civil engineering, not because he liked it, but because it seemed the least obnoxious. He plugged diligently during his four years and graduated in 1898. Later he was instrumental in having a course in business engineering established at Tech, and he had the honor of giving lectures himself in that course.

During the vacations of his college years he worked at road-building, acting as time-keeper and later as assistant to the engineer in charge. This was healthy outdoor work and fitted in with his college course. It was not the work he hoped to do later, but quite welcome in the circumstances.

From the time he was a little boy Roger Babson was always working at something, not solely to get money, but for the joy of accomplishing something. There is a certain strain in New Englanders which is as near perpetual motion as anything yet discovered. They are born on the move and generally die in the harness. This strain was strong in Roger Babson; he was happiest when in motion, doing something.

Tech graduates almost invariably know where they are going after graduating; there is a job waiting somewhere. But young Babson had no intention of building bridges or railroads. He had the itch for business and the call of the investment center was the loudest in his ears. Massachusetts boys with this longing usually make tracks for their own "Street" which is State. It isn't as big as Wall Street, but the tickers tick just the same and there is a stock exchange. Also it is a well known fact that if anybody wishes to float a bond issue or sell a mess of stock, the sea around Boston is one of the richest in the world. Babson Senior would have kept his son in Gloucester (there were several good opportunities there for him) but young Babson meant to fly his own kite. He was twenty-three years old and the world was his oyster; perhaps it could be opened on State Street.

He tried for a job in every banking and investment house in Boston, but it happened to be a depression year and they were firing, not hiring. One day, when he was about discouraged, he spotted an advertisement in a newspaper which called for the services of a young man with an investment house. There was no address given; applicants had to write to a post-office box number.

How young Babson went after this job is a fine example of persistence and initiative. He wrote five or six letters, but no request came for his services. Most young men would have given up in disgust, but he turned his wits on the problem, determined to see the man who hid behind an anonymous box number. He got to the post office early one morning and parked himself beside that box number! Sherlock Holmes couldn't have done better. Soon along came a boy for the mail and on the big leather bag he carried was the firm name, E. H. Gay & Company. Young Babson now followed the bag to the office. And finally he got inside to see Mr. Gay. He got the job and went to work that very morning.

This connection did not last very long, although the young investment clerk worked very hard and managed to sell quite a number of bonds. But he was a young man of ideas and considerable inquisitiveness; this very inquisitiveness finally got him in bad odor with his employers. In fact, they fired him one day while he was in New York at the firm's office in that city. It was a hard blow because he had done his best and saw no reason why he should be let out.

It was a temptation to go home and indulge in a breathing spell—as many a young fellow has done in a similar situation. But young Babson did not want to go back to Gloucester, like a dog with his tail between his legs. It would look like a licking—and he didn't feel like being licked. Instead he suddenly decided to stay in New York and go into business for himself. He had found out that bonds could be bought much more cheaply at the market than from the Boston investment houses. Hence he thought he could undersell the Boston houses, working through the mail. He hired an inexpensive office and went to work, typing his own letters and gathering his own information and prices. Some success came; he might have made something of the venture. But he realized that there was too much New England in him to become a New Yorker. He wanted to go home—and home meant that peculiar atmosphere linked up with the blue Atlantic Ocean and the rocky shores thereon. No good to grow anything on except the joy of living, as every real New Englander knows.

Before returning to Boston, however, he opened an office in Worcester (he was taking the return in easy stages!) and ran it for a time. But soon he was back in the old Hub of the Universe, this time entering the employ of C. S. Cummings & Company. This was just after the turn of the century when there was a great boom in street railway promotion. The old horse cars had gone, and everybody wanted to ride on the "trolleys." Also every locality in New England wanted its own line.

There was lots of money to be made in selling the bond issues of these street railway companies, and young Babson became very successful as a salesman in these securities. The firm also sold government and municipal bonds. It was a valuable experience for the eager young business man. He learned a lot about what went on behind the scenes. In the few years he worked at this job he learned much about what made the wheels go round, what made the big financial machine tick. It was not to be his big job, but that job was dependent upon the knowledge he was getting. The experience was also valuable for the acquaintances he made.

One thing always bothered young Babson; he liked activity but he loathed *wasted* activity. His observant eyes often noted people in business, running about with papers, like chickens with their heads chopped off. Another thing that annoyed him was duplication of efforts; why do a thing over and over again when once was enough? Still another thing that upset him was wrong information. All around him he saw evidence of this, some of it willfully wrong and some just plain dumb. It was this opinion, gathered through his early life in business, that later was to determine his whole career. He meant to set people right; in other words, to take the humbug and uncertainty out of business.

In 1900 he married Grace Knight and the two made their home in Wellesley, Massachusetts, a town about fifteen miles from Boston. Young Babson gave everything he had to his business. He was young and strong, or thought he was, and there were so many things he was interested in. His earnings grew and the future looked rosy.

But he was not as strong as he thought he was. One day in the fall of 1901 he caught a severe cold while away on business. It refused to yield to treatment and he became worse. People in those days used to "work a cold off," instead of going to bed, with the result that many died. He was stricken with an illness, although he did not know its true nature. Finally, after lying in bed for several months, he demanded a verdict from the doctor. He got it. Tuberculosis.

Only one who has had a death sentence pronounced upon him can know how this unfortunate man felt. Young, the whole world before him, married to a charming girl—and those dreaded words staring him in the face.

There were only two courses open—succumb or fight.

Babson elected to fight, and with the real light of battle in his eyes. There would be no half-way measures; he would tackle the thing just as he would a big business proposition—thoroughly, efficiently. Fortunately he had made a little money and had saved it.

He and his wife, who had been a trained nurse, went to work. He lived and slept in the open air, ate the most nourishing foods. The only work done was the job of getting better. He eventually became strong enough to travel and he and his wife went West, where the climate was supposed to be more conducive to a cure. But he finally came to the conclusion that air is air, no matter where it happens to be. So back to the East he went, where he felt he belonged.

The days went on and slowly he regained strength. All the time he lived and slept outdoors. And all the time his brain was turning around, even more active than before. What was the way out? What was going to happen to him? If he kept on like this, he'd be crocheting or knitting or talking to himself.

Naturally his mind ran to his old business. He began to devour the financial news, monthly reports of railway companies—all the endless "gossip" of what was going on in the business world. It was fascinating when those figures and statements meant something. In every banking establishment some clerk had to be doing that same thing—sorting and analyzing the grist that came in with every mail. A man to every office, and not always a suitable man at that.

Here was an idea. Why not have that analysis made by one man, a sort of human clearing-house, instead of by many? It could be done better by some expert who could devote all his efforts to that particular thing. And there was no reason why *he* could not do the job! He could get reports, analyze them, tabulate them and sell the service to the banking houses for less than it cost them in clerk hire to get the same result. Such a job could be done in his home as well as in the city. It was an idea, anyway, and he decided to have a go at it.

And so the Babson Statistical Organization started in the modest home of the man who conceived the idea. He figured that to make even a worthwhile start he should have eight subscribers, and the price should be $12.50 per month. With a capital of $1200., a typewriter, adding machine and office supplies he ventured on the idea.

His health was now sufficiently good to allow him to make trips from Wellesley to Boston. For weeks he tramped the streets of Boston, trying to get the needed eight subscribers. He got one—then another—another. And finally he had, after combing the city, seven signed up. To get that eighth one was like pulling teeth—the prospect's teeth! But at last he did succeed in getting it and the work began.

It was still necessary for him to work in the open air. When it was cold he wrapped himself in a specially designed and heated blanket; the stenographer also had to use a blanket. On cold days she had to wear mittens. To work the typewriter little hammers with rubber tips, were designed, and she struck the keys with the tips.

The first year Mr. Babson had his original eight clients but no more. But the second year he boosted it to twenty-seven clients, and the third year saw forty-two on the list. The service was eminently satisfactory, giving the desired information which previously had had to be done by some employee in each office. The once-sick man had put it over. The thing which had seemed such stark tragedy had really opened the way for a tremendous success, a success in spirit as well as in business. It was a grand fight and the success was deserved.

Other ideas came, were perfected and put on the market. Many men have "ideas" but few of them ever get into circulation. Generally they are like Clem Hawley's "dee-vice" in "The Old Soak"; they get talked about but only that. Mr. Babson had a positive genius for seeing a thing in his mind and, once having seen it, giving it breath and life.

Soon the infant had outgrown its clothes and also its nursery. New quarters had to be procured for the lusty child, and these were found in a building in the public square of Wellesley, over a fruit market. But this did not suffice for long. The business, with new services added from time to time, soon bulged out of the rented office suite and this time it got a building of its own, a three-story one of brick. The Babson Statistical Organization was on its way—a sort of distant relation of the financial world rearing its head in a quiet Yankee town.

There was no stopping it now. One building followed another with startling frequency, as the years passed. The growth went up the street and back into the rolling wooded country to the south. A radio station, WORL, reared its towers to the sky. And everything arranged neatly, with vast lawns and trim driveways setting it off. This is the part seen by the eye. And when you see the splendid lay-out there is no doubt in your mind about the magic of it. That it all grew from one man's idea, dreamed on a sick bed, makes it still more wonderful.

To go into all the various branches and activities of this huge organization would take far too much space. But a few high spots can be mentioned. The development of the Babson Reports and the Babsonchart, which advise when to buy or sell; the Service Department and Clients' Conferences; the Babson Institute, Webber College, Radio Station WORL, the American Public Welfare Trust and the Gamewell Companies.

The Babson Statistical Organization sells protection. Mr. Babson says: "My business is your protection,—financial protection, fire protection, burglary protection and health protection." It is the largest organization of its kind in the world. Mr. Babson also was instrumental in developing such statistical projects as Poor's Manual Company, the National Quotation Bureau and the Standard Statistics Bureau.

The Babson Institute was established in 1919. It is, as might be supposed, a school of business administration carried on as a business man would have it. It trains young men for business life; it is a highly intensive course and covers the essentials of a course in Business Administration in one year. Students punch a time clock—in at 8.30 and out at 5. They have a desk, secretary, dictaphone, telephone and adding machines. During the course they visit factories, banks, ship-building yards and many other scenes showing varied industries in actual performance. The Institute is for young men only.

Later, Webber College at Babson Park, Florida, was

established for young women who wished a similar training. Both these institutions of specialized learning were
successful from the start, and many young men and young
women have graduated from them. Webber has a unique
feature in that the students are taken to Florida for four
months each year.

In the largest building on the Babson Institute Campus
there is under construction the largest relief map in the
world. On a curved surface, exactly proportioned to that
of the earth itself, is portrayed the topography of the
United States and Southern Canada, based on Government surveys. It is sixty-five feet across. To look at it,
one has to stand on a gallery fifteen feet above it. It is
being made in sections about two feet square, each square
being fitted into its proper place as it comes from the
hands of the artists and modelers. It will give the effect,
when done, of looking down on the country from a height
of about twelve miles. Everything is done in proper relief
and in natural colors.

Much of Mr. Babson's work shows the inspiration and
guidance of the scientific principles laid down by Sir Isaac
Newton, including especially Newton's law of action and
reaction. In recognition of this influence, the Babsons
have made a collection of Newtonia which is probably the
finest in the world. It includes all the editions of the
Principia and Opticks published during Newton's lifetime
and most editions published since his death.

During the World War, Roger Babson forsook his
thriving business, bought a house in Washington and
went to work for Uncle Sam. He directed the Bureau of
Information and Education in the Department of Labor,

interpreting the Government's war plans to American labor.

To set down all the activities of this busy man would be impossible. And during the time this book is in the process of being set up and printed, undoubtedly he will have started two or three other new activities.

Speaking of books, Mr. Babson has found time (how we don't know!) to write thirty-nine books. Aside from this tremendous amount of authorship, he has written hundreds of articles for magazines and newspapers. And on top of that he has given many lectures, both in person and over the radio.

The Babson story is an inspiring one for all young men, especially to any young man who gets a severe blow and who feels the end of the world has come for him. This man could have felt just that way when illness struck him down. But he took his breathing spell, and, as the old Irishman said, "spit on his hands and took another grip o' the pick!"

There is no doubt that Roger Babson has had a sincere desire to help people as he went along in his amazing business career. The statistical venture in its earliest days was aimed to help people invest their money wisely. He knew that nothing could stop them pouring their money into the stock market, but he could teach them to pour it efficiently, and to get something in return except a headache. He made money doing the job—but nobody knows how much he made for the many who followed his teachings. He didn't mind if the sheep gamboled, but he could stop their gambling. In other activities, such as the American Public Welfare Trust and the Gamewell Company, he has aimed to help people to healthier, safer and happier living.

Not so long ago the main street in Wellesley was just a countrified thoroughfare, a beautiful suburban street with graceful trees arching over the road. The tempo was of the horse and buggy age—and it didn't look as if any business would ever grow on those wide sweeping lawns. But now the south side of that same street presents an amazing change. There is nothing suggestive of a transplanted Wall Street; the picture is rather that of a college lay-out—something the size of Amherst or Williams. The buildings are widely spaced, surrounded by lawns and drives. It is very well done, a lovely grouping in a lovely town.

As was suggested in the beginning of this sketch, there was magic in the career of Roger Babson. No one could look at this huge plant, which grew from the idea of selling service to bankers for $12.50 per month into a business of millions, and believe otherwise. Five hundred years ago, as has been said, he would have been in a tough spot as a worker of black art with his figures and prognostications. Now—well, we'll probably erect a statue to him some day for all the efforts he has spent for the good of humanity.

EARL D. BABST

A LAWYER WHO BECAME AN INDUSTRIALIST

EARL D. BABST

EARL D. BABST

A LAWYER WHO BECAME AN INDUSTRIALIST

EARL D. BABST comes from a pioneer Ohio family of bankers and lawyers. It is easy to see how this atmosphere, created by his forebears, led young Babst to take up the study of law and later to become interested in business. Crestline, Ohio, was the place of his birth and the date was July 6, 1870.

His preparatory education comprised a course in the Crestline public schools, which, finished, was followed by a two year interlude in the Babst Banking House. But his education was not finished. He entered Kenyon Military Academy at Gambier, Ohio, where he spent two years. But going through a couple of years of "shoulder arms and squads right" failed to whet an appetite for the life of a soldier. However, military discipline and exercise were of value, both in character and body building. He was graduated from the military academy in 1889.

In the same Ohio town is Kenyon College and here he spent two years. At the end of this period he moved farther afield, selecting the much larger institution of the University of Michigan at Ann Arbor. He was graduated from the University of Michigan in 1893 with the degree of Ph. B.

Now he did an unusual thing. Wishing to take up the study of law he entered the law school of the University of Michigan. There was just one large lecture-room in the law school in those days. A lecture would be given for first-year men, and the following hour one for second-year men, throughout the day. Young Babst simply went to the lecture-room and remained there. He wanted to cram two years work into the space of one—and succeeded. Not only that, but his marks were high.

In this high-pressure method of education he had not suffered from overwork and in no sense was he one of those over-emphasized pluggers who keep their noses in a book interminably. But he had a keen mind and had trained himself, even at this early age, in the art of concentration. It was mental exercise for him, something far different from mental drudgery.

Now came that period which is so often an interlude of bewilderment and discouragement to young lawyers. Where to start, how to start? A mere diploma and a prepossessing appearance are not enough. Hard-headed clients want some guarantee of success—and that means a record of achievement.

For a start young Babst picked a city in the State in which he had received his higher education, Detroit. At that time Detroit was nothing like the city it was to become. There wasn't a single automobile in it. It was just a city of general business, well situated, and having about 200,000 population. Still 200,000 persons milling around in one locality seemed to indicate the need of the services of a lawyer or two—and so the young and ambitious Babst hung out his shingle

We often read (generally in fiction) how some budding lawyer sits in his lonely office for years, waiting patiently for some client to knock at his door. But young Mr. Babst had no such probation to serve. On his very first day in Detroit, after getting settled, he fell in with that heaven-sent boon to all lawyers, a man with a problem he could not solve himself. This man owned a magazine in Babst's native State of Ohio, and he had come to Detroit to buy another magazine to combine with his own. The publisher needed somebody to look after the legal end of the transaction and so Babst got the job. He did his task so well that sometime later the publisher arranged with him to conduct a department in the magazine dealing with legal problems.

In law, as well as in every other profession and art, there is a cardinal principle. It ought to be well known but even after all these centuries have passed, many are still unaware of it. That principle is nothing but this: do any job, no matter how insignificant, as thoroughly as you know how. Young Babst knew it, had known it for some time. He had determined that every case presented to him would be handled to the best of his ability, regardless of the work put in on it. He was wise enough to know that even if he lost money on a few such cases, the time and effort would pay good dividends. He soon proved this to his own satisfaction. One day a man came into his modest office with an age-old problem—a bill to collect. Every lawyer knows what these things are. Just routine work with no dramatics or a chance for oratory in court. Many lawyers figure that a letter worded to scare the debtor into fits (or frantic payment) is enough for such a picayune legal case.

But Mr. Babst did nothing of that kind. And the bill

itself was for a mere three dollars! Of course the client really wanted satisfaction, not three little dollars. The young lawyer took the case and proceeded to expend as much energy on it as would have been appropriate on a big corporation suit. The case did have a few complicated points and Mr. Babst spent hours in the law library, getting the exact solution. When he finished there was no guess-work, no bluff, no mere depending on a letter to a debtor. He had a complete case and knew exactly where his client stood. The bill was settled.

Not long after this he got a much better case, and all because of his unsparing efforts on that first one. The man who had the three-dollar case told somebody else about the young lawyer who was so thorough, and that led to the more important assignment. This was an illuminating demonstration of what thoroughness amounted to, and for Mr. Babst it showed a distinct path to follow in his future career. He determined to spare no efforts on any matter that came his way. This plan bore fruit. While clients did not rush up his stairs and batter down his door with business, the growth was satisfactory. Slowly, but with a sound foundation, he built his professional edifice.

He had not been in his adopted city long when something happened which might have caused him to take the fork in the road which so many lawyers take, that of politics. It came about this way. In 1896 the burning political question was that of free silver, the famous sixteen to one scheme. A young and powerful orator by the name of William Jennings Bryan preached this gospel and became the leader of the Democratic party and its

candidate for President of the United States. His epic
speech which ended with the words, "You shall not press
down upon the brow of labor this crown of thorns, you
shall not crucify mankind upon a cross of gold," set men's
hearts aflutter and many there were who followed him.

However, young Mr. Babst's keen and logical mind
saw flaws in the scheme, and he proceeded to do something about it. At that time he was living in a boarding
house. Across the long table the conversation was always
brisk and sometimes heated. "Please pass the butter"
was a prelude to "Well, why isn't this tariff idea the right
one?"—and many were the good-natured arguments
around that table.

Young Babst took the side of the McKinley gold standard (we were on it then!) and soon gathered a little
organization of young fellows who believed as he did.
From the boarding house it spread to the precinct, then
to the ward, then to city size. Before the campaign was
half under way, it was State-wide. And Mr. Babst was
happily and busily engaged as a vital member of the
speakers' bureau. Here was a chance that would have
led to a political career, but he elected to stick to his own
profession without outside diversions.

It was a couple of years later when an incident occurred which altered the course of his business life. One
day in 1898 he was traveling on a train to Chicago.
Nearby in the Pullman smoker, sat two men, earnestly
conversing. The subject of their talk seemed controver-
sial, even troublesome. Occasionally they looked over at
Babst, who was even then a figure that attracted interest
and confidence. Finally the two men got into conversa-

tion with him. They were both lawyers and when they discovered that he was one, too, they put their intricate problem before him, the question that had so absorbed them. What would *he* do with such a nut to crack?

This was a sort of game and Mr. Babst smiled as he mulled it over. Then he outlined a course which he would pursue in the matter. The two men nodded, considerably impressed. They hadn't thought of that particular way out. Before leaving the train they asked for his business card and said that he might hear from them again.

He did. They were counsel for the National Biscuit Company, and not long after this event the Company sent for him, with the result that he was appointed counsel for them in the West. It proved to be a contact with far-reaching results. It put him on the path which unerringly drew him towards the world of industry.

He held this connection for a couple of years, administering his duties from his Detroit office. All the time he was building up a substantial practice, and also interesting himself in the city affairs. The first rumblings of the coming great industry in Detroit were making themselves heard. Quaint vehicles were scudding about the side streets and several future great men in the world of industry were performing openly as smudge-faced mechanics. However, young Mr. Babst was not interesting himself in automobiles. But he was growing up with the city, giving a good deal of attention to civic matters. He became a director in the Citizens Savings Bank and helped to found the Detroit University School.

In 1902 he left Detroit to go to Chicago, there to become a member of the law firm of Green, Peters and

Babst. This firm was counsel for the National Biscuit Company.

At this time we can stop and consider something which was to engage a lot of Mr. Babst's attention, the grocery store. Now we know the grocery store as a ship-shape place, big or little, with rows of labeled cans and packages arranged on shelves. We go in and say to the grocer that we want a can of Humpty-Dumpty molasses, a package of Domino Sugar or a box of Uneeda biscuits. We mention brands, not just articles. We know what we want, get what we expect in weight and quality.

But the grocery store of the early 90's was a far different affair. The sugar was kept in big barrels, just sugar, and people often accused the grocer of adding sand, just as they say the milkman waters the milk— generally in fun, of course, but sometimes not. And speaking of milk, that, too, was vended in a different way. It came in large cans and the grocer, when he carried it at all, dipped it out in a measure. Rather unsanitary, but then people didn't know about germs in those days. Pickles came in barrels. Crackers came in barrels—very handy to the unsanitary fingers of Tom, Dick and Harry. Molasses was kept out back somewhere in a barrel, far too adjacent to the kerosene barrel sometimes. Everything was kept in bulk, weighed or measured out by the grocer. (People used to accuse the poor man of including his thumb in weighing, too!)

The package was making its appearance, however. A package with a printed name on it. Grocers were slow to welcome such an innovation—and you may imagine the numbers of Toms, Dicks and Harrys who resented the possible demise of the cracker barrel and the prune box!

There was a weak spot, however, in the business of getting out an expensive box or package, advertising the brand and trying to make something of it. Other firms would copy the name, get up a similar package and reap the rewards of the original company's endeavor. Nobody could or would do much about it.

The firm which Mr. Babst represented was in this fix. They were one of the first to get out a cracker in a box. It was called Uneeda and the box was the same one you see today—blue with white letters. Women liked to buy these Uneeda crackers. There were no dirty (or kerosened) fingers to touch the crackers inside. It was a good cracker and a fine name. That name took the fancy of everybody as it was one of the first of its nature.

But alas, there were copy-cats! Such imitators as Uwanta Biscuit or something equally near appeared. The National Biscuit Company was not the only sufferer. Other firms who got out original articles were imitated by people who wanted to make an easy profit on the other fellow's work and brains. There were laws to stop the practice but it was expensive to bring suit. The laws needed pointing up, too. Somebody had to be a pioneer in this business of stopping what you might call "plagiarism" in goods.

It became Mr. Babst's job to do something about this intensely irritating and costly situation. Now he knew his law; a bit of reading would get him all the facts and what citations there were on that end. But he had an urge to do more, what you might call in the arts "getting local

color." He went to the source, the grocery store itself.
Hundreds of them. He talked with grocers, learned their
opinions and business problems. He studied the customers who came in the stores. In the less sophisticated
spots he saw the old cracker barrels and kerosene barrels
still in use. He poked into things, kept his eyes and ears
open. It was that old idea of his—thoroughness, the same
procedure used in his extra-research in the three-dollar
law suit of his youth.

With all that information and background he went to
work. He brought suits, in the name of the National
Biscuit Company, against scores of infringers against
their trademark and design, in every Federal district
court possible. Such a pleader knew all the sides to the
question, and there was no standing up against his well
prepared cases. The Company won in every instance.
It became not only bad manners to copy another's hard-
earned trade-mark, but somewhat dangerous. Life for
the copyist, who expected to get rich on another's pioneering, became slightly more than hazardous; at any
moment a distinguished looking and quite competent
gentleman might descend upon him and his stolen trade-
mark with results dire and swift.

The situation became much better through these efforts of the tireless Mr. Babst, not only for his own
company but for others who wished to establish special
brands of goods. The trade-mark became something
reasonably safe. It was most important work and we
see the value of it every day.

In 1906 Mr. Babst went to New York City to become
Vice-President of the National Biscuit Company, suc-

ceeding his old law firm as general counsel. In the next few years he devoted a lot of his time to fighting infringements, as mentioned above, and in studying methods of merchandising. It was a new world; all the time he was getting more into industry and farther away from law. In 1910 he gave up most of his legal duties to devote himself more to the business side of the company. He kept up his traveling and the study of the grocery business. It was an ever-interesting study and in his thorough, painstaking way he was learning its many intricacies and peculiarities. Why did some grocers fail and others succeed, with the same standing start? Why did some brands attract more customers than others? What did the people want? What did the grocers want? All this investigation was getting him somewhere. It made him an authority on the business, one of the largest businesses in the civilized world and one of the most essential.

In 1915 he left the company he had been with so long, and went with the American Sugar Refining Company to become its President. If ever there was a basic industry, sugar surely is one. Next to salt, we just have to have it. And Americans are the greatest sugar consumers in the world. In the year 1935 the sweet-tooth of America demanded 6,359,000 tons of sugar. Tons! The American Sugar Refining Company in 1915 when Mr. Babst became its president, was the largest sugar refining company in America, as it is now.

As we stopped before in our story to look at the old time grocery store, let us pause a moment to learn something about sugar. We take the pleasant tasting stuff for granted, but once upon a time it was not so common. People sweetened their tea and coffee (when they had them) with anything sweet, syrup, honey, or drank it plain. As time passed and merchandising methods grew better, sugar became more common.

Most of us have a vague idea that it comes from the sugar cane, a tall reed-like plant that grows in the Tropics. Other things give sugar, as the sugar beet, maple tree and so on. But the bulk of it comes from the sugar cane and most of what we get comes from the West Indies. A comparatively small amount of cane used in our production is grown in Louisiana and eastern Texas.

The process of refining has not changed greatly in the last hundred years. The raw sugar comes to the refinery in sacks; it is not as dark as brown sugar but the color of straw. It is washed in spinning centrifugal machines, then melted down, next mixed with diatomaceous earth and passed through cotton duck filters and bone char. Next it is crystallized in vacuum pans, then roughly freed of syrup in other machines, and finally fried in hot air in the revolving tunnel of a granulator.

To sell that innocent looking virgin-white stuff would seem to be one of the soft jobs in this world. There is no argument entailed in selling it, no missionary work; everybody loves it and just has to have it. But the business itself can have plenty of grief, and the few well-informed knew that Mr. Babst had his hands full in his new job. One editorial writer on a newspaper in a sugar producing State wrote that he undertook what was probably the hardest job in America.

When Mr. Babst assumed charge he found his work cut out for him. He discovered among other things, that his company was faced with nearly two hundred suits, amounting to approximately $200,000,000 brought by Louisiana planters, by ouster suits instituted by the State of Louisiana, by special legislation directed against it, and by a dissolution suit brought by the Federal Government. These were the legacies left by those who had controlled the biggest sugar company in the country, in its early days.

It was Mr. Babst's job to straighten out all these difficult matters, and during the next few years he was very busy doing it. He succeeded in his usual thorough way. However, there were other matters besides law suits that the new President had to attend to. As in his beginning with the Biscuit Company he went out to study the retailing world of his product, the grocery store. He traveled everywhere, visiting grocery stores big and little. He visited over a thousand of them in person, and sent out trained investigators who studied several thousand more.

The company had experimented somewhat with packaging. It had two brands, Domino and Franklin. But in many stores the old method of vending sugar from a barrel was still the custom. Mr. Babst studied all the business that went on around that old sugar barrel. How much waste was there? Did the accommodating clerk add just a wee bit more than a pound every time he weighed out an order for a customer? How much string was used, how much time was consumed in weighing

and putting it in a bag? And how about accidents, as
bags of sugar falling on the floor and bursting open?

Mr. Babst got all his figures and facts and proceeded
to change the situation. Sugar for the customer was to
be supplied in attractive two-pound and five-pound car-
tons, with the name and trade-mark plainly printed
thereon. Sugar would mean Domino (not a nameless
barrel) to the millions of housewives who visited the
grocery stores of the land. The grocers were not slow
to see the advantages of the package. It was not long
before the old sugar barrel was an antique in most places.

Mr. Babst had scarcely become acquainted with his
new duties when the whole business was turned upside
down by no less a thing than the World War. If you
are old enough to remember that you will recall the
sugar-less days and meatless beef-stews and gasoline-less
Sundays. Sugar was one of the important commodities,
although most people had never bothered to consider how
much they depended on it. The millions of soldiers, not
only Uncle Sam's but those of all the Allies, had to have
sugar. As we have discovered sugar has great energy-
building properties. So whole shiploads of the precious
stuff had to go overseas for the millions of fighting men.

This item in the grocery store got more attention
than all the others put together. Selfish and unpatriotic
people schemed to get hold of more than their share
and to hoard it. It was a tremendous job to regulate all
this intricate and bothersome business, and to Mr. Babst
fell all the trouble entailed. The American Sugar Refining Company was by far the biggest of the sugar

companies and he was its boss. For two or three years he had to handle this extremely difficult allocation problem.

But if the War brought its problems, peace brought even greater ones to the man who presided over the destinies of the big sugar company. This was partly due to economic causes, and partly to hysterical hoarding. People, denied sugar for so long, went crazy and bought needlessly. The price of sugar rose after the War to dizzy heights, later to fall to alarming depths. And with the steep and sudden decline in price came a troublesome train of conditions. Business men, threatened with losses, either refused to accept their commitments or to pay for shipments which they had ordered. Industry was confronted with wholesale repudiation.

Mr. Babst had to take a stand that caused a lot of comment. He insisted that contracts be lived up to. The whole principle of business was at stake. If a contract was not a contract, then business might as well throw up its hands. Suits were brought in instances where buyers refused to live up to their agreements.

In 1919 Mr. Babst's company branched out from the field of refining sugar to add that of production. It purchased the stock of a Cuban corporation, the Central Cunagua, with 100,000 acres of land, a railroad, a huge sugar mill, and a whole town. Later another large tract of land was bought and a new central built; also two small islands were purchased for sugar growing.

The troubles which descended on the American Sugar Refining Company through the heritage of early practices, through the War and its aftermath of crazy prices,

were all overcome. Mr. Babst proved a competent
helmsman over this craft which had to ride out so many
storms.

The sugar business is not as sweet as its name would
imply. The crop itself is unstable. One year it may be
a bumper, the next hurricanes and bad weather may cut
it down alarmingly. Then too, the margin of profit to
the refinery is very small, when viewed in pounds. The
"spread" as it is called, is never much more than one
cent a pound. Out of this the refinery has to pay its
costs. The profit per pound ranges from one-tenth to
one-quarter of a cent per pound. But, of course, there
are a great many pounds in six and a half million tons!

Mr. Babst once quoted a saying of Josh Billings as an
example of thoroughness and accuracy. The homely
humorist-philosopher once wrote: "It's better not to
know so many things than to know so many things
that ain't so!" Truly, Mr. Babst has pursued that policy.
Only the statement in his case should have an addition.
Earl D. Babst first learned a few things well, then kept
on adding many things known well.

BRUCE BARTON

AUTHOR AND ADVERTISING GENIUS

(Photo by "Acme")

BRUCE BARTON

BRUCE BARTON

AUTHOR AND ADVERTISING GENIUS

THIS is the story of a man who might have been a number of things. We call such a man a jack-of-all-trades and usually, as the proverb says, he is a master of none. But this man has shown he could be a master of several—and so we shall have to call him a jack-of-all-successes, or a master-of-many-trades, whichever you like.

At any rate, he could have become a very good minister (and he does do a bit of preaching with a pen); he could have become a good professor of history (and once started to be one); he could have made a fine salesman (and has sold many things); he would have made a fine executive (and is one); he is an outstanding advertising man; and he is an author in several media as editorial, essay and article. Altogether it would have been pretty easy for such a man to have landed in some shipping room or perhaps at the helm of a freight elevator, with so many things attempted. But instead he upset the usual result and became successful at all the endeavors he tried.

We could begin his story with the date of his birth, which is the generally accepted way to start a biography. But there is something rather interesting about one of his ancestors, and so his story will be mentioned first. But for the flip of a coin or a quirk of conscience, Bruce

Barton might have been born in England and stayed there. However, this ancestor willed otherwise, and his adventure is good reading.

He was an English soldier and wore the violent red uniform of King George the Third. On the night when our own famous Paul Revere made his great ride to Lexington, this hated British soldier was patrolling the hostile streets of Boston, no doubt thinking himself something of a blade and possibly strutting his stuff for the demure belles of Beacon Hill.

The next we hear of him was at Lexington where he participated in that reverse-Marathon and ran all the way from Concord back to Boston. The embattled farmers didn't get him, however, and he lived to fight again six weeks later at Bunker Hill. Once again he came out whole. The war settled down and Private William Barton began his odious job of chivying the mad patriots all over New England.

After awhile something happened to him, to his point of view. Possibly he fell in love with New England, or perhaps his love for the cause of the under-dog got the better of his loyalty to King George.

Anyway, one night at sentry-go on the east bank of the Hudson River, he determined on a bold course. He removed his scarlet coat, took off his heavy marching boots—and silently walked into the river. Across that wide black stretch of water could be seen the feeble flames of the Continental camp. The Rebels! Enemies to his majesty, whose uniform he had just abandoned. With sure, bold strokes he covered the distance, came up on the bank and confidently entered the camp with his hands aloft.

The hard-bitten American soldiers looked him over, listened to his amazing proposition. He made no bones about it. He was sacking King George and joining up with George Washington's men if they'd have him. The men took him to an officer who listened to his tale. In those days foreigners were not looked upon with too much suspicion; this dripping wet Barton person looked pretty husky and his sales-talk was first class. Thus, speaking "literally," was the first Barton offering for publication and, as the editors say, his offering was accepted.

He was no spy or deserter for gain. He just saw something that seemed right and proper and went after it. He saw service at Trenton, Princeton and Monmouth. And so loyally and gallantly did he conduct himself for his adopted country that he was appointed an officer. The war over, he settled down, married and raised a family. The sword he carried is now a treasured possession of his descendant, Bruce Barton.

Bruce Barton was born in Robbins, Tennessee, August 5, 1886. His father was William E. Barton, at that time a circuit rider in the service of the American Missionary Association. When Bruce was three years old, he witnessed his father receive his diploma from Oberlin Theological Seminary. Later his father became minister of the Congregational Church in Wellington, Ohio, and after that in Boston, Massachusetts. Then came a call to Oak Park, Illinois, near Chicago.

Like so many boys, Bruce wanted spending money.

Even as a youngster he had a business man's vision; he tried for more than a mere paid for assignment.

One of his very early ventures into business was quite creditable and worthy of a more mature youth. He had gone on a visit to the farm of an uncle in Ohio. His uncle had a sugar bush and in the season he made quite a lot of maple sugar. Bruce tried it, thought it was so nice that people around Oak Park, who didn't have any sugar bushes, would be glad to buy it. He worked out a scheme, telling his uncle that he could get him a better price for his sugar in Chicago than in his own locality. The uncle agreed and Bruce got busy. He sold a lot of it, and later arranged to get a larger supply from other farmers. For several years while in school he made around $500. each year in this way. When he began this venture he was only twelve years old.

When in high school he met printer's ink for the first time. A neighbor had bought a couple of wobbly newspapers, put them together in a none too healthy unit and started to publish. He needed an editorial "staff" and hired young Bruce (who had had a vast experience on his high school paper) to be that "staff." It was a weekly and the writing, editing and so on took three days. Bruce worked three afternoons and three evenings for one dollar a day. It was confining work and had to be done after school sessions. It was none too happy a connection for a young fellow who wanted to go to shows and parties. When his chums and girl friends were away at dances and good times, he had to plug at his job of writing and editing a grubby little paper that nobody seemed to want to read. Yet, to his credit, he stuck at the business for three years. All he got out of it was three dollars a week—and an education that no college could possibly give!

He "retired" as he said himself, disillusioned at the grandeur of the newspaper game, when he was fifteen. But there are two things that, once met, never release their hold on you. Printer's ink and actor's grease paint. Inoculation with either of these is for life. He did not intend at the time of his retirement, to return. But we shall see.

Through with high school he entered Amherst College. And there he spent four happy, busy years in that picturesque old New England institution.

And now came the accident or incident that had a great deal towards determining the course of his life. He had planned, after graduating from Amherst, to enter Wisconsin University where he had a scholarship, and there to take up the study of history with a view to teaching. He had an idea that the life of a college teacher was just what he wanted—interesting work, academic atmosphere, long vacations and a whole year of travel now and then.

As commencement time drew near he was brought down by a grippe germ; he had overworked and his resistance had become too low. At the time his classmates were voting that he was the most likely man in the class to win success, the doctor in the hospital was picking him out as the most likely to die. But he licked the germ and finally began crawling around in the sun.

On Baccalaureate Sunday, lying on the grass in the sunshine trying to sleep, which he couldn't do at night, he noticed a rusty looking man wandering aimlessly around the campus. Nobody paid any attention to him.

Something told Bruce that the stranger must be an old Amherst man back for a look at his alma mater—and something urged him to get up and speak to him. Sick as he felt, he disliked the idea of an old grad feeling the later generation lacked the manners to be hospitable. He dragged himself over and spoke to the stranger.

It turned out that Amherst was not his college but he was a member of young Barton's own society, so the young man took him to the frat house. The man signed the visitors' book and Barton was then glad he had approached him. He was William E. Curtis, of the Chicago Record-Herald and he was in the East writing a series of articles on the New England colleges. This was most interesting to both of them, as Barton was president of the student body. Later Mr. Curtis published a statement from the young student and ran his picture in the article.

That chance meeting and the resulting article changed the course of young Barton's life. A man named Chapman read the article, was impressed by it, and sent for Barton.

"You ought to have a year of business experience before going on any further in an academic atmosphere," the man told him, when they met.

Bruce Barton, potential professor of history, stared at him. What good would a year of business be to a teacher? Still, it promised an interesting experience. He always liked to accept a challenge or an offer and anyway, he was only twenty and what was a year?

The man talked on. He owned three magazines, a weekly, a monthly and a farm paper. Printer's ink again!

And he had sworn off the stuff five years before! But
the magazine man had something else besides advice to
offer; a job at $25. a week, and Barton took it.

Then began as busy a year as this young man ever
experienced. He was hired to solicit advertising, and this
proved very interesting. Barton loved to meet business
executives, and the gamble of wits incidental to captur-
ing an advertising contract was the most interesting game
he had ever played. Big names had no terrors for him,
and soon many of the Chicago captains of industry had
the experience of meeting an earnest bright-eyed whipper-
snapper who assured them that their rosiest future lay in
spreading their names in the three modest magazines he
represented and of which they had probably never heard.

One day his boss left for New York in a hurry. After
he had gone there was consternation in the office. No editorials had been written! And professional magazines
could not go to press with a large, almost empty white
space saying "Compliments of a Friend." Hardly.

"Listen," said the old foreman. "I am waiting for editorials and if I don't get 'em, there'll be a hole in the
magazine. Where are they?"

Young Barton looked around. Nobody would or could
take the responsibility. He moved over to a desk, slid
the typewriter around towards him, and waved the foreman back to his world of type.

"I'll do it," he said. "Give me an hour or two."

The paper was put to bed a few hours later, *with* editorials. Barton didn't know whether his score was a home
run or—no runs, no hits, one error! But later the boss
returned from New York and read his paper. And from

that day on he was always too busy to write any editorials. Barton wrote them.

Times were not too good just then; a panic—or what they thought was a panic—was knocking business over and out. The staff was skeletonized, and soon the young man who had come in for only one year of business experience, was doing about three years in one. He did most of the editorial work on the three papers. And gradually took over the shameful job of writing what should have been bought from contributors! He wrote editorials, special articles under half a dozen names on every conceivable subject, advice to farmers, answers to readers' letters and whatnot. It was just one of those jobs that can't be done—and this twenty-year old lad loved it!

But even his ardent efforts didn't save the ship. When magazines start to fold up they collapse quicker than a withered accordion. Young Barton saw them go and he was now free to go on with that scholarship. But something had happened, he found. He had had a taste of the business world, and teaching was no longer so attractive.

Sometime before that an advertising firm in New York had made him a flattering offer to come with them. But he did not feel he had had experience enough to do justice to an eighty dollar a week job. So he passed it up.

For a time he went through an experience that was both chastening and hardening. He worked in a construction camp in Montana. There was, too, an interlude on a farm in Michigan where he milked cows and cut hay. It was a time when he was far from printer's ink, but it was just the thing for him. There can be too much ink.

A few years later he did go to New York, with the firm

of P. F. Collier & Son. He was soon made assistant sales-manager in charge of the book selling department. This was a great organization with 32 branches and over a thousand salesmen. At that time they were launching Dr. Eliot's Five Foot Bookshelf. The new assistant sales-manager wrote the ads himself which have made it famous, ads which will live after him.

Besides copywriting and organization, Mr. Barton went out on the road himself. He sold sets of books. It was on one of these trips that he happened in a town where Billy Sunday, the famous revivalist, was preaching. This preacher was one of the most colorful speakers that ever lived, and Bruce Barton went to see and hear him. He himself knew something about preaching; he had heard many ministers since he was a toddler.

Now he saw one that was a revelation. Billy Sunday could startle the most blasé audience out of its placidity. Bruce Barton listened, enchanted, and later sought out the evangelist. He went away and wrote an article about the dynamic preacher, and sent it to Collier's magazine. It was accepted and printed.

John Siddall, editor of the American Magazine, saw the article and liked the way it was written. He sent for Mr. Barton and asked him to do some articles for the American. He coached him, trained him to write in the particular style needed by that magazine. He became very successful in turning out interviews and articles.

This was a turning point which Mr. Barton might have taken. Many men, tasting this kind of success, are tempted "to leave the world" like a sort of monk, and write. But about that time the Crowell Publishing Company sent for him to take on the editorship of a magazine they were launching called Every Week. It was about the shape and size of Collier's and sold for three cents, the lowest retail price charged for any magazine.

The new magazine grew very fast; in a couple of years the circulation shot up to 600,000. Mr. Barton wrote the editorials himself. They were his own individual type and people liked them; they were philosophical, really common-sense sermons.

Every Week suffered an unmerited fate and was abandoned by its publishers. But the editorials went on, salvaged from the wreck, only they were published by the Redbook Magazine. Mr. Barton wrote these regularly every month for seven years; they were always to be found on the first page of reading matter.

The World War came along and Mr. Barton tried to get in it but could not. However, he took on a publicity job for one of the relief organizations. He worked as hard at this as he had at any of his other jobs. In this connection he became associated with two other young men who were to join him later in a famous partnership, Roy S. Durstine and Alexander Osborn.

The war over, all three young men were out of a job. It was a time of great uncertainty but not hopelessness. Those of an adventurous turn of mind found plenty of opportunity to "start something."

These three young men did just that. They pooled their resources, which were mostly brains and ambition, and started the advertising agency of Barton, Durstine and Osborn.

The first assault for business drew blanks. Just telling

people you were now in the advertising business didn't exactly bring in a rush of orders. But they kept on. They had ideas and demonstrated the fact. In 1920 the new firm stood 23rd in the amount of business done among the agencies. In 1926 it stood 5th on the list and that was an achievement that could hardly be described in words. The advertising world realized there was a new element in its midst, and even the general public, little familiar with the personnel in this mysterious business, began to hear of the doings of B. D. & O. The initials sounded like a railway and it was just about as speedy! In 1928 the firm of Batten & Company was merged with it and now the initials were even harder to say. B. B. D. & O. But that is what advertisers call it. The concern occupies a commanding place in the advertising world; it employs six hundred persons of a very special type, and numbers among its clients many of the largest business concerns in the country.

That is, in very brief form, the story of Bruce Barton, the business man, the man who can take a product like a shelf of books, a motor car, a food product, and put it before the public via magazine and newspaper pages so the readers see it in a new and compelling way. The art of advertising is very intricate and difficult to analyze. Many men have been artists in it, men not always in the advertising business itself. Bruce Barton has the rare art, the ability to do this thing; to influence the progress of products, as it might be called, through presentation in words and pictures.

In all these busy years of building up a great advertising agency, the preacher instinct had not been dead. It was only sleeping. And in 1924 he decided on an action that had given him many hours and days of thinking. He wanted to write his own conception of the life of Jesus. He had, in a way, been turning it over in his mind ever since he was a small boy. And the idea had become strong in him that most people had a radically wrong picture of the Saviour. He was sure of it. And to a man of his training, such thoughts had to be put down on paper.

He wrote it. Anyone reading the first few pages would realize at once that it was dynamite. It was too strong meat for many minds; but excellent for those who liked the truth even at the expense of seeing some age-old beliefs shattered.

Mr. Barton showed it to one editor who knew at once that his "fan mail" would be too full of brick-bats. He didn't have the courage to print it. Then Mr. Barton submitted it to a woman, Gertrude Lane, editor of the Woman's Home Companion. She was neither scared nor pessimistic. The book came out in serial form in that magazine under the title of "The Man Nobody Knows."

Letters came in by the sackful. Some were pretty violent, but more were full of praise. But the publication went on, and when it was finished serially, it was put out in book form. In eighteen months 250,000 copies were sold. Later it was a best seller in England and all English speaking countries. Then it was translated into German, Spanish, Italian and Swedish.

Later Bruce Barton wrote another book in similar vein about the Bible, called "The Book Nobody Knows." This, too, was a best seller. It took plenty of courage to do these two books. He got many unpleasant letters about them. But he knew in his own heart that they should be written, that in the long run they would do good rather than harm.

An advertising man is unfortunate in one sense. He can't sign his name to a creation like an artist, a composer or an author. The public often admires what he does but they don't know his identity. Bruce Barton has hammered out on his old typewriter (his original machine, by the way) countless ads and slogans with which the reading public is familiar.

He coined for the United War Services the slogan now used by the Salvation Army, "*A man may be down but he is never out.*" That, incidentally, is a lot more than a slogan; it is a message that has brought new spirit and hope to thousands of men, men who needed to hear it darned bad. It was Mr. Barton who first likened insurance to *A Rock In a Weary World.* And he created for General Electric Company the theme, now widely used by many utility companies, that any woman who does work that could be done by an electric device is working for $\frac{1}{4}$ to $\frac{1}{3}$ cent per hour.

Bruce Barton would be loath to consider himself a sort of legendary figure in the business world. But he has come to be just that in the eyes of many young men. They have heard of his phenomenal success in the advertising business, have heard of the brilliant campaigns he has originated. More than any other man he has put romance in the advertising profession. And, whether he likes it or not, he has become a target for many young men to shoot at.

BERNARD MANNES BARUCH

OF WALL STREET AND WASHINGTON

BERNARD MANNES BARUCH

OF WALL STREET AND WASHINGTON

O NE day in the late 1880's a tall young man presented himself for physical examination preparatory to entering the Military Academy at West Point. He had passed the written examination with flying colors. And a single look at him seemed to imply that the physical test would be a waste of time.

He was three inches over six feet, straight and hard as nails, and his flashing blue eyes had the glow of health and intelligence. Seldom did candidates more fitted for the college of soldiers present themselves. Moreover, this upstanding lad already had a reputation for fighting and pugnacity, qualities not exactly ignored at the Point. In addition his father had been a distinguished army surgeon in the Confederate forces during the Civil War. In short, he looked to be an admirable specimen for a future general in Uncle Sam's Army.

But to the surprise of the young man, the physician finally shook his head, explaining that in spite of his excellent physique, he was deaf in one ear, and that fact would keep him out of the Point. Then the young man remembered. In a college ball game not long before, he had banged out a long hit. He sprinted around the bases, arriving at the home plate at the same time as the ball thrown from the outfield. A close decision.

Arguments followed and then a rough-house. In the mix-up the home-run hitter was hit himself—on the side of the head with a ball bat. That blow had given him the deaf ear.

And that little thing kept one Bernard Mannes Baruch from the possibility of bearing the title Major General in later years. Mr. Baruch often thought of that, when he was Chairman of the War Industries Board and providing the sinews of war for other major-generals.

Bernard Baruch was born in Camden, South Carolina, on August 19, 1870. He was the second son of Doctor Simon Baruch, who had emigrated in 1855 from Schwersen, Poland, to the United States. The father, brilliant and industrious, was graduated from the Medical College of Virginia. The ink on his diploma was hardly dry when his adopted state joined the colors it had elected to raise. This was his new home, these people were his people, and into the Confederate Army he went, there to serve faithfully and brilliantly the full four years.

He saw a lot of hard service, and was captured three times; first at South Mountain in the Antietam campaign, second at Gettysburg, and again at Thomasville, North Carolina in April, 1865. It was a post-graduate course in a way, because the young surgeon became an expert on the treatment of gunshot wounds; the field was his laboratory. From the experience he wrote a paper on the subject which was a standard work for many years.

The War ended, he settled down in Camden, to take up normal life again. Those were trying days for everybody in the South. There was plenty of practice for the young physician but little money. However, he married a charming girl, Belle Wolfe, daughter of a planter; money would come when conditions were better. Belle Wolfe was of distinguished ancestry. Her father was a wealthy planter of Fairfield County, South Carolina, who lost everything including his home, in the War. Belle was a girl in her teens when his house was burned over their heads. Her American ancestry goes back to 1690 when Isaac Rodriques Marques, a Spanish-Portuguese Jew of education and substance, came to New York. He was a merchant and a ship owner. His descendants remained in New York until after the Revolution, in which they fought. Her branch then settled in South Carolina sometime prior to 1800. Thus on one side of the house, Bernard M. Baruch is descended from a family nine generations in America, and on the other side, his father's, he is the son of an immigrant.

Bernard was the second child born to them. The middle name, Mannes, was given in honor of a friend of his father's. Two other boys were born. When Bernard was about ten years old the ambitious doctor decided there was more opportunity in a larger city, and a city in the North. The family moved to New York City, a wise decision. The Doctor's talents were soon recognized. He became professor of Hydrotherapy at the College of Physicians, Columbia University. He specialized in this subject; his treatments were adopted at the famous spas at Saratoga. Doctor Baruch diagnosed and helped to perform the first appendicitis operation of record. Medical history gives him more credit for the origin of this operation than it does to any one else.

The Baruches got along. But like so many scientific men, completely wrapped up in their work, the Doctor was no money maker. However, the boys went to school and to college. Bernard entered the College of the City of New York in 1884.

He was a first class student, so good that he spent less time than anybody else in the class in study and yet managed to get superlative marks. His brain worked fast and accurately; he had the faculty of boring straight into a thing and seeing it for what it was, a faculty that was even more pronounced in later years.

He was no less proficient athletically. Football at that time was a pastime for the Big Three and his college did not have an eleven. This was unfortunate for Bernard, for such a sport was just made for him. However, he did excel at la crosse, boxing and baseball; in the latter he played first base and he was an out-standing batter. His physique was admirable for boxing; he was well over six feet tall, quick as a cat, strong and courageous.

He had his moments while in college. Once he was called up on the carpet by the President of the college to explain a fistic encounter with a fellow student. It was a good fight and ended when young Baruch knocked his opponent down the steps of the college building. Such a thing generally meant expulsion. But Baruch had been called a name no real man can stand, and he just had to fight, expulsion or not. The President was stern and laid down the law, but young Baruch could always charm anybody with his smile and use of words, and he succeeded in this instance. Indeed, recognizing his peculiar talents, the President suggested West Point might be just the college for him; there the use of fists was not frowned on at all. The suggestion was taken seriously by Bernard, with the result mentioned above.

He was graduated from the College of the City of New York in 1889. And now here was this big lad, with the body of a gladiator and a fine brain, ready to go out into the world. His father thought there was nothing better to be than a doctor. But his mother knew the long waiting in that profession. She suggested business instead of a profession. Sometime before she had taken young Bernard to a well known doctor of phrenology, for the purpose of having the youthful bumps analyzed. The doctor looked him over—or rather his head—and gave the verdict: he would make a fine business man but a poor doctor. Perhaps the doctor knew his bumps, but his subject was never entirely satisfied with the choice of career he ultimately made. He rather regretted not having become a doctor and, as a matter of fact, he expected to be one up to the time he graduated from college. That last summer he attended classes with a cousin who was studying medicine, and spent a lot of time in the dissecting room.

However, it seemed best to try business. His entry into the world of industry was via a glassware firm, and the pay was three dollars per week. There wasn't a thing interesting in it for young Baruch; nothing ever happened and nothing could be made to happen there. But more attractive businesses were all around him. If glass dishes and plates failed to excite him, there were other things and he would get into them. His errands sometimes took him into the financial district and for some reason this locality was just packed with thrills. There were great names staring at him from the signs on the buildings, names that he was constantly reading about in the newspapers. The house of Morgan was a particularly interesting building. Young Baruch liked to look into the windows, imagine what was going on inside. It was not long before he knew two things— that glassware was not for him and that stock-broking was.

He managed to get a job and a little experience with an old banking house. But there was no action there; no money either. A better opportunity soon came. Through his father he got a job with the firm of A. A. Housman & Company and he went to work for five dollars a week. He was in!

The eyes of many men, young and old, have centered on that magic district, Wall Street. It has always meant the Promised Land, El Dorado of the modern world. But the keen eyes of Bernard Baruch saw more than most of them. He had the happy faculty of seeing it as something more than a place to work in, a place to gamble in. It really was the symbol of many interesting businesses scattered throughout the country; in itself it was nothing, but it represented everything tradeable in the United States. It was the most romantic business of all.

Young Baruch knew he would have to master a good

many things before he could do what he wanted. He must acquaint himself with many dry facts and figures, the statistical groundwork. But there was something else. He had to cultivate something more important than figures—Men. He would have to get to know the right kind of men, men who could teach him the things he wanted to know. He had the best commodity to exchange in the world—personality. He had no money, but he did have charm, intelligence and in his face glowed courage and daring. It took a lot to impress those hard-headed business men of Wall Street. But young Baruch soon showed that he could impress them.

At this time he met a man named Middleton S. Burrill who took a great interest in him. Mr. Burrill was a lawyer and a member of a distinguished New York family. He took considerable interest in Wall Street affairs, however, and was an extraordinarily skillful amateur speculator. He gave young Baruch much sound advice and help. Baruch met other speculators, and the greatest of all was the famous James R. Keene. Keene also took a fancy to the up and coming young man who could ask so many sharp questions. It was a case of one shrewd mind meeting another and being drawn to it.

His firm liked him. He was their one clerk who seldom had to consult files for information before answering a customer; he carried most of the answers in his head, the result of poring over all sorts of financial reports and journals. After he had been with this firm a couple of years he felt he was worth more salary and asked for it. They countered with an offer of a partnership, a one-eighth interest, and he accepted. He got the better of the bargain, making $6000 for himself as a partner, over twice as much as the salary he had asked for.

Cautiously the young brokerage clerk essayed a few flights in the market on his own account. He was so sure of himself and his ideas that he borrowed ten thousand dollars from his father. This he lost in a few deals that turned out wrong. But this did not discourage him for long; he still had faith in himself and a determination to recoup the loss.

In 1898 he made a large commission by arranging the purchase of the Liggett & Myers Tobacco Company for Thomas Fortune Ryan, which the latter merged with the American Tobacco Company. A little later Mr. Baruch made a big profit in selling a certain steel stock short. Now he was well out of the woods and had paid back the money borrowed from his father.

Mr. Baruch now decided that he might as well make all the money that came from his own ability and when he was twenty-nine he bought a seat on the New York Stock Exchange. Soon his name was well known in the financial district as a shrewd speculator.

In 1901 he made a big killing in Amalgamated Copper. In his opinion copper was too high; he analyzed the company and saw no reason for the price of the stock. So, against the advice of Keene and other big operators, he began to sell it. In this he showed his perception was more shrewd and accurate than that of men who had been playing the market for many years.

Then he found out that the Guggenheims needed two smelters on the Pacific Coast in order to combat the encroachments of the Rockefeller mining interests. They had made ineffectual efforts to buy these smelters. Baruch went out to the coast and bought them. It was a fine piece of industrial diplomacy and strategy, evidence of which Mr. Baruch had given in the Liggett & Myers deal for Ryan. The Guggenheims paid him $1,000,000 for his work. Baruch turned around and wrote two $300,000 checks, giving one each to two persons who had helped him in the matter. He said they had earned this because without their help he could not have swung the deal.

His career was not only brilliant, it was steady. At no time did he ever suffer when he crossed swords with the greatest traders in Wall Street. He had ways of getting the most accurate information, and when he got it he played it for all it was worth. He seemed to know just when to get out of the market after he had made his profit, something not known by every speculator. Keene, whose opinion ought to be as good as any, said he was the smartest trader of his time.

He was a millionaire by the time he was thirty. He had suffered a few losses but that was all in the life of a speculator. Generally he was right, as a speculator has to be. He once said, "I'm a speculator. And what is a speculator? A speculator is one who plans for the future and acts before that future arrives." Again he said that a speculator was an observer and "that he observed."

Up to the coming of the World War the life of Bernard Baruch was simply that of a man remarkably successful in the building of a great fortune. He had made it alone, and in the most difficult of arenas. At any stage of the game he could have been tripped up and ruined, but Mr. Baruch was always smart enough to take care of himself.

His active career in Wall Street was from about 1895 to 1917. He was a member of the Stock Exchange for twenty years, from 1897 to 1917, when he resigned because he felt that he should do so when he entered official life. The early part of his career was concerned principally with speculation. The latter part with industrial development. This is a side of his business life that is little known because Mr. Baruch during his active days, was never on a board of directors, or never an officer of a company, even the companies which he controlled or owned outright, like Texas Gulf Sulphur. He would never serve on a board of directors, although he was asked many times to do so, because he was still in the speculative field and he said a speculator had no business on a board.

The large industrial undertakings in which Mr. Baruch was a big factor were Texas Gulf Sulphur, Utah Copper, Intercontinental Rubber Company and Alaska Juneau Gold Mining Company. All of these were pioneering efforts. Texas Gulf Sulphur enabled the United States to retain control of the world sulphur market. The Utah Copper Company by the development of the Jackling process for mining porphyry low grade rock doubled the world output of copper. Intercontinental Rubber showed that rubber could be made from the guayule plant. It was the beginning of a development which Mr. Baruch believed eventually would enable American

manufacturers to grow their own rubber in Mexico and
in other parts of the United States. Alaska Juneau was
a pioneering effort which achieved success when gold
was profitably extracted from ore running 80¢ to the
ton, a thing that would have been called madness a few
years before.

Mr. Baruch had met Woodrow Wilson just before
the latter was nominated in the summer of 1912. He
had gone down to Princeton to see the New Jersey Governor, not much interested. When he came away from
the visit he declared that he had met one of the few
great men of the world. He was greatly impressed.

Neither did Mr. Wilson forget. Early in 1917 he appointed Mr. Baruch to a position on the Council of
National Defense. His part of the big job was that of
head of the raw material division. Mr. Baruch threw
himself heart and soul into the job and he was very
successful in getting things done. He had never been
in politics, knew and cared nothing about such things.
He only saw the job at hand and bent every effort in
getting it done. There was nothing in it for him; in
fact, he lost money by leaving Wall Street and going
to Washington. There were fortunes to be made in the
Street during those War years, even by brains far less
capable than Mr. Baruch's. But he elected to be one of
those ardent disciples who followed the light of the
Princeton Professor. It was a great light, and Mr.
Baruch saw it perhaps more clearly than any other.

In 1918 President Wilson appointed Mr. Baruch to
the Chairmanship of the War Industries Board. This
is a dry sounding title and carries none of the glamour

and color of—say that of major-general! But Chairman Baruch had more power in his position than ten major-generals. In fact, he had more power than any other man except the President himself.

It was a tremendous undertaking. Mr. Baruch had autocratic control over every industry in America. This great Board had to function not only for us, but for the Allies as well. It had to keep things regulated and keep them moving in the right direction with all possible speed. Other wars had been fought with the horrible spectacle of thousands of soldiers sent to their deaths through the inefficiency of home officials. It was up to Mr. Baruch to see that this did not happen again. And it did not.

Red-tape he met with lightning-like shears. Anything incompetent, human or otherwise, that got in the way of his great machine was speedily removed. He worked all hours; in fact, there were no hours. He stayed on his feet as long as he could stay awake, then slept to get strength for another go at it.

He hired an entire floor of a big office building for himself and staff. One day one of his secretaries complained that they needed more room and no more rooms were to be had. "All right. Buy the building," ordered Mr. Baruch. He spared neither himself nor his fortune. At one time he paid out of his own pocket the expenses of a mission to Europe to study the distribution of materials sent across the ocean. He also put up money to establish a hospital for the workers of the Board during the flu epidemic.

What Bernard Baruch did as Chairman of the W. I. B.

is history. He did not work for his own interests, and he actually lost much of his fortune in taking on the duties. But he did vision the larger part of the picture. Not for an instant did he forget the millions of boys over there, depending on him for everything they had to fight with. There could be no falling down on the job, and there was not. It was a fine unselfish performance, and those who like to criticize Mr. Baruch should remember it.

The War was over. It was a time of going home. At the time there were several thousand girls in Washington, employees of the W. I. B. Many of them had come from points far distant, to enjoy both the work and the excitement. Now they were through and Mr. Baruch was worried about them. So he offered to pay their railroad fares home. There were many who accepted and it cost him quite a lot.

After the end of the War came the Peace Conference at Paris. President Wilson went over and with him went Mr. Baruch as adviser. That great gathering in Paris made history—some sort anyway—and Mr. Baruch saw it made. He thought it was wrong to bear down too hard on Germany, not because of any kindly feelings towards the Germans, but because it was not good business. He argued that an utterly crushed nation could hardly be expected to make good on reparations, that half a loaf was better than none. He viewed the proposition with his Wall Street eyes and saw that a too heavy foot on Germany's neck meant all liabilities and no assets. He thought, too, that the United States ought to have some security or guarantee for the great war debts—and this didn't make him any more popular with the Allied diplomats. But the great War President trusted and admired his adviser. And later, when Mr. Wilson was stricken and lay ill in bed for months, Mr. Baruch was one of the very few who were allowed to see him. Their friendship ended only with the President's death.

The end of the War saw a great let-down to both soldiers and those who had worked as closely with them as had Mr. Baruch. It was difficult to see things in the old way. Speculation in the greatest market in the world now seemed flat. He had been in public life, had seen a larger sphere of action, and now had no taste to tie himself to a ticker again. There was as much to do as before, only more leisure to do it in. He still wanted to help.

His interest centered in the great question of agriculture, and the vast army of men engaged in it. They needed help and he meant to give it to them. After the Administration changed hands he had no office with sweeping powers, but he did have a knowledge of how to get things done, and a force of men who liked to work with him. In spite of his connection with Wall Street the farmers liked and trusted him.

He gave a great deal of time and effort to the case of the tobacco growers at one time; he worked out a campaign to take the surplus off their hands and saved them from a bad situation. He was appealed to by the Kansas State Board of Agriculture and again he answered with a plan which was not only successful in solving their problem, but helped in other parts of the country. For these efforts and many others in the far-mers' behalf he charged no fee. The game was enjoyable for itself.

He did not reopen his offices for ten years after the War was over. The new interests took him all over the country and an office was superfluous. Farmers were not the only ones who availed themselves of his uncanny wisdom. He was a Democrat but the succession of Republican Presidents were not above asking his advice from time to time.

Mr. Baruch has always kept himself in fine physical trim. He is as straight today as when he fancied himself destined for a career at West Point. There is an amusing story about him, which happened during his stay in Washington during the War. One day while walking out of a restaurant, he was imprisoned in a revolving door opening on the street, by three young college men who thought of having some fun with him. They kept the dignified official trotting swiftly around with the door for several minutes, to his great disgust. Finally they released him. He was angry and began to lecture one of the youths, who looked like a football player, and who had been drinking. The husky youth bristled and growled, "You needn't get sore. If you're looking for trouble, you can have it."

Things looked squally for a minute, but just then a bystander who had known Mr. Baruch for years, stepped up to the young belligerent and whispered, "Young fel-low, you'd better let that grey-haired man alone. He's got a punch like a mule, and I've seen him hit a man so hard once he almost changed his religion!"

The young man noted the glitter in the Baruch eyes and also his powerful athletic shoulders and decided to take the advice. He walked away, muttering.

Mr. Baruch had made a good sized fortune and after the War years, decided to enjoy it; he had no inclination to spend all his time piling up dollars. He had bought a huge estate in his native state of South Carolina, and to this he often went for rest and hunting. This big country estate of 17,000 acres is called Hobcaw Barony and is located in the Georgetown coastal region. There are within its boundaries islands, rice fields, timberlands, pine woods and marshes—a diversified and beautiful sweep of territory. The first owner of Hobcaw was Lord Carteret, who held it as a royal grant. Later the Huger family held it for generations, but after the Civil War it passed out of their hands. Mr. Baruch bought it up piece by piece, until he got it all together again.

Mr. Baruch has been called "The Mystery Man of Wall Street," a title probably given him by many who could not understand how he did the successful things in his career. To them he was like a magician who pulls rabbits out of silk hats—only he substituted dollars for rabbits.

He could have held many high offices in the service of his country, but rich men are not supposed to make good public servants for some reason as yet unknown. He himself felt he ought to decline the offer of President Wilson to be Secretary of the Treasury on that account. The President could not understand this viewpoint. Nor could a great many other people who felt that Mr.

Baruch would have made an outstanding public official.

Mr. Baruch once said, as he discussed his life, "I've had a full and varied life. If my call should come to-morrow I'd have nothing to complain about. During my younger days in Wall Street I had contact with the older financiers and with the great railroad barons—the ferocious, cigar-chewing men who drove back the frontier with every blow on a spike. Then years later, I was in Washington during the most stirring period of the War; after that I went to Paris and saw the statesmen of a dozen flags sew the map of Europe into something that they hoped would hold together. All this came to me before I was forty-eight. Yes, I've had a vivid life and I've no reason to envy any man."

In 1934 Mr. Baruch announced that he was going to quit Wall Street and move his office uptown, in order to get more leisure in which to think and reflect on public affairs. He wanted to write his memoirs, too. He does his writing at Hobcaw Barony and at his home on Fifth Avenue, where he has his study on the top floor. This study and Hobcaw are highly inaccessible places. There is not even a telephone connection with the outside world at Hobcaw.

In some ways Mr. Baruch's career has been unique. When the ship of state has been skidding around, those in power have not hesitated to call him in and ask him to help. This tall, smiling, keen-eyed man could always be depended upon to take up a tangle, look it over and promptly straighten it out. He knew what made the wheels go round, and, when they stopped, what would make them go again. If the United States had any such office as consulting-physician and business-manager there is nobody in the country who could fill it better than Bernard Mannes Baruch.

GEORGE BRUCE CORTELYOU

SECRETARY TO PRESIDENTS AND
CABINET OFFICIAL

(Photo by Blank-Stoller, Inc.)

GEORGE BRUCE CORTELYOU

GEORGE BRUCE CORTELYOU

SECRETARY TO PRESIDENTS AND
CABINET OFFICIAL

B OSTON was in gala attire one day in the early
1880's. Flags hung from every mast and pole,
colored bunting was festooned on the fronts of the
buildings, people thronged the crooked, narrow streets,
waiting. The center of attraction seemed to be around the
old Railroad Station on Kneeland Street. Here thousands
of people had been milling around since early morning.
The reason: the President of the United States was paying a visit to the city and everybody wanted to see him.

Near the main door where President Arthur was due
to come out, stood an eager faced young man. He was
very handsome, tall, with coal black hair and remarkably vivid eyes. He was a student at the New England
Conservatory of Music. Now this young man had seen
celebrities before; the great of the music world, of which
he was a humble part, poured into Boston, and he had
seen and heard many famous musicians. But he had
never seen a President of his own country. He wondered
just what such a high and mighty personage would look
like.

The great man came and the crowd surged around him.
Bands played and whistles tooted and the people cheered
frantically. The police and soldiers cleared a pathway to

the waiting carriage but it was slow progress. The young man who had come to see the spectacle managed to work his way near. His keen eyes noted everything, the President, his party, but especially another man who seemed to have more to do than anybody else. It was the President's secretary, F. J. Phillips.

Our young friend watched this man, found out who he was, and finally when there was a halt in the proceedings, pushed his way close to the carriage and spoke to him.

"You—you're the President's secretary, aren't you? That must be wonderful. I'd like to have that job some day!"

Mr. Phillips smiled down at the eager-eyed young fellow, and nodded. Then the carriage pulled away, leaving the young man staring after it.

The name of that young music student was George Bruce Cortelyou, and it seemed a strange ambition for a future musician to have. About the nearest a musician ever gets to a President is in one of the army or navy bands that sometimes play in Washington.

The incident must have made quite an impression, for soon after this young Cortelyou was busy studying stenography. The career of music was abandoned. Of course he had no definite idea of where the thing would land him, but it seemed likely that a young man who possessed a knowledge of shorthand would have an entering wedge into the business and political world. And that was about all this quiet but confident young man wanted— an entering wedge. The rest he felt he could supply.

George B. Cortelyou was born in New York City, July 26, 1862. Cortelyou is a French Huguenot name and his

ancestors had come to America from France in early
Colonial times, probably during one of those migrations
of Huguenots resulting from the severe persecutions in
the seventeenth century. His father was a successful business man and numbered among his friends such men as
Horace Greeley and Thurlow Weed.

Young Cortelyou attended public schools and later entered Hempstead Institute on Long Island. Here he met
a Miss Hinds, daughter of the principal of the school, and
some years later she became Mrs. Cortelyou.

From Hempstead he went to the State Normal School
at Westfield, Massachusetts, although his father had intended that he should enter Harvard. After this he went
to Boston, to take up the study of music for which he had
an aptitude.

But as we have seen, the musical career was given up
and he had bent his attention on the mastery of stenography. He had a remarkable brain and a facility for
mastering almost anything he turned his attention to. He
attained such proficiency that soon he was appointed instructor of stenography in a school in New York City.
But it wasn't teaching and it wasn't music that this
young man was destined for, although he would have
gone far in either. Two things explain this man's remarkable aptitude for successfully fulfilling almost everything
he might turn his hand to—the Yankee genius and his
French Huguenot blood. The combination has produced
many remarkable people.

For a time Cortelyou was a stenographer-reporter in
the New York Supreme Court. Here he made a name for
himself, with his speed and accuracy in shorthand, and

by his many other efficient qualities. He was a striking looking man, one that attracted attention in whatever gathering he happened to be. He was tall, broad-shouldered and athletic in figure, despite the fact that he never participated in any sport. His eyes were large and expressive, and under a close-clipped moustache was a firm, determined mouth. His black hair was brushed straight back from a high intelligent looking forehead. And his clothes always appeared to have just come from the tailor's. Certainly he was a distinguished and individual looking man, and later the cartoonists were to have a subject which even their art could not make ridiculous. No matter how preposterous other figures were in the cartoons (not excepting Presidents!) that of Cortelyou was always spick-and-span and proper.

In 1889 he was appointed a stenographer to the Post-Office Inspector for New York City. This was the Government at last, although not Washington! But the hands of fate were reaching out for this personable young man, apparently buried in a dingy post-office building. He worked at this job for two years, always efficient and dependable. Then he was appointed confidential stenographer to the Surveyor of the Port of New York. In that same year came the opportunity to go to the city where secretaries to Presidents live—Washington, D. C. But the job assigned to young Mr. Cortelyou was only that of stenographer in the office of the Fourth Assistant Postmaster-General.

Before taking this job he had a chance to become private secretary to the famous Thomas C. Platt, which would have been a good connection, but somehow Wash-

ington called to Cortelyou and he turned down the offer
of the New York boss.

It was now a case of being a little toad in a big puddle.
Washington was full of big shots and Cortelyou had seen
enough of public life by now to realize just how much
chance he had. First, he had no political pull at all.
Neither did he have any social influence. He would have
to depend on his own abilities—plus a bit of luck.

But though he seemed buried in a great government
machine, he determined to fit himself for anything that
might happen in the way of promotion. It seemed to him
that a knowledge of law would be a distinct asset. To
get it he would have to devote his nights to study, attending to his job in the daytime. He took his degree of
Bachelor of Laws from Georgetown University and that
of Master of Laws from Columbia University.

And now he was ready for opportunity if it knocked
at his door. Things had been known to turn up, even in a
place like Washington with its thousands of ambitious
and self-seeking men.

In 1892 Grover Cleveland was elected President of the
United States for the second time and shortly afterwards
the "open season" was declared on Republican office
holders. The Civil Service was not there to help them;
it was this same Grover Cleveland who was to give that
movement meaning and stability.

But for some reason Cortelyou was not one of those
turned out. His boss, the Fourth Assistant-Postmaster
General liked him and appreciated his qualities. His
name was Robert A. Maxwell.

The story goes that one day, sometime later, at a

cabinet meeting, President Cleveland said, "I wish you gentlemen would bear in mind that I want a first-class shorthand man. Some of you must have the right kind of man in your departments, and I wish you would look around and let me have one."

The Postmaster-General, Mr. Bissell, replied, "I believe I have in my department the very man you want. He's a handsome young fellow, smart as lightning, and as methodical as a machine. And above all, he's a gentleman."

"That's the kind of a man I want," said Mr. Cleveland. "Who is he, and where is he, and when can I have him?"

"He's a New Yorker named Cortelyou," said the Postmaster-General. "I'll speak to him and we will send him up to you tomorrow."

Cortelyou appeared next day. Mr. Cleveland looked at him, seemed to approve of him. But the young stenographer had something on his mind.

"Mr. President, it's a great honor you have conferred upon me. But I can't enter your service under false pretenses. I am a Republican. I have stayed on only because Mr. Maxwell requested it."

Mr. Cleveland, a bluff and hearty man, replied, "Good Heavens, my boy, I'm not interested in your politics. What I'm interested in is whether you are a good stenographer. And Bissell says you are."

Some will say that was luck playing into the hands of this stenographer. But if he hadn't prepared himself for just such a promotion, luck would have passed him by. At last he was in the White House, a member of the

Presidential staff. And he determined that nothing could stop him now.

Young men who have dreams don't always supply the other ingredient—work to make the dreams come true. But Cortelyou had both ingredients. He was faithful, he fitted himself in every conceivable way for any promotion that might occur. He plugged, he kept his mouth shut, and he never dodged responsibility. There were efforts made to displace the Republican blacksheep in the Democratic fold, but if ever there was a rock in the White House, Grover Cleveland was it. He liked his very efficient stenographer and in his service the young man remained. As a matter of fact, Mr. Cleveland thought so much of him that he recommended him to his successor on his retirement from office. This is one of the few instances where a Republican got his start through a Democrat.

Again the political pendulum swung in 1896 and William McKinley, a Republican, was elected President. House-cleaning came again but Cortelyou was by now a fixture; he became assistant secretary to the new President. Only one step away from the job he had cast such longing eyes upon on that day in Boston.

A few years after this ill health compelled the secretary to the President to resign, and Cortelyou was promoted to the coveted post. Thus it came about that this silent, hard-working young man, who had never served any apprenticeship in politics, who possessed neither backing nor influence, and whose name was utterly unknown to the vast bulk of his countrymen, became Secretary to the President.

Even in those days of the last of the old century, it was a post almost as exhausting as that of the Chief Executive's. The Secretary had to act as buffer between the President and the public. He had to possess great tact and diplomacy, had to sift out the ones who should see the President from the ones who were time-wasters. There was, too, a large clerical staff to direct and a tremendous routine business. Practically it was an "all-time" job; there were no hours when the secretary was not subject to call.

Cortelyou was very much in the public eye now. If the politicians hadn't known him before, they did now. He was always on the job and there was nothing his keen eyes overlooked.

Soon the Spanish-American War came along and from the day the battleship Maine was blown up in Havana Harbor until Spain surrendered, Cortelyou was indeed a man-of-all-work. All during the hot summer he worked day and night. The telegraph office in the White House became a War Chamber, and there were hourly meetings of the Cabinet, twenty-four hours a day. Cortelyou was President McKinley's right hand man, always cool when others blew up, always ready to help in any way. Later in the Philippine Campaign and the Boxer trouble he was the same efficient, hard working man.

And then one day in September, 1901 came the tragedy that stunned the whole nation. President McKinley had gone to Buffalo to attend the Exposition. There had been talk of assassination some time before; one attempt on his life had been made. But McKinley had been a soldier in the war, was without fear and decided he was in no danger.

On September 6th the President was driven to the Temple of Music, where a reception was held. There was an opportunity for the public to meet him. After the line of people had been going up to shake his hand for a time, a young man stepped up in his turn. The man's hand was bandaged and as President McKinley smilingly reached out to greet him, two shots came from the bandaged hand of the fellow. He had concealed a short pistol inside the bandage.

The President staggered and fell back into the arms of his secretary. And it was to him that the mortally wounded man spoke, saying, "Cortelyou—my wife—be careful —don't let her know."

The assassin was overpowered. It was Mr. Cortelyou, the cool and efficient, who now took charge. He ordered the stricken President taken to the hospital and placed him under the surgeon's care within an incredibly short time after the shooting. And it was he who so thoughtfully arranged for the interview between the wounded President and his invalid wife. From that day until Mr. McKinley was laid to rest, it was Mr. Cortelyou who arranged everything. The amount of work and strain he underwent was terrific and towards the end he was near the breaking point. But outwardly he was the calm, well poised man familiar to those who frequented the White House. After the funeral ceremonies he rushed to Washington and an hour after his train arrived, he was seated at the side of the new President, ready as ever for duty.

An iron man. And truly an iron man was needed to keep step with the new President, Theodore Roosevelt. Mr. Cortelyou was retained because Mr. Roosevelt had known him and thought highly of his ability.

Of course the habits of the strenuous Teddy are known to everybody. It was his keenest delight to wear down his friends in any sort of endeavor. He was tireless himself and many a companion had to go to bed after an experience trying to keep up with him. But there is no evidence that he ever made his equally tough secretary quit. And strangely enough, Mr. Cortelyou ignored all forms of athletic endeavor. His sole exercise was his work and the walk to and from the White House to his own home.

One day in the spring of 1902 two newspaper correspondents went to the White House to interview President Roosevelt. There had been a good deal of talk about an appointment that might be made in the Cabinet, in case the man then holding the post was removed. The President told the correspondents there was no truth in the reports, that the man would stay. But the newspaper men persisted and wanted to know who would be his successor, "just in case."

President Roosevelt turned on his heel in his impulsive, characteristic fashion and called out, "Oh, Cortelyou, step here a moment." Then he said, "Whenever a vacancy shall occur in the Cabinet it is my purpose to appoint Mr. Cortelyou if he will accept, and I want that distinctly understood."

Mr. Cortelyou smiled and went back to his desk. The correspondents published what the President had said but

few people believed it. Cabinet posts were not usually
filled by promotion from the secretarial ranks, especially
by men with no political influence. That wasn't to be
believed.

But not long afterwards a new department was created,
the Department of Commerce and Labor. It was to be
an important department, one of vast scope, and the man
who headed it would have to be a most capable official.
President Roosevelt surprised everybody by appoint-
ing his Secretary, George B. Cortelyou to that post. And
the ex-stenographer, without any pull or influence, became a full-fledged member of the President's Cabinet.
Pretty good for anybody who as a young man had
thought the post of Secretary to the President a sufficiently high place in the sun!

Once again Mr. Cortelyou took on brand new duties.
The new department employed about ten thousand at that
time in its various branches. A score of scattered bureaus
were placed under its jurisdiction, reorganized and simpli-
fied. The new head weeded out politics, cut red-tape and
did an excellent job of it.

In 1904 President Roosevelt made another of his surprising moves. He appointed Mr. Cortelyou Chairman
of the National Republican Committee and manager of
his campaign for re-election. This exacting job had always been held by politicians skilled in the art of cam-
paigning, but Mr. Roosevelt wanted Cortelyou. As usual
he conducted his assignment most efficiently. Mr. Roosevelt was returned to office. Then Mr. Cortelyou got his
second Cabinet position, that of Postmaster-General.
Here were new duties, an entirely new business to learn,

and with his usual quick mastery of problems he succeeded in this position, as he had in all the others.

In March, 1907 he was appointed Secretary of the Treasury, his third Cabinet post. No other man in history has held three Cabinet positions. It was a remarkable achievement, and still more amazing because it was made by a man with no political influence. There was never any doubt about Mr. Cortelyou's ability, even in the minds of those politically against him. Sticks thrown at him invariably turned out to be boomerangs.

He ended his political career when Mr. Roosevelt left office. He had been holding down positions paying only a tenth of the salary he could have commanded in private enterprise. He had received scores of tempting offers to go into business and now he felt he should do this.

The long and varied service performed had been well done. He could retire from public life with a fine record. In the book "Forty-two Years in the White House" by "Ike" Irwin Hoover, there appears on one page a list of "bests," under the heading "We Elect." And beside the caption "Best Secretary to the President" is the name of George Bruce Cortelyou. That is quite an honor, to be thus selected by an unbiased observer who had seen many Presidential secretaries.

Other opinions were equally satisfactory—and here are what three Presidents said of him:

Cleveland: "I class Cortelyou and Lamont as two of the brightest young men I have ever known."

McKinley: "Cortelyou is a wonderful fellow. He never loses his head."

Roosevelt: "Cortelyou has a remarkable knowledge of public men and public questions. He is invaluable."

Many men go into public life after years of service in business, as Alvan Fuller, Andrew Mellon, Bernard Baruch and others. But Mr. Cortelyou reversed the process. He made his mark in public life first, then went into business afterwards. Of course this has its drawbacks; nobody likes to sit in the grandstand after he has had the fun of running with the ball. The spotlight has its glamour.

But Mr. Cortelyou had had plenty and now he wanted to see what business was like. There were many big concerns that wanted him. But the Consolidated Gas Company of New York got him. This was and is one of the biggest public utility companies in the world, the second in the United States. It supplies gas, electricity and steam power to Manhattan and outlying sections. It serves millions of customers.

At that time the big gas company was in bad odor with many of its customers. The company had not learned the now generally accepted course of service and goodwill. The gas and juice were supplied and that ended the company's concern.

Mr. Cortelyou found a strange lack of cordiality and interest of his employees towards the public they served. It was hard to find out why. So he took to going about by himself, asking thousands of questions, and seeing many people. He changed the dingy looking payment stations where people went to pay their bills into attractive offices. He taught his thousands of employees how to be so pleasant that barter in gas and electricity was a positive pleasure to the public. It took time and patience. The result was a complete right about face from the old careless service to an up-to-date one.

The career of George Bruce Cortelyou is the complete answer to the statement so often heard by young men (and older ones for that matter), "Oh, I've got no pull. There's no chance for an unknown fellow in a great big system; you're lost." There were times when he was only one among thousands, all trying to get their feet on the ladder to fame and fortune. What did he have that the others did not? We grant him a superior brain and a perfect set of nerves and muscles—but all the rest he supplied. He prepared himself for every contingency. He could wait (a most valuable asset), he kept his mouth shut, and he had a confidence and determination to succeed at any task, no matter how awe-inspiring it might be. In his heart he must have been scared a good many times at the new and unknown assignments put up to him. But he never showed it. He was a good industrial soldier and grew into a good industrial general.

JAMES DRUMMOND DOLE

WHO BUILT A GREAT INDUSTRY OUT OF PINEAPPLES

(Keystone View Co.)

JAMES DRUMMOND DOLE

JAMES DRUMMOND DOLE

WHO BUILT A GREAT INDUSTRY OUT OF PINEAPPLES

WE are familiar with the story of the country boy who leaves the farm, goes to a big city, and carves out a successful career for himself. It is an old story. But the story reversed is not so common.

James Drummond Dole was born in a city; to be exact, Jamaica Plain, Massachusetts. Jamaica Plain is one of the many suburbs of Boston, and it is safe to say that no cows have been seen there for a good many generations, and if it ever did have farms, it was long ago.

His father, Charles F. Dole, had no connection with farming either. He was a minister and his church was in that same suburb of Boston. The boy, James, grew up in the pleasant district of the Old Hub, lived the same life as any other lad, with ball playing in local fields, bicycling and the like. His orbit was distinctly of the city with no suggestion of agriculture. He attended Agassiz Grammar School, and later Roxbury Latin, a famous preparatory school.

Yet in spite of his environment this young fellow felt the call of the soil; he always wanted to grow things. There was an unescapable urge to plant, to cultivate. For several years, when he was in his teens, he experimented with a small vegetable garden, learning a lot about soil, planting and the care of growing things. Had the farming urge been a mere passing fancy, these summer sessions with potato bugs, beetles and all the other pests of agriculture would have cured him. But no such thing happened; he still wanted to make agriculture of some sort his life work.

After preparatory school days at Roxbury Latin he entered Harvard, graduating from that university in 1899. But before that, as far back as 1896, his eyes had been turned on the far distant land of the Hawaiian Islands. A thing as simple as a prospectus, extolling the delights and benefits of agriculture in those semi-tropical lands, planted the idea in his head.

There was a reason why young Dole was ready to consider the Hawaiian Islands as a possible spot for him to investigate, if not do more. His father's cousin, Sanford B. Dole, was Hawaii's leading citizen, head of the Provisional Government. When the people of the Islands overthrew the Government of the Queen, this Yankee from New England, known and admired by the Hawaiian people, was chosen to be their leader. He was the first President of the Republic and later, when the Islands were annexed to the United States as a territory, he was appointed Governor. So young Dole knew something about this land, knew it was a Paradise, that it had a delightful climate, that it had a wonderfully rich soil. Surely there must be an opportunity for a young man in such a place. If anybody could make a living at farming in the stubborn, rocky soil of New England, the chances of success in a place with a much warmer climate and a soil not worked out would be much greater.

But there was the question of leaving his parents, his home, the land of his birth and all his friends. There was some troubled thinking, balancing the assets against the liabilities of such an adventure. But one day he said good-bye to his father and mother, boarded a train, and left them for the West. At San Francisco he took a steamer and finally one day he landed in the Islands about which he had thought so much. Hawaii. Honolulu. How different it all was from everything he had known.

At the time there was a coffee boom on in the Islands. Sugar was the main crop, but for some reason young Dole was not interested in sugar; he wanted to be a pioneer, to start in something new. And coffee was new to the Islands. He studied it, and after some investigation, decided that he did not want to become a coffee planter. Still he was in no hurry to make a decision on the larger problem of becoming a farmer of something in this new land which had begun to have a strong fascination for him. Possibly there was a hunch that opportunity for him was there, even though he could not quite see it.

One day he learned of a piece of homestead land, located out at Wahiawa that was to be sold at auction. He went out, thought it had possibilities, and bought it. He was now a farmer, an owner of land in Hawaiian Territory.

Now to see what this rich soil and wonderful climate

would do. He planted all the vegetables he had known in his native land, using New England as a sort of yard-stick; perhaps beans, cabbages and tomatoes would grow twice as big. But as an experiment he also planted some-thing with which he was unfamiliar—pineapples.

Those queer looking things had been introduced to the Hawaiian Islands only a few years before, in 1890. Some plants had been brought from Florida and others from Australia, to see what they would do in the rich soil and mild climate of the Islands. They did very well, producing fine, sweet and juicy fruit. A few years later a planter named Captain Kidwell shipped a few cases of the canned fruit to San Francisco. This was the begin-ning of the industry.

Young Dole saw in this ugly looking but luscious tast-ing fruit a possibility. The local territory as a market was out; anybody could grow them there who wanted to take the trouble. But he visioned that biggest market in the world, the United States. Pineapples were not cultivated there, but an appetite for them could be!

The pineapple itself presented a difficulty or two. It ripened with a rush. Picked ripe it would be rotten before getting to the market of the United States; the steamer service in those days was poor. And picked green, it would not ripen and become sweet as some fruits did, namely the banana. How then, to get the fruit, in its sweet and delicious fullness to the big market. In cans. That was the big idea.

As is sometimes the case with big ideas, the author of this one discovered that somebody else had had the same one. There was a firm already selling canned pineapple in the United States, the fruit coming from the West Indies. However, further investigation showed that the fruit was picked green, canned—and the matter of sweetness left to the consumer.

So young Mr. Dole's idea was slightly different. Pineapple with its own natural sweetness, and pineapple picked before that sweetness came were two very different things. He would can his ripe, on the spot—and no matter how long it was in transportation, it would be just as nature intended it to be when the customer five thousand miles away opened it.

It was a fine idea, but there was an anchor deep in the mud before his ship of industry could shove off. Capital. It took money to buy even simple machinery to start a small cannery. Also some special knowledge; young Mr. Dole's four years stay at Harvard had taught him nothing whatever about canning. Also, he had made a false start in planting; he had used lime to de-acid the soil, only to discover that the pineapple was one of the fruits that thrived on that very acid.

When in doubt a New Englander generally goes home. Both the things he needed were there—capital and knowledge. In that compact little section of the United States he could dig up both. So back home he went, with his fine idea.

Boston is supposed to be one of the best spots on earth in which to float a scheme. But for some reason most of the friends of the optimistic Mr. Dole could not see a fortune in such a simple thing as a little known fruit put up in cans. That was their bad judgment; if they had had sense enough to go in on the ground floor, now they would be—but that is getting ahead of the story.

Mr. Dole left his homeland once again, but little richer than when he had arrived. The funds he had hoped to raise were much too meagre for a decent start. On the long train ride across the continent he could see failure staring him in the face, and, worse luck, failure because of insufficient backing, not because of the lack of soundness in his idea.

But in San Francisco luck smiled on him, far more sweetly than it had in his native Boston. He talked of his scheme again and a wholesale grocer listened, liked it, and invested sufficient money for the start.

Once back in the Islands Mr. Dole started things moving. He had got his specialist in canning, a man from Maine who knew about canning fish. With the simple equipment for a start—a few Chinese field workers, a force of fifteen all told—the venture got under way. Young Dole worked day and night, and at all the tasks involved. He worked like a Chinaman in the fields, he ran the paring machine, he operated the canning machine, packed cases; was, in fact, man of all work. It was terribly hard work, but all of it enjoyable; he could see something ahead perhaps denied to others.

The first year's pack was a disappointment, not in the quality of the product but in the amount done. By the hardest kind of work Dole's little company packed 1893 cases. However, the product was well received wherever it was introduced. It now became a question of getting more land, more pineapples planted, a general growth all around.

The following year, 1904, the pack came to 8810 cases, a good increase. In 1905 it jumped to 25,022. And in 1906 it was 31,934. The next year saw a fine jump, 108,000 cases. The idea was sound, and the Dole pineapple in cans was becoming known for its fine individual flavor.

However, in 1908 there came what seemed like overproduction. The goods did not move fast enough in the market, and there was a still bigger crop of new pineapples looming up. Mr. Dole had an idea that the key to the situation lay in educating more people to try the new product. At that time comparatively few people used pineapple; and those who did, used it too infrequently for the peace of mind of those pioneers in the Hawaiian Islands. By then there were competitors, you may be sure. There are never any competitors when the new thing is tried; the onlookers are always willing to watch the first fellow risk breaking his neck. When he accomplishes what he sets out to do and success smiles on his daring, they are all delighted to come in.

However, Mr. Dole was not peeved because of this. In fact, he had brains and gumption enough to help them all out of the hole together. He formed an association of all the pineapple growers in Hawaii. Together they would launch a big advertising campaign, telling the world not about Dole pineapples, but all the Hawaiian grown pineapples. This was the first movement of this kind—a sort of one-for-all, all-for-one campaign in advertising.

The association sent out competent salesmen, especially to those sections of the United States where pineapple had not gone too well. Advertisements were placed in magazines and newspapers, telling of the goodness and virtues of the product. Over a million pamphlets, with recipes, were sent out. The result: the huge stock was moved with such celerity that there was no doubt about what to do with the coming crop.

After that there was never any serious difficulty in disposing of the stock. In 1912 the pack came to 500,000 cases, and six years later it was over a million. In 1923 it was two million cases and in 1926, three million.

Practically all of the special machinery used in packing pineapple originated in the Dole cannery works. There came a need for some piece of machinery, and the need was met. Original methods in cultivation were used. The Dole concern pioneered in this. They used paper mulch in growing the young plants; this prevents the growth of weeds and at the same time keeps the soil soft and the temperature uniform. Many things had to be learned, by patient experimentation and painful error.

Once again Mr. Dole had to go through a period when everybody thought he was wrong; to put through a gigantic scheme with not much more help than he got in his first venture in Hawaii. However, this time he succeeded in selling enough stock to start the venture, over a million dollars worth.

Perhaps, to the general run of people, the idea did not seem any too bright. What Mr. Dole intended doing was to buy an entire island, the sixth largest in the Hawaiian group, and plant it with pineapple. This was in 1922 when pineapple was quite well known everywhere and the demand very good. That part was all right.

But this island of Lanai! It was the black sheep of the group, quite different from the others with their luxuriant growth. To be sure, it did have *one* luxuriant growth, of giant cactus spreading all over the island, and prohibiting the growth of anything else. Nothing but this stubborn, prickly, useless plant. Sugar planting had been tried and it had failed. A few cattle eked a precarious living on this unattractive island. Poor cattle and cactus. No wonder everybody out there doubted Mr. Dole's wisdom.

But he knew what was under that cactus. It was the finest black, virgin soil, running down (as they discovered later) to a depth in places of one hundred feet. Enough to bury Jamaica Plain and most of Boston!

Mr. Dole had his way, bought his Cactus-Paradise and started to root the pest out of it. Giant tractors were used in teams, hauling great chains which dug up the cactus plants. They curry-combed that island until the last of the evil was destroyed, leaving a perfectly nice island covered with the richest of black soil. And everybody had said Mr. Dole was wrong. He was not wrong. He knew both his soil and his pineapples—and pineapples are a very temperamental plant.

Still he wasn't done. More millions were poured into developing the island. There was nobody there in the beginning, and several thousand workers would have to be housed and taken care of. Furthermore it would have to be made an attractive place to live in or the people would leave. So up went buildings by the hundreds— houses, stores, a huge auditorium for movies, concerts and holiday festivities. It was a crowd of mixed nationalities that would live there, and they would have to be kept contented. Radio telephones were installed. Other things established were a golf course, tennis courts, a hospital and a schoolhouse.

But how about a harbor, scoffed the wiseacres? Lanai had none. And the Pacific was anything but pacific in that quarter at times. How were steamers to be loaded with the millions of pineapples? Answer that, Mr. Dole, they said.

He did. He dumped 116,000 tons of rock into a huge breakwater for protection against rough water, and dredged a channel sixty-five feet deep. Lanai, the "Ugly Duckling" of the Hawaiian group, was de-cactussed, housed and beharbored. And ready to grow more pineapples than any other place.

The first planting took place in 1924. And by 1930 the Lanai crop was equal to the yield of all the rest of the Hawaiian plantations combined!

The industry has kept on growing. The Dole plant in Honolulu can can over one million pineapples in twenty-four hours, and has done even better than that.

Mr. James Drummond Dole is the man who gave us pineapples. His was the idea, his was the pioneering work, his genius kept it going.

All from an idea of a lonesome boy in a far off land, too proud and stubborn to go home and bury himself in a job under someone else.

Ideas! The grandest thing in the world. Strangely

enough the same opportunity exists today; young men have the same chance that this lad from Jamaica Plain had. In 1900 there was the same old refrain, "Oh, there's no chance now; everything has been done." It was the same a hundred years before that, and it will be the same a hundred years from now.

Nobody asked James Dole to leave his home and go to an island five thousand miles away. Nobody showed him a picture of a pineapple and told him there was a fortune in it. Nobody told him about the can to hold its sweetness. Nobody told him to buy a derelict island and dig dollars out of it. When he did all this—there was "nothing new under the sun, no opportunity for a young fellow."

There is a saying, "To the victor belong the spoils." There is a better one, with less tarnish on it: "To the creator belong the spoils." James Dole created. He took a few ingredients, assembled them with care and brains, and built a thriving industry.

CAPTAIN ROBERT DOLLAR

WHOSE SHIPS PUT A GIRDLE ROUND THE WORLD

(Keystone View Co.)

CAPTAIN ROBERT DOLLAR

CAPTAIN ROBERT DOLLAR

WHOSE SHIPS PUT A GIRDLE ROUND THE WORLD

WHEN Robert Dollar was twelve years old he went to work in a machine-shop. The hours were long and the work confining to a lad just the age to revel in outdoor play. His first week's pay was sixty cents. After awhile he was allowed to run a lathe and this was rather fun. Still his mind would dwell on other things; he wanted something else than spending his life within the walls of a noisy, ill-lighted factory.

Whenever he could get out of the hot, metal-smelling place he would make tracks for the water front, near which the shop was located. And here, for that boy of the keen, blue eyes, was real life.

Ships! Aberdeen clippers with their teakwood planking, fastest things on the Seven Seas. And now and then a sharp-nosed rakish thing with an immense spread of canvas, audaciously challenging the ships of his own Scotland—a Yankee clipper. All sort of ships came and went. They sported the flags of every country. He used to dream about going to some of them, especially the one represented by that flag with the red and white stripes and the blue-starred field. The boy never tired of browsing about in this part of the town. He would talk for hours with the old sailors, or rather listen to the wonderful tales they had to tell.

"Some day," he would often murmur to himself, "Some day I am going to own one of those ships. And I am going to sail it around the world!"

It was no idle dream. Before he got through he owned more ships than could have found docking space in that little port of Falkirk. Ships of size and grandeur that were undreamed of by anybody at that time.

Robert Dollar was born at Falkirk, Scotland in 1844. The town is almost due west of and not many miles from Edinborough. It was in his blood to follow two things—lumber and the sea. His mother's name was Melville and the men of her family had been to sea for generations.

One of his mother's uncles owned a little lumber yard in the town and Robert's father was manager of it. The Dollars lived over the office of the yard at first, but later they moved out a bit, and had a house with a garden. There was a school of sorts in the town and to this Robert went for a time.

When he was nine years old his mother died, and in spite of his few years, the blow struck deeply. His father, unable to stand the grief, took to drinking, a course of conduct that filled young Robert with loathing. He made up his mind there and then that he would never touch liquor, and he never did.

But the father was not long a widower; he soon married a young woman of the locality and took her home to his children. She was very kind to Robert and he thought a great deal of her.

Wages were low and it was impossible to keep the boy

in school. When he was twelve he went to work in the machine-shop, which was a few miles distant, at the port. His schooling days were over.

The following year his father, tired of the grind and poverty, decided to try his luck in the new country across the ocean, the land about which he had heard such wonderful tales. So he and his wife and two sons took passage on a sailing vessel and some weeks later landed in Quebec. From there they went to Ottawa. Money was scarce and young Robert had to find work to help out. He got a job in a stave-factory where he worked twelve hours a day for the princely salary of six dollars per month! The land of opportunity was a delusion in everything but scenery; it was harder to make a living in than the old one.

The stave-factory job didn't seem to promise much. Robert was growing taller and big-boned, and he wanted to find something with more action and better chances. He learned of a lumber cutting expedition starting north from Ottawa and managed to wangle a job as cook's helper. He had heard it might be tough but he preferred taking a chance to standing still.

He was right about its being tough. The crew of lumberjacks left Ottawa in the fall in birch bark canoes and struggled for ten days up the Gatineau River. There were frequent rapids and long hard portages. Sometimes they got wet to the skin. They made camp deep in the heart of the woods, woods that seemed as old as Time itself. It seemed a wonderful life to young Robert Dollar; it was so clean everywhere, so majestic.

The men quickly built a big square cabin of huge logs.

There were no bunks put in and everybody slept on the ground with his feet towards the fire, which was always going in the center of the enclosure. The smoke went up through a hole in the roof—some of it!

Most of the men were French-Canadians and spoke only French. Young Dollar kept his ears open and picked up the language. The men worked very hard, from dawn until dark—and the cook's chore boy worked *after* dark.

It was a hard life, but a healthy one. He washed never ending stacks of dishes, brought in quantities of wood for the cook and for the fire. He cleaned the stables and helped with the oxen. In his spare moments he learned the art of swinging a woodsman's axe. Sometimes he got an opportunity to try his hand with a rifle, and the results helped the menu; game was plentiful all around the camp.

The "salary" was only a little better than that of the stave-factory, but of course, he got board and so the ten dollars a month was all velvet. Robert saved his money from instinct; he knew the lumberjacks blew theirs in when the season was over, sometimes in one big orgy. But he knew enough about life by now to appreciate what money meant.

In such surroundings you can imagine that sometimes there was a little trouble. The lumberjacks were rough men and naturally sparks flew at times. The menu especially got on their nerves, in spite of their voracious appetites. It was pork and beans, pork and beans, pork and beans—until they hated both hogs and beans.

One day, after about a month of this monotonous fare, the salt ran out. That was the last straw; they could stand the endless beans, beans, beans, but tasteless ones were altogether too much. One of the jacks, a Swede, jumped up and grabbed the young cook's helper around the neck, demanding salt. Robert, startled, scuttled back into the kitchen, telling the story to the cockney cook.

"Salt it is, young feller? Well, there is only salt enough for the foreman. Tell 'im that, me lad."

Dollar went back and told the Swede. The man lost his temper completely, crashing one fist on the table and sending the dishes flying. Then he swung another blow at the hapless young Dollar. The boy staggered and went down.

When he got up again his blue eyes were blazing and every inch of his tall, wiry frame was trembling with anger. His hard fist shot out and snapped into the Swede's jaw. Startled, the fellow set himself and gave battle. But the air was full of angular arms, strengthened by months of hard work. Back and forth struggled the two; big, slow moving ox of a man against his much younger but faster opponent. The encounter was short but lively. And it ended in a draw. Dollar had held his own. In that brief interval the chore-boy became a man— and was accepted as such by the rough lumberjacks who admired his nerve.

It would seem that his time was completely filled with work, but now and then he did get an interval all to himself. He realized that what schooling he had managed to get was very precious; he determined to hold it and to do what he could to augment it. Naturally there were no books at the temporary camp and but meagre writing materials. But he did manage to save some odd pieces of paper and from somewhere he got hold of a pencil. At every opportunity he went over the problems of arithmetic which he remembered from his schooling; he wrote sentences and jotted down other remembered things. And there was always his Bible to help, a book which he constantly read.

One afternoon the owner of the camp arrived on a tour of inspection. His name was Hiram Robinson. He poked around the camp, finally coming upon a gangling figure, bent over a bit of paper. Curious, the man came up behind him to see what was going on.

"What are you doing, boy?" he asked.

Robert had heard nobody come in and he was startled. "Why, sir, you see, the cook don't need me just now and——"

"So? Show me what you are doing."

The boss looked at the columns of figures, checked up the answers. He passed the paper back to young Dollar, and went on his way. There was no criticism, so the boy thought it was all right. He kept on with his figuring and writing.

But Mr. Robinson did not forget the instance. The next year he was sending another crew of lumberjacks to a camp up the river, miles from any white settlement. He called in young Dollar and told him he was to keep the camp accounts.

"But, sir, my writing is not good enough, and I can't spell very good."

"That's all right," smiled his boss. "I've been asking about you. You speak a little French and you're smart. You just go ahead and do your best."

He was seventeen then, tall and muscular. Such a life

either made or broke a boy. He could handle an axe
with the best of them now, and he picked up a lot about
the business. For a lad this job was a big responsibility,
as he had to keep the time of each man and figure out
his pay; there could be no chance for disputes about this.
He had to keep accurate account of the cutting, too.
There was, also, accounting for the canteen from which
the men bought various articles such as tobacco, clothing
and the like.

He determined to do his new work to the best of his
ability. It was hard, sometimes exhausting. Much figuring had to be done at night, and his eyesight suffered
from having to work so many hours by the uncertain
light from the flickering fire, the sole illumination. He
would nod over the endless task, wanting the sleep which
everybody else around him was getting. But doggedly
he kept on with it. And at the end of the season he had
the satisfaction of knowing he had done well. He was
chosen to do the same job for the next couple of years.

For five years he worked with this company. Of course
there were unusual adventures, things that weren't in the
book. Up in the Canadian backwoods they still tell how
Robert Dollar rescued a Georgian Bay lumber camp from
starvation. Savage storms had cut off the camp from its
weekly supplies. Dollar summoned a handful of men,
burlapped the hoofs of half a dozen horses and started
up a frozen river for relief. A terrific storm arose before
they had gone ten miles. The men threatened to mutiny,
but they were helpless to return without Dollar.

He set off alone on snowshoes. The fury of the storm
increased and he was blown along the ice and hurled

against a snow bank, stunned. When he recovered his senses he found his right arm broken. He had to get on in spite of the pain, to stay would mean the end. Through the snow and wind he toiled; again he was tossed into a drift by the gale. He was all resigned to perish, but made one more feeble attempt to go on, and finally stumbled from the ice to land.

Finding a ragged shelter behind a knoll he waited hours for the storm to die down, then, with his clothes as stiff as metal, he fought his way to a small village. Later he led a rescue party which located the men and horses huddled in mid-river, half frozen to death. The camp got its supplies.

The year he was twenty-one he got his first pioneering job. The firm had bought the property of a bankrupt lumber company located three hundred miles up the Du Moines River. Young Dollar got his orders. He was to go up there, take over the property and crew, run things, and then bring down the winter's logs via the river.

He went up and took over. There was the usual hard gang of lumberjacks, ready to take advantage of any new boss, especially a young one. But Dollar knew the tribe by that time. He could snap out his orders in either English or French, and they soon found out he was the boss. It took a strong man to keep these men in line but he did a good job at it.

In the drive down the river there was trouble in plenty. Jams came and it was young Dollar himself that often got them free. It was hard, dangerous work but he got his logs down safely.

Then he was made foreman of a camp of forty men.

As the seasons went on his pay rose, first $26. per month, then finally $44. per month. Most of this he saved. He never had any serious trouble with any of the crews, young though he was. And somehow he had the knack of getting an immense amount of work out of them.

In 1872 came the opportunity to try out what had long been in his mind. His savings permitted him, with the help of a partner, to buy some timberland and go into business for himself. The section he bought was in newly opened country some distance north of Toronto.

Everything went well at first and he was in line to make a nice profit on his first venture. But he held his logs too long, hoping to get the top price. A severe panic hit the United States and before he could help himself, he had lost his market. He lost all his savings, $2500. and was compelled to give notes to his men for wages. To pay off his indebtedness he took a job as manager of a group of lumber camps. In three years he had cleared himself of debt.

A little later he found another partner with some capital, and a fresh start was made. He finally had eight lumber camps, and now he was really getting somewhere. In 1880 he managed to get a market for his lumber in England, where big timber was needed. He cut pine twelve by twelve, which required the destruction of the largest trees. Lumbering seemed to offer some chances to experiment, and Dollar began to look into the matter of cutting corners, something he continued to do all his career. He cut the middleman's profit out by shipping his logs direct to the large cities in the north of the United States. He sent lumber down by ship and raft to Quebec, where he sold to the exporters. Soon he decided he could export too; he chartered a sailing ship to England and sold a cargo of lumber to a Manchester concern.

Of course there was a great deal of traveling to do between camps, spread out all over a large district. Often he went on foot, through snow, covering long distances this way. He always wanted to see things for himself; his own eyes were better than a carload of reports.

In 1882 he came down to the United States and as soon as he could do so, became a citizen of our country. His lumbering operations now centered around Marquette, Michigan. He set up sawmills in the forests and cut big timber for the export trade; smaller sizes he sold in the United States. Lumber was not his only interest. He made a fine profit on a large tract of land which he bought.

In 1888 he sold his interests in Michigan and moved to San Francisco. He built a home for his family in San Rafael.

Robert Dollar had been of the opinion that it might be cheaper to own a ship or two of his own than to charter them. Chartering a ship cost quite a sum and there was no way of dodging it. Naturally the owners of a ship charged a neat profit for its use; why couldn't he save all that? He needed ships, would always need them. Since he had come to the West Coast he was operating in redwood, cutting down great trees a thousand years old, and also sugar pine. Shiploads of this stuff were going up and down the coast—and maybe some day they would be going farther!

So he bought a steamship. It wasn't very big—260 tons—but it was seaworthy and staunch. It rejoiced, for some unknown reason, in the name of Newsboy. The little ship was the first vessel of the to-be-famous Dollar Line. It soon sported the dollar-sign on its busy little smoke stack. The dollar-sign by the way, had been used on the big logs for some time.

This was a proud acquisition for Robert Dollar. The boy who had haunted the waterfront of Falkirk, dreaming of ships, now had his own. And he could get aboard, if he liked, and go to any of those far away ports which had so thrilled him when he hobnobbed with the old tars in his boyhood.

That was only a start. He built or bought other ships to carry his cargoes, sailing ships and two steamer-schooners, the Grace Dollar and the Robert Dollar; these were 500-ton vessels.

These ships soon had a chance to pay big dividends. The Klondike Gold Rush began in 1896 and the Dollar ships were on the coast, ready to go north to the magnet that drew thousands of eager men. Captain Dollar had bunks fitted in the ships and entered this highly profitable trade, carrying passengers and cargoes of provisions and mining equipment. He bought another wooden ship of about 1500 tons for this service, and all these vessels made money for him.

One afternoon as he sat in his dock-side office, studying the manifest of a coastwise schooner, a tall, extremely handsome stranger entered.

"They tell me," he began, without introducing himself,

"that a man may get passage on your ships to the Orient."

"Sorry," Captain Dollar replied. "Not on one of my ships."

"Well," the stranger smiled whimsically, "if you don't cross the Pacific now you should—if you have vision."

Captain Dollar sat upright, staring at the visitor. "Ships for the Pacific trade are costly and riskful," he said, after a pause.

"Ships are romance," said the stranger, laconically. "The farther they sail, the more romance."

He departed after dropping his card on the Captain's desk. It said—Bret Harte.

This was a startling encounter, and for a reason. Captain Dollar had been thinking for a long time of just this thing. The Orient was a land which fascinated him. Once the Yankee ships had done a great business in the Far East. Those hard-bitten adventurers who sailed from Salem and Boston had driven in the wedge; since their days of magnificence, trade had languished. Captain Dollar knew how those old-timers had operated and he felt he could do the same. They had solved the two-way problem by buying cargoes themselves and selling them on their return at a handsome profit. No profitless return home in ballast for them.

It was not the habit of this man to plunge into a thing without thought. He had the ability to think years into the future, weigh every contingency. This new idea needed a lot of thought. But finally he felt he was right and went to work. He bought his first big steamer, the Arab, of 6500 tons. And in 1902 he went over to prepare the way.

At that time American shipping was at a low ebb, mostly due to the discouraging shipping laws of the country. There were three lines plying between the Orient and the Pacific Coast, only one of them American owned. None of them carried lumber.

Captain Dollar sent over a cargo of lumber to China which he sold at a profit. But when he tried to get return cargoes his competitors had cut the rates, which would force him to carry freight at a loss if he tried to meet their figures. In China he had noticed some oak railroad ties of good quality and he learned they had come from Japan. He sailed to the island of Hokkaido, where he discovered they were being turned out, and saw the chance to do business. The ties were first-class and cheap. He brought a few of them back to the United States and got an order for great quantities of them from the Southern Pacific Railroad. This proved a profitable venture; he sold many shiploads of the ties, and also many other cargoes of sulphur, mahogany and other hard woods.

Captain Dollar went places himself, arranging for return cargoes which made the business profitable. He was fond of saying, "Never come home in ballast or your voyage will bring you a loss. Always take a full cargo both ways, even if you have to buy it." Countless times he did buy goods with the sole idea of keeping his ships profitably loaded. And the things he bought were many and varied—iron mines, timberland and merchandise of all sorts. He was more than a shipper; he was a trader.

Nobody remembers just when he became known as "Captain" Dollar. As a matter of fact he never was a skipper. But the title fitted him like a glove. He was six feet two inches and very straight, with the ruddy skin of a seafaring man, and white hair and beard. As he acquired ships, knowledge of them came to him. There was nothing from keel to topmast that held any secrets for him.

Once he wanted to build a couple of wooden ships with particularly big hatches for his lumber carrying. Lloyds, the great insurance firm of England, would not pass ships of such a design; they claimed the hatch construction would weaken the vessel. But the far-seeing Captain had gone to them prepared. He had had a working model made of the proposed ships and these he laid before them. He explained how the huge lengths of lumber went in the hatchways, and demonstrated with sticks cut to size. Also he had figures and dimensions of what he wanted to build. The experts at Lloyd's went over the figures and the model; they were so impressed with all his knowledge and preparedness that they told him to go ahead. He did and the ships turned out to be perfectly satisfactory. It was a slow process convincing the Chinese, who had seen many examples of the white man's "honesty," that he would treat them fairly. But there was something about him that inspired their trust. He was scrupulously honest in all his dealings with them, and this resulted in lasting friendships with many of them. No matter how much trouble came to the unfortunate country in revolutions and wars, Captain Dollar's position was always secure.

Ill feeling came in 1907 between Japan and China and our own country over various immigration questions. In

1908 Captain Dollar, who was chairman of the Oriental Department of the Pacific Coast Chamber of Commerce, organized a party of business men to tour China and Japan, and try to set things right. Speeches were made in the key cities of both countries with happy results. Captain Dollar himself was a fine speaker, convincing and interesting.

As the years went on Captain Dollar never rested on his oars. Every year he made trips to his many ports of call, arranging for cargoes and business. He traveled thousands of miles on both land and sea, always looking for a chance to build up trade for his ships. Once, in the Philippines, he signed up to take 10,000 tons of copra per year for three years, a great risk because he had to guarantee the buyers a set price, regardless of whether it rose or fell. But the venture turned out well; it developed into a trade in copra that ran to some $22,000,000 per year.

During the World War he was one of four shipowners called in to help in the colossal muddle that had arisen. Shipping was frozen and something had to be done. President Wilson called for immediate action. Captain Dollar and his three fellow shipowners drafted the Emergency Shipping Bill in a little less than three hours and the next day Congress passed it. This bill allowed American citizens to register under our flag foreign ships for foreign trade only.

While the war went on Captain Dollar made some shrewd trades in ships. One vessel he bought for $340,000. and a little later sold to the Japanese Government for $800,000. Sometimes he would find a ship that others did not want and fix it up so it would bring a good profit. He was very clever at this, often seeing possibilities in a ship that eluded others. He had an idea that after the war was over, there would be a slump in shipping, that many ships constructed under the stress of war would be thrown on the market. This opinion was so strong that he sold many of his own ships, making excellent trades. There would be lean times in the shipping business soon, and many fine bargains after that—and he wanted to be in a position to make the best of both situations.

All during the war his ships were busy, and so was he. He built an immense electric sawmill on Puget Sound near Vancouver. He carried coolies for the British Government with his ships, destined for France. His ships were made over to do this work as well as to carry freight; otherwise they would have been commandeered by the British Government, as many of them were under British registry.

After the War there was a slump in shipping as he had foreseen. But before the great depreciation in ships came he had sold almost half of his own for good prices. Now he could buy in again when the bargains came, as he knew they would.

In 1920 he started a round-the-world freight service from here to China and Japan, down to Singapore, through the Suez Canal to New York, thence by the Panama Canal to the Pacific. For this service he had bought four big freighters from the United States Shipping Board. These ships did well enough, so he bought three more. They were well built, a fact of which he was very well aware.

He was seventy-seven years old in 1921 and he was still going strong, traveling all over the globe, arranging for business for his ships. He said at the time, "You can't get business by staying at home. The man who sits at a desk may get business in boom times but not otherwise."

One of his big ventures at this period was establishing himself in the trade up the Yang-tse River in China. He built a great wharf at Shanghai, and three huge warehouses, costing $800,000. He opened offices along the River at Hankow, Ichang and Chungkung. Three riverboats were started on the upper Yang-tse as freight feeders for his sea going ships. He ran them up 1600 miles farther than any of his competitors had ever gone before, opening up an immense new region. The River was infested with bandits who loved nothing better than to loot a boat rich with cargo. To cope with these he had a steel boat built and equipped with armor-plated bridge, and extra powerful engines. These river-boats were run under the American flag. There was a little trouble with the bandits at first, but finally the company put a couple of Marines on each boat, and that settled the bandit question.

The opening of this river was a benefit to the Dollar Company, but it also greatly helped the country which had been nothing but a great provincial section before. Thousands of Chinese found employment in the factories built, the stores opened and all the varied activities that the venture gave rise to. One of the Dollar Company's enterprises was the establishment of a feather factory near Shanghai. This plant employed one thousand persons gathering and preparing feathers for the American market.

Captain Dollar was almost eighty when he embarked on the biggest venture of all. For a long time he had been thinking of a great passenger and freight service to circle the globe. So far his service had been all freight.

In 1921 his fleet, all under the American flag, was composed of thirteen steamers and ten sailing vessels, with a dead weight capacity of 134,038 tons. All of these ships but two were named after members of his family. The Dollar ships flying the Dollar emblem were known all over the world.

The first step in this passenger business was made for the Shipping Board. The Pacific Steamship Company was operating seven or eight 10,000-ton passenger steamers for the Shipping Board. The service was not paying, so the Dollar Company was employed to run them. This gave a splendid opportunity to learn the inside of the passenger service. The Company ran the line for three years. At one time the Dollars tried to buy the ships but could not get them at the figure they wanted to pay.

But in 1923 they bought seven ships that had been running from San Francisco to the Orient. They were called President liners on account of the names they bore. They were splendid modern ships, 522 feet long and of 10,000 tons, equipped for first-class passenger service.

The idea was to put them all in service at once, running them all one way—always west, in an endless chain around the world on a regular two-week schedule. It was an innovation in shipping and even the experts said that it would not pay. The first ship left late in 1923. Captain

Dollar and his wife, who had always traveled with him, went ahead in another of his ships, to arrange for freight and business.

From the first the service was successful. The ships were always punctual, arriving and leaving on schedule time. Beds were installed instead of bunks and everything was done to serve and please the passengers. Two years later five more of these big liners were bought. And finally the company built two new ones, larger than the others, the President Coolidge and the President Hoover.

Captain Dollar died May 17, 1932, at the age of eighty-eight. He had been active all his life. His last public act was the making of an address to a crowd of young people two weeks before his death. He had worked thirty years longer than most men. The first half of his life was crammed with unbelievable hardships; the latter half was no less busy even when success was his.

It is a very brave man who at four-score years stakes everything on one gigantic venture, as he did in the matter of the round-the-world service. Not many would dare take such a risk. And very few have enough ambition at that age to want to do such a thing. He loved his ships, he loved the sea, and he loved all the intricate and romantic business that goes with ships. That was why he never tired of it, why he was young in purpose at eighty.

HARVEY S. FIRESTONE

AUTOMOBILE TIRE MANUFACTURER

HARVEY S. FIRESTONE

HARVEY S. FIRESTONE

AUTOMOBILE TIRE MANUFACTURER

IT is interesting to note how many inventions came about and how many fortunes were started because somebody became irritated about something. It has happened a good many times. Thoughtful men, becoming annoyed at some discomfort or clumsiness in the mechanics of living, sat down and evolved an improvement—and a new business enterprise was started.

In the so-called gay nineties, when salesman Harvey Firestone was driving around the country every day, good or bad, he suffered from one thing, just as every other road traveler did. Many salesmen traveled from town to town by horse and buggy, and those buggies were equipped with steel tires. The roads were bad and every time the wheels struck a stone, the rider got a good percentage of the shock. At the end of a day's drive, the rider felt as if his spine had been under treatment from a small but busy pile-driver.

Young Mr. Firestone loved horses and driving, but he also liked to be comfortable in the pastime. So he had his buggy wheels fitted with cushion rubber tires. Such things were new; in fact, in every place he traveled, even in the big cities, his was the only buggy so equipped. While these tires had no air space, they did give a more comfortable ride and they were silent.

Little things often alter men's lives and these tires of young Firestone's played a great part in moulding his. He did not invent such tires, nor was he the first man to apply them to wheels. But he did a good deal about introducing them to the public, a public which, at that time, was not so ready to accept new-fangled ideas as it is now. The young salesman, driving about the country, much too alert and restless for such slow-poking travel, dreamed his dream, and when he got the chance put that dream into action. It makes quite a story.

Harvey S. Firestone was born on a farm in Columbiana County, Ohio, December 20, 1868, a bare sixty miles distant from Akron, the city in which he was to make such a success. The statement "born on a farm" often brings up a picture of poverty, but the Firestone farm was nothing of the sort. It was a very good and prosperous farm, and the senior Firestone, Benjamin, was a man who was both well informed and successful in farming.

Young Firestone had that early advantage of gaining a healthy body in such fine country surroundings and life. There was considerable cattle raising and he acquired a good knowledge of animals, especially horses. He began his education in a small country school at the age of seven. He was a good pupil and his teachers liked him. Later he attended a very good high school in Columbiana and graduated.

He could have stayed on the farm and turned his energies in that direction, but already he had come to the conclusion that business offered a better opportunity than farming. He did not know it but he was entering an era of business which was to have many golden chances, probably the greatest the world has ever seen. Within the next two generations came our most remarkable progress in inventions with their resulting businesses.

So Firestone, like so many boys, left the farm to seek his fortune in the fascinating world outside, the world of men and cities. To prepare himself in the fundamentals of business, he spent a few months at a business college in Cleveland. This training and the life in a larger city sharpened him, made him more avid to get into some of the opportunities which he saw all around him.

He wanted to enter the employ of a relative, Clinton D. Firestone, who operated a carriage factory in Columbus, but there was no place for him there. However he did get a start, through this same relative, and soon we find him keeping books in the coal business of John W. Taft, also in Columbus. This connection lasted only a few months, owing to the closing out of the business and young Firestone was out of a job, almost at the start of his career.

However, he had made the acquaintance of a man named Jackson, who had some idle money and who wished to get into some sort of business. The business decided on was that of manufacturing and selling patent medicines, lotions and flavoring extracts. In those days the sky was the limit to which anybody might go in promisory medicines; almost every ill could be cured by one single concoction—according to the label on the bottle.

The business got under way and young Firestone went out to sell the small Ohio towns with this array of goods. But patent medicines were successfully sold in only two ways—from the back of a wagon by an expert medicine man or doctor, or helped by an advertising campaign. The new line was not advertised and Firestone had no success with the medicine, which probably was both harmless to patient and disease. But he did learn the art of selling; the extract and lotion went well.

However, the venture began to peter out after a few months. There was no advertising and too much competition. The firm had to close up and again Firestone was out of a job. It looked like failure but it wasn't; what he really obtained was a post-graduate course through experience. Shortly after this he entered the employ of his relative, Clinton Firestone. At first he was a bookkeeper, then he managed to get into the selling end of the business, finally getting the district outside of Detroit.

He did very well. But the fine buggy business was doomed; the cheap machine-made buggies were flooding the market and soon the Firestone Company, which made only high-priced hand-made buggies, had to close up. Once more young Firestone was in the ranks of the unemployed through no fault of his own.

But if buggies had thrown him off, now buggies were to pull him back on his feet. Those tires. Firestone had the only rubber-tired buggy in Detroit, in a territory and a country filled with buggies. The average back-yard in America had more buggies and wagons than they will ever have motor cars. Buggies, Concord and piano-box, surreys, phaetons, coaches and what-not, all having hard steel tires. Firestone got to thinking, really thinking about this problem. Rubber tires were good, so why not supply others with them? There was an idea for a business and a new one in his part of the world.

He had a little money but not enough. But now he knew a lot of business men and he was not long in finding one who would go into the business with him. They looked around and finally bought an old run-down factory in Chicago for $1500. cash and started in business. It was simple. The solid rubber tire came in long strips from the rubber factory. The proper lengths could be cut off and then cemented to the steel rim. There was no great art in it; just cleanliness and care. Business was good at the very beginning, as everybody wanted a set of rubber tires, once they got a demonstration. And the alert and energetic Mr. Firestone saw they got that.

There was no trouble getting orders but there was in getting credit and sufficient cash to keep going. Firestone not only sold tires, but he had to sell stock in the company, something much more difficult. The little company, called the Firestone-Victor Rubber Company, grew in spite of the difficulties, grew to the point where it was possible to buy out a rival. Firestone raised the money for this.

Later the company consolidated with another company, using a more up-to-date rim. These mergers and acquisitions now resulted in quite a sizable and important concern. So important, in fact, that a tempting offer by another company to sell out could not be turned down. The Consolidated Company paid Firestone's company $1,254,-000. Firestone's share was $45,000. in cash, which was good after only four years in business and from an initial investment of only $1000. Much better than farming, for instance.

Mr. Firestone could now rest on his laurels, get a job or

go into business for himself. But it was not long before he was, as we used to say in a certain childhood game, "getting warm." He had located in Akron, Ohio, having become interested in a small tire department operated by a company that made other things as well. Now he was in the very heart of the rubber world. Tires were only a small part of that world but they were growing more important all the time.

It was not long before Mr. Firestone met a man named James Swinehart, who had worked out a device for holding tires on the rims by means of wires. The idea was satisfactory and the tires stayed on under stress and strain, a novelty at that time. A company was formed and a factory building found. In August, 1900, the new firm, the Firestone Tire & Rubber Company, came into being.

The organization was composed of one shift of twelve men. Firestone was treasurer and general manager. For the first few years the company had to buy its tires from other concerns in Akron. The Firestone part of it was the fastening device (no mean part in those days) and the service of putting them on the wheels. These, of course, were solid tires of cushion rubber. The little company lost money at first, although it did plenty of business. As they only gave service and applied the fastening device, the profits were small. Finally it showed a little profit, a sign hopeful enough to indicate the wind was in the right direction.

Firestone had been convinced for some time that to make any satisfactory showing the company would have to make its own tires; there was too little profit in buying them from other companies. So a larger building on the outskirts of Akron was bought. More money came in from one source or another, through the efforts of the indefatigable young tire maker. A reasonably efficient equipment was installed. The machinery was second-hand but fit to use. At least tires could be made—and the company started in to make them.

They made a good tire and the fastening device was superior to any other. Then they found a way to cure the rubber in long strips, a distinct improvement over the customary process at that time of curing each completed tire. These strips were sold in reels and the dealer saved a great deal in the amount of stock he had to carry. He no longer had to stock the various sizes in demand, owing to the difference in wheel sizes. This, and other improvements, brought the Firestone product into prominence and made it a serious contender to the other older tire companies. Of course, all this was connected with the solid rubber tire for pleasure carriages and trucks. But in several cities there were some quaint looking contraptions appearing in the streets, deafening the ears of human beings and scaring horses—queer things that were soon to revolutionize the rubber tire business. The horseless carriage was actually here, men were being arrested for going twelve miles an hour in the things, and before long the whole face of America would be changed.

Firestone realized from the first that automobiles were more than a toy, that they would be perfected and that a better and different kind of tire would have to be designed for them. They could not stand the vibration from hard tires with their delicate machinery. It meant the pneumatic tire which up to then had been used for bicycles and racing sulkies. Under the heavy weight of an automobile these tires would blow out.

However, pneumatic tires had to be supplied for the new vehicles. Firestone decided to try his hand at it, but there was a snag at the very beginning. It seemed that everybody could not make tires who wanted to. The clincher type tires could only be made through the permission of the Association which controlled a very sweeping patent—and clincher type tires were the only ones in use. Mr. Firestone applied for a license to make them and was refused. So then he did a thing typical of him. If obstacles were placed in his path and they could not be removed, he simply went around them. He got in touch with a man who had evolved a straight-side tire which seemed to be a satisfactory thing. Firestone decided to manufacture this type. He hired a tire-maker and started in, making, testing and trying to better the product. Those early tires of his (and everybody else's) were crude and often undependable. Sometimes one would stand up very well, and the next one would blow out. The rubber varied and there was no way to help this. But they kept trying, and after a year of hard work and many disappointments, the Firestone factory began to turn out a tire of its own pattern which worked fairly well. That was the day of the fabric tire and even the best was none too satisfactory.

Long before the Firestone factory was really equipped to handle large orders for the new pneumatics, Firestone succeeded in interesting Henry Ford, who was getting out his first large order, two thousand cars. Firestone demonstrated his tires and got the order. But there was all sorts of irritating trouble which arose during the production of this very important order; delays and trouble with the rims and flanges, getting men who knew how to build tires which then were made by hand. But eventually the first big order was successfully completed, and those first Firestone automobile tires went out on the road to make good.

But even good tires would not fill the bill satisfactorily if they could not be serviced on the road. The standard pattern was clincher and so Firestone had to make clincher type, in spite of the fact that he was refused a license. He went ahead and dared a possible lawsuit, but nothing came of it, as the patent was proved invalid. More trouble did come down on his head though, through rims, so much that he decided he would go ahead and make his own rims. From this start, a thing of necessity, grew the rim factory of the Firestone Company.

The Company was now fully launched into their part of the new industry which was moving ahead so rapidly. Soon there were more makes of cars on the road than there are now. There were some weird tires, too, and several years went by before really dependable tires came on the market.

The Firestone Company moved steadily ahead, in spite of various troubles which beset it at times. The first year, 1900, it did a business of $110,000—and lost money. Four years later sales jumped to $460,000. In 1907 the figure was $1,600,000, and in 1910 the remarkable figure of $5,000,000 in sales had been reached, with profits of $1,394,835.

New buildings had to be erected to take care of such

phenomenal growth. The name Firestone on a tire meant something. Racing cars used them and they were sturdy enough to come through these gruelling contests, frayed and burned, but still standing up. The motorist has always paid a lot of attention to tests made in racing, and Firestone was clever enough to see this. Of course, he had to have the toughest kind of a tire or the tests would have been worthless.

There were boom times in the tire business, during the World War and the two years following the Armistice. The Firestone Company had grown with the years. In 1920 there were 19,800 employees—quite an increase over the twelve that had started work on that August day in 1900. In 1919 the company produced 4,000,000 tires and made a profit of over $9,000,000. The company had increased its capitalization to $75,000,000. Several times it had outgrown its buildings with the result that enormous new ones had to be built.

Methods changed with the great increase in business. After 1912 tires were made by machinery instead of by hand, with the result of more satisfactory uniformity, better tires and lower costs. Wages grew and so many tire-makers and would be tire-makers came to Akron that houses had to be built for them.

But boom times always precede a depression. In 1920 Mr. Firestone was called home from a European vacation with the unwelcome news that tire sales everywhere in the country had practically ceased for some unaccountable reason. Great quantities of raw materials which had been ordered were constantly coming in, had to be paid for. Everybody in the organization seemed demoralized at the sudden violent slump in business. The captains and lieutenants in the Firestone army were incapable of doing anything about it; it was a situation solely for a general, and it had to be General Firestone for a time.

He refused to be stampeded or disheartened. There were cars, the people had to drive them, every time a tire went around a little bit of wear took place. It was certainly foolish to think that people would stop using tires. But something had to be done to get an immediate and sizable movement going in those immense stocks of tires, in the factory and in the distribution centers.

The answer to the problem was something known to any little merchant—a sale. But Mr. Firestone knew it would have to be a *good* sale to do the trick. Something so good that the public simply could not resist. So he announced a cut of 25 per cent in tire prices—and that was certainly something to make any motorist sit up and take notice. Such an opportunity might be snatched away at any moment; the public was quite familiar with price fluctuations in fuel prices, so why not in tires?

Anyway, the public answered. New tires were put on the road and the old spares thrown away. The Firestone sale, announced by banners and signs at every distributing point, was a great success. In two months the Company sold $18,000,000. worth of tires and the situation for the Firestone Company was definitely saved.

Naturally the other companies did not like such drastic price cuts. Some people do not like profits cut away, even if such tactics save the ship. But it mattered little to Mr. Firestone what they thought about him; when he had a job to do he did it, no matter what the consequences were.

One of the major irritations of the tire business has always been in the rubber itself. It is not a native product, and probably never will be. Prices have varied in the last few years from as low as fifteen cents a pound up to three dollars, a vacillation entirely too great for the stability of any American industry. Several countries have aspired to control this product, with the idea of possessing a monopoly, among them England, Holland and Brazil.

Mr. Firestone thought something might be done about this and in 1923 sent investigators to various parts of the world where rubber is known to grow—Mexico, the Philippines, Panama and Liberia. Rubber is satisfactorily grown in all these places, but Liberia answered the purposes of Mr. Firestone better than any of the others. Liberia is a sort of colony of the United States, in a sense, and it seemed to be a country where a business venture might be conducted without threat of revolutions and molestation.

In 1926 one million acres of land were leased for ninety-nine years. And thus began one of the most romantic episodes in American industry.

One of the first problems was to organize a large labor force in this far off country, where the average annual temperature is eighty degrees with high humidity. About one hundred Americans and twenty thousand native men were recruited for the work. Most of the plantation labor came from native tribes of the interior, men who finish a hard day's labor with dancing to the beat of tom-toms.

Such a vast undertaking excited much interest. It was the first organized industrial effort Liberia had ever seen. Natives walked miles through the jungles to see what was happening. To retain any regular force, there was no question as to how the native workers must be treated. There must be no repetition of Congo treatment here. The company made no contracts with labor. The men were paid individually and they could leave any time they liked, just the same as in this country. Once the natives saw they would be treated fairly, there was no question about getting enough help.

Not all the acreage could be planted at once, of course. The first year 15,000 acres were planted with rubber trees. Rubber seeds and seedlings were imported from all parts of the world's tropical belt and scientific research experiments in plant propagation were being carried out on a large scale. Seedlings from Sumatra were imported, a very difficult journey of 12,000 miles being necessary.

At the time of the Firestone venture in Liberia there were no passable roads. Now, through the company's pioneering and engineering, there are good roads in the vast area, and the way to its plantations is accessible. Since the Company came, Monrovia, the capital, has installed a modern electric light plant and telephone system. Bungalows have been put up for the white employees and their wives. The natives live in two-room houses which replaced the native mud huts used for years. For the native boys, the company has provided a trade school.

A subsidiary company, known as the United States-Liberia Radio Corporation, operates radio stations in Liberia and at Akron. This offers a direct service to the public between the two countries.

The Firestone Company has built and equipped a power plant which provides ice, cold storage and electric light for the whole area. A system for running water and a sewerage system have also been set up. There is a big electric machine shop capable of repairing all mechanical and motor equipment in the area. It is truly remarkable what a magical transformation has been made in this country, which was nothing but a wilderness a few years before.

Everybody is familiar with the old proverb, "Big oaks from little acorns grow." Certainly this applies to the company which is the subject of this sketch. The little acorn was the rubber-tired buggy which hauled the thoughtful young Mr. Firestone over those country roads in the early nineties.

And the oak? The Firestone Company now consists of two great tire plants, a steel rim plant and a battery plant in Akron; a plant in Hamilton, Ontario; another near Buenos Aires, and one in France. Cotton, which is hardly less important in the industry than rubber, is taken care of by a mill in Fall River, Massachusetts. And of course, that really important department in far off Liberia. Somehow that Liberia plant captivates the fancy. Outside of the daring of the venture there is something else; it has brought hope and the joy of a more complete living to thousands of really forgotten black men. This sort of fruit is the sweetest kind which sometimes grows on the trees of American business.

Mr. Firestone likes to think of himself as a salesman, and of course he is. But a study of his career brings us to the conclusion that he is a very good general. In all the panics and depressions he has always emerged with flying colors; indeed, he does rather better under adversity than in times of peace. That master-stroke in 1920 was truly Fochian.

When the depression of the thirties becomes history we shall be able to look back and appreciate the concerns which were depression-proof, those that, like ships, headed out to sea to ride it out, rather than scuttle for home. But more important and thrilling is the story of the *men* who were depression-proof. Such a one is Harvey S. Firestone.

ALVAN TUFTS FULLER

AUTOMOBILE MERCHANT AND STATESMAN

(Jaimeson Studios)

ALVAN TUFTS FULLER

ALVAN TUFTS FULLER

AUTOMOBILE MERCHANT AND STATESMAN

BOYS of the nineties had a different type of athletic hero than they have today. At that time football was played only in the three major colleges, aviation was unknown, and boxing was more the business of bruisers than sportsmen. Baseball was about the only sport that produced athletic stars in that day, and every lad had his "gallery" of pictures of these heroes, thoughtfully supplied by a manufacturer of cigarettes.

However, there was another kind of athletic figure which captivated every boy's fancy in those colorful days of the nineties. Bicycle racers. Their kind has long since been forgotten. They were nothing whatever like these six-day grinders or those others who now flash about tiny saucer tracks behind spitting motor-pacers.

The bicycle meets of those days approximated the big football classics of the present in interest. The gay-clad riders at Waltham and Charles River Park meant the same to boys then as did Lou Gehrig, Jack Dempsey and Bobby Jones of a later day. Those bike racers were definitely the boys' particular heroes in the nineties and naturally enough every lad had a terrific urge to grow up and straddle a racing wheel.

It was in the very heart of this exciting scene that Alvan Fuller was born. In the public square of the town he lived in, Malden, Massachusetts, there was the start of an annual classic known as the Linscott Road Race. It had about the same color and interest as the present B. A. A. Marathon, and the distance was only a little short, twenty-five miles, to Waltham and return. This event was one of the first, if not the first, of its kind in the United States.

As a very little boy Alvan never missed this race. His eyes popped at the thrilling sight of the several hundred athletes who shot away, to pedal for glory. The whole town, as well as a good deal of Boston, crowded the streets between Malden and Waltham to watch. The hours passed, everybody at white heat, wondering which of their heroes would come back first, humped over his handlebars, tearing his heart and lungs out on those old hundred-pound wheels. It was a tremendous event and made a great impression on that little boy. Of course there was no doubt about what was in his mind; some day he would grow up and be one of those bike racers.

Later came the oval track, banked at the turns, and now there was no waiting for the crowds. The whole thrilling scene could be watched—all the various events, the novice, the sprints, the handicaps (always full of spills) and the pursuit race. The band played the Washington Post March, there were bags of peanuts to munch and flags to wave. Altogether, it was a Roman Holiday, the likeness of which has never been duplicated.

Bicycles were the one driving power of the boys of the nineties. They lived on their wheels (when they could afford one) and nearly every ambitious boy wanted to grow up and become a racer. Naturally this boy of Mal-

den had visions of fame, too, and he was determined to
succeed. The bicycle was going to have a lot to do with
it—but not in the way he thought.

The Fullers were not well to do, although they came of
a long line of fine New England stock. Peter Tufts, from
whom the future Governor got his middle name, was a direct ancestor, who came to this country in 1642. This
Peter Tufts gave the land on which is now located Tufts
College at Medford. Alvan's mother's name was Flora
Tufts. Another early ancestor was John Fuller, who came
over from England in the ship "Abigail" in 1635 and who
settled at Ipswich. Alvan's father was Alvan Bond Fuller
and was a veteran of the Civil War.

Young Alvan entered the public schools of Malden and
in his play hours amused himself on a velocipede which
had been given him by an uncle. It was the pride of his
young life, this three-wheeler, and he spent many hours
scooting back and forth on his sidewalk. Sidewalk?
There was no sidewalk to him; it was a bicycle race
course!

There was a fly in the ointment, though. In the neighborhood was a much bigger boy who was something of a
bully. One of his stunts was to wait until eight-year-old
Alvan came whizzing along on his velocipede and then
suddenly lay down a big piece of lumber which either
stopped progress or toppled the rider off his machine.
Alvan's eyes blazed and all his instinct called for retalia-
tion. But there had been edicts about fighting—and anyway, this bully looked as big as a house. It would be best
to ask about the proper course.

His family listened to his tale of woe. It was too bad,

of course, but every neighborhood since the time of Adam had had an overgrown bully who teased little boys. Better stay in his own yard or try some other street. But somebody, noting the belligerent look in the little boy's eyes, said, "Well, why don't *you* get a stick yourself?"

There was an idea—and one to his liking. Little as he was, the gladiator spirit was well defined in him. So Alvan went out to the barn and got himself a bit of wood, too—not shaped like a vehicle-stopper, but more like a shillalah—one of those nice sticks with a lovely hard knob on one end!

Now for Mr. Bully! He stuck the shillalah under his arm, got on the velocipede and started down the sidewalk. Out came the grinning nemesis, licking his chops. He threw down his chunk of wood as the little rider came up, roaring at the little fellow's discomfiture.

Then his roar changed to a bellow. The air was suddenly full of shillalahs, coming from all around a blazing-eyed mite of dynamite. The hulking coward covered his head to ward off the shower and got a few in the shins. Then shrieking, he took to his heels, leaving the scene definitely in the enemy's hands. Very young Alvan Fuller had won his first fight and all by himself. Never again would he dodge a scrap or ask anybody's advice on what to do about it.

School days were not long for him. He did negotiate the grammar school, but at no time did he threaten to set the educational world afire. There was no money to send him to high school or college and so at the age of sixteen Alvan went to work.

He got a job in the shipping department of the big rubber shoe company in Malden, called the Boston Rubber Shoe Company, and his pay was $7.50 a week. The hours were long, seven A. M. until six at night. Not very much time left in which to become something—say, a bicycle racer. Yet the young man had his dreams.

He told of his sensations years later. He said, "As a boy of sixteen on my way to work in the rubber factory, with my dinner box under my arm, the idea came to me that, perhaps, some day I would become Governor of my State! There was a reason. The words of Dick Whittington had made a great impression on me. My mother had read those stories to me, so when I used to go to work and I would hear the bells of Malden ringing, I recalled the Bow Bells dinning in the ears of Dick, bidding him turn back to London. They seemed to say, "Turn again, Whittington, Lord Mayor of London." So—I thought those Malden bells might be saying "Turn again, Fuller, Governor of Massachusetts!"

Conceit? If so, it was the right kind. There is nothing ignoble about conceit that has any backing—and the resolution of a boy of spirit is certainly good backing. There was something very inspiring about those early morning bells, and, as he said, they seemed to speak to him, tramping to his drab work in the shipping room.

What to do about it? He was no scholar, and anyway, academic education was not for him. But there was always business of some kind. What did he know? Well, there were—bicycles. All around him he saw interest in bicycles; they had taken a strong hold on the people. The newer machines had pneumatic tires, light tubular-steel frames and now could be propelled by women and children.

He began to tinker with bicycles. He learned how to repair them, how to set the tires in shellac, how to mend the erratic tires themselves, how to paint up the used machines and make them look new. Every night saw him at work on this venture. Soon he knew all about bicycles and his back yard began to look like a carnival on wheels. What a motley of names, too. Rambler, Stearns, Pope, Union, Orient, McCune, Columbia. Every blessed one of them signifying some star racer or even a group of racers. It was fascinating work and midnight always came too soon.

He sold a few. And now came the big idea. He would have a store! A bicycle store was, next to a racing track, the most fascinating thing on earth. He had seen them. The wheels stood in racks, diagonally parked, and customers came in and looked them over, sat on them and tried them out. Opportunities were plenty, too. To those who did not know how to ride you could give lessons.

There was a back yard to the Fuller home and this answered the real estate part of the problem. With the help of an uncle, Alvan built a small building, paying for the lumber out of his savings. All this was done at night and on Saturday afternoons.

It was a proud moment for the young merchant when the final lick of paint went on that modest, one-story building. And now into it went the Ramblers with their bright copper rims, the baby-blue Columbias, the orange Stearnses and the black Orients. Alvan was about burst-

ing with pride and excitement. On the front of the building he put up a sign reading "A. T. Fuller."

Bicycles then brought a good price. For instance, the
Orient brought one hundred dollars, new; the Saracen
seventy-five. Stearns was about the same. Some fancy
ones ran up to one hundred and twenty-five dollars. Used
bikes were priced according to age and condition.

Young Fuller sold all makes. He was a very persuasive
salesman and knew what he was talking about. People
around Malden liked his brisk, business-like manner and
they bought bicycles of him. In his first year he sold 104
machines, exactly two a week. This was good business.
The profit on new machines was quite good, and of
course, there were by-products such as pumps, graphite,
tires, kits, and so on.

The Fuller bicycle store never faltered on its march.
The hand that guided it was a young one in a field of
much older ones, but it was a master hand nevertheless.
He frequented the race tracks, loving that indefinable atmosphere, and its acquaintance with the great in bicycling. In those days bicycling was a world in itself, not
just a sport.

He inaugurated the custom of giving a sort of party in
the store every Washington Birthday. This was the signal
that winter was over; peoples' thoughts were turning to
spring and cycling. This custom of Washington Birthday
open house has continued to this day; the automobile
concerns of Boston keep open and invite the public to
come in and look over the new models.

The second year in business (the rubber shoe connection had been cast aside) young Fuller sold 364 bicycles—

almost one for every day in the year. This meant a lot of work, more than appears on the face of it. People then shopped for bicycles as they do now for cars. It was easy for anybody to become all snarled up over the problem of whether to own an Orient, a Stearns, a McCune or any other—and it was young Fuller's art to straighten out their minds. One per day was a splendid performance. It also involved taking timid people out in the street and teaching them the business of equilibrium. There was a lot to it.

In 1898 when he was twenty years old, he opened a store on Columbus Avenue, Boston, where, for some reason, bicycles had their habitat. He was in a nest of dealers, but that didn't stop him. Soon he tripled his previous mark, selling around a thousand machines a year. This, with all its side-lines, was very good business.

It was sometime in 1897 that he began to be interested in a thing that was breaking into the bicycle business. For some reason, the motor car was first taken up by the bicycle people, probably because the "corn-popper" or motor-pacing machine had been in use on the tracks. At least, most of the bicycle manufacturing concerns began to look into the matter of the horseless-carriage.

It was a period of great promise but not many men saw its real potentialities. The queer, sputtering contraptions might be good as curiosities, but few could see them as vehicles for general use.

Young Fuller saw something, at any rate. But he was a salesman, not an inventor. He had no intention of shutting himself up in a shop, like Ford, and sticking at the problem until he made a car. The first machines were coming from France, as that country was far ahead of all others in motor vehicle building. So the youthful bicycle merchant sailed for France one day and went shopping. He came back to Boston with two de Dion Voiturettes. These early de Dions were quaint to look at, part bicycle and part vehicle. But they would go, go fast enough to scare the wits out of anybody at that time.

These de Dions were the first automobiles ever brought into the Port of Boston. Mr. Fuller soon claimed his frightful creatures from the customs house and proceeded to give a show. Soon the streets of staid old Boston echoed to the "put-put-put" of the French horseless carriages. Horses went up on the sidewalks and old ladies sought smelling salts. The tiny, crooked streets of Boston were even then more cluttered than now, with a few lines of horse cars left and innumerable trolley cars to make traffic interesting.

Mr. Fuller sold his two cars soon after he got them. But the time was not ripe to go into the automobile business right then; there was too much to be done by American pioneers before that. The bicycle business was still good, and for some years the bulk of the public would propel themselves about or ride on trolley cars.

But things moved rapidly as the months went on. Horseless carriages began to appear from various parts of the country—the Winton, the Rambler, the Stevens-Duryea, and a steamer or two. Soon the Cadillac had a showroom in Boston right opposite the Public Gardens. But Columbus Avenue was to become the first Automobile Row; the Fuller bicycle store was right in the path of the coming automotive cyclone.

Mr. Fuller was soon in it. He took what cars he could get. They were weird examples of the coachmaker's art. There were Metz Buckboards from Waltham which were certainly the lowest cars (in altitude) ever made. There were cars that had doors in the rear, and others that had their engines amidships. There were no windshields and the only thing stream-lined was the driver's face! It was a hectic atmosphere and its early phase closely resembled the "hoss-trading" marts. What lies were told about those early cars!

In 1903 young Mr. Fuller made an acquaintance with a new car that he liked. It was sturdy, and under the hood was an engine that looked very shipshape and efficient. It cost more than most of the other cars but it seemed to be just the thing he had been looking for. It was the Packard. And that was a very important alliance—Alvan Fuller, twenty-five years old and the aristocratic car, a mere infant. He decided to handle it in Boston, certainly a locality where a high-priced car would sell if anywhere.

From the first he was successful with it. It had a powerful four-cylinder motor and the body lines were handsome; the radiator lines were the same as today except for the present backward slant. Soon he realized that bicycles and motor cars were not quite the same thing. You said good-bye to a bicycle when sold, but the automobile proved to be an acquaintance just made; it needed things from time to time, no matter how good it was. And so service was born.

Mr. Fuller's idea was to sell a car so good and keep it so good, that it would stay on the roads for years. The school of "sell 'em quick and sell 'em often" seemed short-sighted to him. He meant to make that "Ask The Man Who Owns One" mean something. The Fuller-Packard service was the best. Only first-class mechanics were employed.

While he was selling against lower-priced cars everywhere, his business grew in leaps and bounds. He soon saw that the new infant was going to need a bigger yard to play in and it was then that he did something that made people say he was everything from foolish to crazy.

He started to build the largest existing automobile sales and service building in the East in 1908, in a section over a mile from even the outskirts of business Boston. The land had been used as a golf links and it was "country." There were no stores anywhere near it and not likely to be any. The big building went up in spite of all the criticism and advice, and was promptly called "Fuller's Folly." All the automobile business was clustered close-packed from Park Square to Dartmouth Street in a totally different part of the city. The wise-acres knew that nobody was going to go out into the country to see Packards, when all the other cars in America were having a daily show near the heart (and pocket-books) of downtown Boston.

The outcome can be put in one sentence. Alvan Fuller with his "Folly" brought the whole business out there with him, without even asking them to come! Automobile Row is now where he put it—and glad to be there. In the old days they used to put the cars inside at night with a shoe-horn; now they have plenty of room.

There is little more to be said about Alvan Fuller's business career. It has gone on and on. He is many times a millionaire. The bicycle-tinkerer who listened so avidly and hopefully to the bells of Malden is probably the most successful automobile dealer in the country. As far as Boston and territory is concerned, Alvan Fuller is Packard and Packard is Alvan Fuller. The original "Folly" building has had to be enlarged three or four times its first size, in spite of the fact that it was once considered much too large.

But Alvan Fuller has been something else to Boston and Massachusetts than a successful business man. He is known in that state as a statesman—and he might just as well have made it national as state.

While he was making his first big success in business, the man in the public eye was Theodore Roosevelt. There was a two-fisted personage that just appealed to young Fuller. He believed in the great Teddy and said so in no uncertain terms. When T. R. jumped the fence and landed outside the sacred G. O. P. boundaries into the more or less wild lands of the Bull Moose, Mr. Fuller also went. He wasn't a politician and didn't want to be, but he liked the fiery ex-President and wanted to help.

He leaped into the fight (and that Bull Moose bolt was one!) and began to make speeches. The outcome was the chance to run for Governor of Massachusetts on the Progressive Ticket. But Mr. Fuller declined. He did not care for public office at that time as his business was taking most of his attention. But several years later he began "lower down" and ran for State Representative as a Progressive and won. He was launched on a career of public office which was to be meteoric.

In 1916 he was elected to Congress. The United States was not in the World War but that event was only a few months away. Mr. Fuller took up his residence in Washington and proceeded to get himself talked about more or less.

For one thing he refused any salary, or indeed, any of the privileges granted to Congressmen and Senators, such as clerk hire, mileage, franking and the like. It was commented upon by some of his peers, and he explained his attitude. As to the salary he said he felt that any man who could afford to should be glad to give his services to his country without pay. And as to the franking privilege, that he considered to be much abused; he even quoted some evidence on the subject that showed up some of the members in none too good a light.

He was elected for another term in 1918. He waived exemption to military service but the government preferred to keep him in Washington. All through the War he voted for every measure that was designed to help forward the cause of our country in the conflict, and he was one of 47 out of 450 odd honored by the country for a hundred per cent record in this respect.

Massachusetts brought him back home to elect him Lieutenant-Governor of the State in 1920. He served for four years; that is, two terms. And then in 1924 the people of his State put him in the Governor's chair, the highest honor they could give him. Dick Wittington had no greater honor.

This is not the easiest job in the world. Massachusetts has had some great Governors and to follow in their footsteps is no light matter. Some of these Governors have been business men, and such was Mr. Fuller. He was no politician in the usual meaning of the word.

In fact, he proceeded to run the State on the same principle as he did his Packard plant. Naturally, as a business man, he employed no man just because he was the third-cousin of some politician and controlled the votes of Precinct 2 Ward Steenth! Hence his appointments were made on merit—and the pork barrel politicians became very wroth indeed and swore to get him at the polls next time. What they forgot was the fact that he had no political machine—but he did have the majority of the voters for him. He had the biggest following of voters of any man who ever ran for office in Massachusetts.

Naturally he made enemies—especially as he ran the state government on a pay-as-you-go system, and refused to run into debt. As a matter of record, he took office with a debt in the treasury and left with a surplus of over five million dollars—a thing that is so rare now that a memento of it should be put in a museum!

He was a good Governor and he worked hard. Even his enemies (rather a large list) agreed that he gave an honest administration, and that he tried to do what was right. He did get into hot water many times, always because he thought something was wrong and should be corrected. He was outspoken and frank, qualities not usual in men in public office. He never beat around the bush or gave evasive answers. And he had a knack of going to the people themselves, thus confounding the politicians.

In the middle of his second term he had to face one of those tough spots that are sometimes the lot of statesmen. His famous predecessor, Calvin Coolidge, had gone

through his ordeal in the Police Strike, to ride therefrom
into the White House. Governor Fuller's ordeal was
much longer than that and had no such happy ending.

Several years before he was Governor, two men had
been arrested and convicted for the murder of a paymas-
ter and special-officer in South Braintree. They were Ital-
ians and radicals, by name, Nicola Sacco and Bartolomeo
Vanzetti. The final determination of the case came before
Governor Fuller under his pardoning and commutation
power.

The case had aroused intense feeling all over the world;
there was plenty of fiery criticism right here in America,
and many people thought the two men were being rail-
roaded into the electric chair because of their radical be-
lief; they had been convicted on circumstantial evidence.

Governor Fuller was "on the spot." By the stroke of a
pen he could have freed the men. But he was Governor of
over 4,000,000 people and he had taken an oath to serve
these people to the best of his ability. He meant to see
justice done, exact justice. And he faced the appalling
task with an open and unprejudiced mind.

He saw everybody who had any light to shed on the
case. He spent hours going over every scrap of evidence
which had been presented at the trial. He appointed a
special investigating board composed of Judge Robert
Grant, President Lowell of Harvard and President Strat-
ton of Tech. The findings of this board agreed with his
own. And finally, after a great deal of time and study on
the case, he announced that he saw no reason why the sentence should not be carried out. The men were electro-
cuted later.

This case is still being talked about. Radicals and fanatics will never forget it. Sacco and Vanzetti are considered martyrs—and so they would be if they were innocent. But the court had found them guilty, the Governor's own commission had found them guilty, and so had the commission mentioned above.

It was a terrific ordeal to go through; telegrams, letters, visits to the state house and all sorts of communications deluged the Governor. It took a lot out of him. What his critics (and they were many) lost sight of was that he was only trying to do his duty, to uphold the laws of the State of Massachusetts, as he had sworn to do. The New England conscience was strong in him; there is no other blood in him. And he went through with what he thought was the right course, regardless of the consequences. His attitude can be explained by his own words which were uttered on the occasion of his inauguration as Governor. When he strode up Beacon Hill on that morning in 1925, he said, "I experienced a thrill such as I had never felt before in my life. I then and there resolved that I would not fail, that I would never betray the trust and confidence which had been placed in me, that I would keep the faith."

In all his public life Mr. Fuller has never drawn a cent of pay for his services. This custom started even with his little check as state representative. It may be a gesture— but what a fine one it is. When everybody seems to be willing to let Uncle Sam or his state or city government take care of him, it is heartening to see somebody who likes the idea of standing on his own two feet. Such a gesture, becoming universally popular, would certainly take the hardness out of hard times, and incidentally, do some sadly needed repairing to the national backbone!

He said good-bye to the State House one day, when his term was up. There were tears in the eyes of this strong man when he left the scenes and faces with which he had worked for eight years. He was still young, only fifty, and it seemed a crime to be giving up the reins.

Since that time he has been mentioned for many high positions, ambassador to various countries, as candidate for Senator, Vice-President, but he is still a private citizen. This is a pity, in view of the fact that so many of his fellow citizens would like to see him in high office again. They trust him, they like his two-fisted character, and he is just the kind of hard-headed business man needed in an age that undoubtedly will be known in history as the Spendthrift Era.

Governor Fuller's career is a fine one for any boy to study. He had, you will note, no help whatsoever. Nobody gave him a boost up, nobody gave him a start in anything, nobody advised him. He selected all the forks in the road himself. He saw the bicycle, saw the automobile, and made them work for him. He saw the opportunity to do something for his fellowmen in public life, did it and accepted no pay for it.

This man's success was his own. He invented nothing. He simply took two useful things and made a tidy business empire from them. It must give him a load of pleasure, this man who once toiled in a shipping room for $7.50 a week, to look up Commonwealth Avenue and see the blue flag flying over his great buildings. In those early days, you must realize, he could have growled to himself in that shipping room, "I've got no chance. Gee Whiz, what is there for me in this world with no college education and no pull." But instead he listened to the bells of Malden and remembered Dick Whittington. And we'd say, without any American brag, that he beat Dick "all hollow!"

FRANCIS PATRICK GARVAN

A LEADER IN THE CHEMICAL WORLD

FRANCIS PATRICK GARVAN

FRANCIS PATRICK GARVAN

A LEADER IN THE CHEMICAL WORLD

THIS is a story of a metamorphosis—of a young man who started out to be a lawyer, did so, and then ran off on a spur track to be an altruistic head of what might be called an industrial incubator. It is a story of a good and continuous battle, extraordinary ability and, rare enough, in industrial history, splendid unselfishness. The man's name is Francis Patrick Garvan.

He was born in East Hartford, Connecticut, June 13, 1875. His father was Patrick Garvan, a paper manufacturer, and at one time state senator in Connecticut.

Young Francis attended the public schools where, with his quick, active mind, he made good marks. His boyhood was the usual one of a lad raised in the more or less countrified atmosphere of a suburban town. Evidently there were cow pastures and the opportunity to roam about bare-foot in the summertime.

Even as a lad he showed signs of the fighting ability he was later to exhibit to such good advantage. He picked no quarrels but if a fight was unavoidable or in a good cause, he sailed in one hundred per cent. In his own words he tells of an incident which happened when he was a boy.

"I remember as a boy fighting from seven o'clock in the morning until noonday, on a hillside in a pasture off Silver Lake, East Hartford, with a boy named Janeway

Brewer. I think I must have got licked, because I don't remember how it came out. All I remember is rage and tears and joy, and my bare feet in the stoney pasture. We sat down and we stood up. We knew no science. We had no audience to goad us on—no audience but the cows we had driven to pasture—and only the dinner bell at the farmhouse was able to end that long, determined fight."

Through with public schools, he meant to have a college education and he selected one in his native state, Yale University. At Yale he was popular with his fellow students and he was also a good scholar. He went in for athletics and proved a fine quarter-mile runner, representing his university at the Mott Haven games in his senior year. He was graduated from Yale in 1897 with the degree of A. B.

Law was the thing that attracted him, and he entered Catholic University shortly afterwards. Then he went to New York Law School where he got his LL.B. degree in 1899. Soon after he entered the law firm of James, Schell and Elkus. Here he showed such energy and ability that one of the partners, Colonel James, recommended him as a likely young man for the reform district attorney's office. Mr. Philbin, the District-Attorney, accepted him and young Garvan, twenty-five years old, was launched into a nine year connection that was to see not only much hard work, but an opportunity to participate in some of the most celebrated criminal cases in the history of the country.

A year after his entering this service, a new District-Attorney came into office, the famous William Travers Jerome, and young Garvan was appointed Assistant District Attorney. During Mr. Jerome's term of office several world famed criminal cases were tried and Mr. Garvan assisted in all of them. At the time the papers all over the country were filled with these trials—that of Mollineux, Dr. Kennedy, Patrick and Thaw. All these cases were intensely interesting and even now make good reading. Such a training was not only interesting but very valuable, and Mr. Garvan made the most of his opportunity. He served nine years in all in the office of the District-Attorney of New York County, part of which time he had charge of the Homicide Bureau (that place so often mentioned in the Mystery Novels!) He also carried on the work of the Bureau of Insurance and Commercial Frauds. The things he saw in these first few years as a legal officer would make a thrilling omnibus book on crime and criminals. Many times he had to face a battery of the cleverest criminal lawyers in the country; the fighting instinct was very much needed in those instances.

After his service in the District-Attorney's office was over he went into private practice, becoming a member of the firm of Garvan and Armstrong, and later of Osborne, Lamb and Garvan. He remained in active practice until that dramatic day when the United States joined the Allies and declared war against the Central Powers.

There was much German owned property in the United States and this, under the rules of warfare, was seized. The President appointed A. Mitchel Palmer as Alien Property Custodian, who was to have charge of the seizure and care of enemy property. To him Mr. Garvan offered his services and a most momentous assignment it proved to be. From that time on Francis P. Garvan was to be in a war, not to be ended on November 11, 1918, but many years afterwards. Long after most of the Generals in that war were dead, and the battlefields covered with verdure, the missiles would still be hurling at the head of Mr. Garvan. He would have to take it, not only from the Germans and their sympathizers, but from many of his own fellow countrymen. But of that, later.

In November, 1917, Mr. Garvan was appointed Director of the Bureau of Investigation of the Office of Alien Property Custodian and manager of the New York office. He served in that capacity until March, 1919. Here he had charge of all the investigations designed to discover enemy-owned property in our country. Hundreds of millions of dollars worth of such property was seized by the office.

On March 4, 1919, Mr. Garvan was appointed Alien Property Custodian to succeed Mr. Palmer. Not long afterwards he was appointed Assistant United States Attorney-General, in which position he had charge of the suppression of communistic activities in the United States, the investigation of the meat packers, and the reorganization of the Bureau of Investigation of the Department of Justice.

The War ran its course. And while it did, much German property was seized. Such things as ocean liners, German owned business and the like. Mr. Garvan put in an extremely busy time. The details were unending. Whole ship crews had to be taken care of, and all the seized property carefully administered.

Now in this immense amount of enemy owned property was something intangible but extremely valuable, much more valuable than any of the ships, businesses and such that took the eye at first glance. Just some pieces of paper—not the kind the German Headquarters tore to pieces when they invaded Belgium. These pieces of paper were chemical patents. There were 4813 of these patents, 281 applications for patents, and a few hundred trade-marks, copyrights and rights under contracts relating to chemical patents. In the rush of wartime such things were hardly considered by most people as very vital. But those unwarlike looking things in figures and technical words were the *most important thing* the United States got out of the World War! And it was Mr. Garvan who saw the light and played the major part in acquiring these patents for the use of American citizens.

Up to and during the War the United States, as well as other nations, depended on Germany for many chemicals, especially those used in dyes and in medicine. Up to the time of the big conflict there were something like six American-owned chemical plants in this country, and these without research laboratories. In the matter of dyes we were absolutely dependent on Germany. The Germans had taken out these patents, not to foster and build up the American chemical industry, but to impede it; they wished to control the market in the United States and, as a matter of fact, had succeeded in creating a monopoly.

President Wilson was greatly interested in the problem, which the War had shown was so important. He gave his approval to the organizing of a non-profit making institution, which had for its aims the fostering of the chemical industry in the United States. This was the birth of the Chemical Foundation Inc., and it was authorized to take over the seized German patents. It was capitalized for $500,000. and $269,850. was paid to the Alien Property Custodian for the patents, trade marks and copyrights. Under the Foundation's charter American manufacturers were enabled to use the chemical patents by the payment of a fee for the non-exclusive license granted.

Attorney-General Palmer, at whose instance the Foundation had been formed, strongly recommended to President Wilson the appointment of Mr. Garvan as the president of the new institution. There was nobody so familiar with the situation as Mr. Garvan, or so well fitted to take the job. His heart was in it and he foresaw its great beneficent powers if properly administered. He agreed to serve without pay. And so Mr. Garvan became the first President of the Chemical Foundation, Inc. It was an experiment that promised much and soon it became apparent that the appointment of Mr. Garvan, who knew how to fight a legal battle as well as anybody else, had been a proper one.

The big War was over—but a fresh one started over the new institution, whose aims were so noble and unselfish. You may well understand that German interests were not going to sit idle while their precious monopoly in the richest country in the world was threatened. They became extremely busy and soon criticism descended on the Foundation in an avalanche. It was contended that the seized patents were worth much more than a quarter of a million dollars paid by the Foundation.

Mr. Garvan, Mr. Palmer and others, were accused of conspiring to defraud the Government of $5,000,000. when the German owned Bosch Magneto Company was sold after the War. Suit was brought but the case was dismissed. Mr. Garvan launched a counter-attack in the form of a statement summarizing the deposition he had made at the trial. He brought charges against the American I. G. Chemical Corporation as a mere subsidiary of the German I. G., against Otto Kahn and Paul Warburg as backers of a German attempt to monopolize the dye industry, against Senator Moses as a worker for low tariffs on German dyestuffs, against Harry Daugherty and Gaston Means, whom he accused of building up a fraudulent case to discredit him.

In 1922 at the instigation of German interests, President Harding ordered the Alien Property Custodian to demand the return of the much talked about German patents. The Foundation refused and the Department of Justice brought a suit in equity for the return of the patents, claiming that the sale was made without due warrant of law, and that the purchase was a conspiracy on the part of certain government officials during the Wilson administration.

But Mr. Garvan unlimbered his guns and fired back. His ammunition and marksmanship were better than that of his opponents, and his case was sustained by the Federal District Court of Delaware in which state the suit was brought. He was victorious in the Federal Circuit Court of Appeals and later in 1926 by the United States Supreme Court.

Meanwhile the Foundation sawed wood. Its activities became many and varied. The charter provided that all profits over and above a small fixed return to the holders of the stock should be devoted to the advancement of the interests of chemistry and allied sciences in useful arts and manufactures. These profits have made possible an extensive chemical education program and countless other movements of benefit to the fast growing industry. It has financed numerous research activities and has distributed thirty million volumes, pamphlets and bulletins of informative literature on the subject of chemistry.

The chemical industry in the United States has bloomed since the days when Mr. Garvan and his Foundation began to look after its needs. Those half dozen pre-war chemical plants have grown to over two hundred with research laboratories. While only two decades ago we were almost dependent upon other nations, chiefly Germany, for our chemical needs, today over ninety per cent of these needs are produced within our own borders. Aside from that, through cheaper methods of production and greater efficiency, we export large quantities of chemical products.

To set down the valuable services of the Chemical Foundation in detail would take a big volume in itself. But a few may be noted. It has financed researches in the following diseases: Common cold, leprosy, streptococci in the blood, whooping cough, muscle diseases, children's diseases, tuberculosis, diabetes, pneumonia, cancer and many others.

The Foundation's assistance in the matter of biological stains has been valuable. Before the war such stains came from Germany; now the various societies and laboratories engaged in this important work in the United States turn out the finest in the world.

Other valuable researches assisted by the Foundation are: research on improved administration and control of anesthesia, bacteriological, pathological, clinical, and historical side of chemo-therapy in relation to disease, radiological research, colloid chemistry in relation to medicine, isolating active principles of vitamins, characteristics of bacteria, behavior of proteins and others.

The Foundation has also assisted in the publication of many chemical journals as: Journal of Physical Chemistry, Journal of Chemical Education, Chemical Abstracts, Journal of the Optical Society of America, the Physical Review, and several others.

It was one of the aims of the Foundation to inculcate a proper understanding and appreciation of the great subject of chemistry, in short, to make Americans "chemically-minded," as the German people were. In view of this the Foundation has done much to get the right sort of literature in the hands of the public. It has published such volumes as "Chemistry in Industry," "Chemistry in Agriculture," "Chemistry in Medicine," "The Significance of Nitrogen," "The Riddle of the Rhine," and others. It has distributed many copies of other books, such as "The Life of Pasteur," "Creative Chemistry," "The Advance of Science" and many others.

Mr. Garvan was married in 1910 to Mabel Brady, daughter of Anthony N. Brady. Mrs. Garvan has been no less interested in the works of the Foundation than her husband. They have given hundreds of thousands of dollars to research in medico-chemical fields. This interest dates from the death of a daughter several years ago, from rheumatic fever. They believe that her life might have been saved had the present large gaps in medical and chemical knowledge been filled.

Mr. Garvan has devoted his life, since the first days of the Foundation, to the freeing of American Chemistry from the domination of foreign interests. No one individual has a record so brilliant and devoted in this great work. In recognition of his invaluable services he was awarded the Priestley medal of the American Chemical Society in 1929, and the medal of that year of the American Institute of Chemists. In June, 1936, the degree of LL.D. was bestowed on him by the University of Notre Dame.

Nobody can estimate the amount of good such a thing as the Foundation can do and will do. At any moment a discovery can be made in one of those research laboratories that will free the suffering of mankind from some dread malady. At any moment some chemist, working in another kind of chemical laboratory, may discover for us some element of warfare that will make the United States so powerful as to be immune from attack by an enemy.

We have this splendid institution now and we should be thankful for it. Thankful to whom? Several men who had a hand in it, as President Wilson, Mr. Palmer and a few others. But only *one* man put his whole self in it, watched it, nursed it, fought for it. That man is Francis Patrick Garvan. Chemistry owes him a lot. And so do we.

MILTON S. HERSHEY

CHOCOLATE MANUFACTURER AND PHILANTHROPIST

(Underwood and Underwood)

MILTON S. HERSHEY

MILTON S. HERSHEY

CHOCOLATE MANUFACTURER AND
PHILANTHROPIST

WHEN the great botanist Linnaeus was asked to give a name to the plant cacao or cocoa, he was offered a cup of chocolate as a sample of the fruit. He sipped it, smacked his lips over the queer, new taste and promptly gave it a name which seemed appropriate. He called it Theobroma, which means "food of the gods," and that has been the scientific name of the plant ever since. The Aztecs in Mexico called it chocolath long before that; it was their favorite beverage. The conquering Cortez demanded three hundred loads of chocolath from Montezuma, emperor of the Aztecs, as part of a tribute he levied. Undoubtedly the inhabitants of the Americas knew about it long before Columbus brought his little fleet to anchor off San Salvador.

Of course some time, somebody had to take this succulent little bean and make a fortune out of it. Anything that was so pleasing to the taste could hardly help making somebody a fortune. Several were made, but the most remarkable one in many ways did not come into being until almost two hundred years after Linnaeus had given this most appropriate name to the plant. And strangely enough, the little bean from the tropics performed its act in a quiet country field in Pennsylvania. How that isolated spot became a thriving and properly beautiful town, and incidentally made a great fortune for one man, is a strangely fascinating story. The man's name is Milton Snavely Hershey.

He was born on a farm in Derry Township, Dauphin County, Pennsylvania, September 13, 1857. This is not far from Harrisburg, a locality of pleasant rolling country and many dairy farms. The Hershey family had lived there for many years, having come over from Switzerland in 1709.

In this quiet and healthy spot young Milton Hershey grew up. He attended a little stone schoolhouse, which never had over twenty pupils at a time, and there learned his three R's.

His first job had nothing to do with either farming or chocolate. He became a printer's devil on a periodical called the Lancaster Farmer. Now the job of printer's devil is dirty and lowly, but there is something about it that is educational. One learns something about letters and type, learns to be very careful with his fingers. So perhaps young Hershey's short stay in the printing office was not entirely wasted time. But the atmosphere, fascinating to so many boys, failed to interest him. He didn't care for ink and type—especially in such instances when he accidentally pied some set-up type and got a proper bawling out; pieing type is sacrilege in any printing office.

His next job was that of apprentice in the confectionery business, working with a product just as sticky as ink but a lot more palatable. He liked this. There was something really interesting in working among the sweet smells and later, in seeing people enjoy the product. Milton

Hershey always enjoyed making people happy and in this early job of his he had a chance to do it in a wholesale manner.

Candy making came easy to him. He seemed to know just how to concoct a mixture that was bound to tickle the palates of the customers. He liked to experiment, to work out a new confection and then watch how it was accepted.

The work was happy enough, but working for somebody else was not. Young Hershey knew his ability and soon made up his mind that he would make his own candy in his own way, and also sell it himself. So he went into business for himself in Philadelphia. Young men went to the city, of course, and there he would make his fortune.

He knew what people liked in the way of candy. Caramels were sure-fire and he could make as good caramels as anybody. It was very pleasant, being one's own boss; but it was also hard work to keep going with so little capital. But one day a trolley car smashed up his precious wagon, and that was a calamity too great for the embryo candy merchant. The first venture was a failure.

A little later he got back his courage and struck out again, this time in New York City. A relative loaned him enough money to make the start. But this venture was no more successful than the first for some reason. He had to close up. And, feeling quite discouraged, he left the big city. It was a definite leave-taking, too, although he did not realize it; never again would he try a big city.

But he knew he was on the right track. His product was good and if the people liked what you made, success just had to come. So he gave up the idea of a great city success and started to make caramels in his native state, in the then small city of Lancaster. This was in 1886.

The Hershey caramels made friends. In fact, they made so many that the young candy-maker could not keep up with the demand. He tried out new things. He made what some people call "blonde" caramels, but he also experimented on a darker brand flavored with that ingredient which was to be such a friend to him later— chocolate. Although he never advertised, those caramels did the job for him. The business grew tremendously, and so did the fame of his products. His venture in Lancaster was quite successful, and the story could have ended right there in 1901. In that year interests seeking to form a trust, bought him out for $1,000,000.

One million dollars at the age of forty-four. That was a remarkable success, all accomplished in fourteen years. He could have retired, enjoyed himself, traveled. In fact, he did travel and decided it was a waste of time.

However, he had an idea or two which he wanted to try out. It was this chocolate. He wanted to do something about that. In 1876 M. D. Peter of Vevey, Switzerland, had produced milk chocolate for eating which was a mixture of cacao nib, sugar, cacao butter and milk. It was different, pleasingly different from the straight black chocolate flavored with sugar. Mr. Hershey had the idea of putting out this new chocolate that he knew how to make, in the form of inexpensive bars—five and ten cents. He had sold caramels in the old days in amounts from penny lots to a dollar a pound, and he knew the enormous amount of business to be done with anything that cost only a nickel.

The other idea that hooked up with this one was geographical. Why not build a proper factory in the country? And what more beautiful spot was there than his own birthplace? People said he was foolish, when they learned of it. It wouldn't work, he was told. Raw materials had to be sent to New York or Philadelphia and the sensible place for a factory was, of course, at points like these. The city was the only place for a factory for all sorts of reasons. And there weren't any good ones for building one anywhere else.

Mr. Hershey listened politely and went ahead with his own plans. He knew the kind of factory he wanted and he knew where he wanted it. In 1903 ground was broken for the first big building in a spot where no industry more intricate than milking a cow had ever been done before. Perhaps it was far from the land where the cacao bean grew, but it was satisfactorily adjacent to a locality where thousands of cows grazed, cows that gave luscious, rich milk. And milk was an important ingredient in the new product he intended to make.

Up went the factory and soon machines were at work turning out the product. The making of candy was no new thing to Mr. Hershey. His idea of the five and ten cent milk chocolate bar was sound. They were conveniently shaped; pieces could be easily broken off without smashing them off on a sharp edge as was the case with some of the early thick chocolate confections. The wrappers were the color of chocolate. They got no advertising and needed none. The chocolate-almond bar captivated the public from its first appearance; that combination is one of the most delectable in the whole gamut of confections.

The Hershey Chocolate Company drew its workers from the surrounding country; there were no highly trained men needed and almost any normal person could learn to run one of the machines after a little training. So well did Mr. Hershey build his great structure that he has never had any labor troubles, never had a strike. Many of the special machines he evolved himself.

The company grew as the years went by, not only in Pennsylvania, but elsewhere. His next step was to go to the source of supplies of a chief ingredient—sugar—and Mr. Hershey bought a great sugar plantation in Cuba. This became a town, too, and is also named Hershey— Central Hershey, Cuba. In the working season it employs 3500 workers and turns out 200,000 pounds of sugar daily.

One of the boosts experienced by this succulent little candy bar was caused by no less a thing than the World War. Explorers had discovered that milk chocolate contained a surprising amount of energy building properties for its bulk. Great quantities were supplied the soldiers. They learned to like it and a 4,000,000 chocolate-eating clientele is no mean asset. The War stopped—but chocolate bar eating, like Ole Man River "just kept rollin' along."

The picture now presented on the site of what once was a simple pastoral scene is truly remarkable. Here are some of the major things of the town of Hershey. A fine new community center, costing $3,000,000, which contains a big library, a swimming pool, dormitory, a hospital, a little theatre and a larger community theatre, two eighteen-hole golf courses, two nine-hole golf courses, one of them for children, the only golf club of its kind in America; the Hotel Hershey, a splendidly appointed hostelry; a big department store; an Indian museum; a roller coaster; women's club building; a 1000 acre park which has a dance pavilion, swimming pool, two athletic fields, a zoo, convention hall, and a sports arena seating 7,000 for ice hockey and 9,000 for other sporting events.

The town itself is an attractive one, with lovely vistas wherever the eye rests. The buildings are handsome and so are the homes. There are no eye-sores of any kind in Hershey. When the factory worker takes a little time out to look through a window, it is something refreshing and beautiful that he sees.

The chocolate plant itself contains thirty connected buildings of stone and concrete, having a total floor area of sixty acres. It employs about two thousand persons in its various departments, and almost as many more in allied interests. This concern is the world's largest chocolate company. One half the business is done in the well known bars. The remainder is divided among breakfast cocoa, chocolate syrup for soda fountains and chocolate covering for candy making. The plant uses 400,000 quarts of milk daily in the manufacture of its preparations.

The office building of the Hershey Chocolate Corporation is windowless, indirectly lighted and air-conditioned, science's latest contribution to aid the worker.

That, briefly, is the story of the business success of this quiet, mild-mannered man. It was a good success, honestly earned. In 1918, when the profits had piled themselves up into an imposing pyramid, Mr. Hershey did something which puts him in a class by himself. At that time he gave almost his entire fortune, something like $60,000,000, to a school for orphan boys. This is called the Hershey Industrial School.

Mr. and Mrs. Hershey had no children, but they were both very fond of them. The dream of doing something helpful for some of those most neglected of forgotten human beings, orphan boys, had been in this man's mind for a long time. As a boy he had had to work hard himself; he felt that boys who had lost their parents were more in need of a helping hand than any other of God's creatures. Perhaps he had seen public institutions and the idea was strengthened by that. At any rate, he decided to do something about it, and as we shall see, he most definitely did.

At present the school has about 950 orphan boys; that is, boys who have lost one or both of their parents. They range from four or five to eighteen years of age, most of them coming from points within the State of Pennsylvania. The boys live in thirty-one separate houses, scattered widely over the charming countryside, some of brick and some being farmhouses; all spick and span, and presided over by house-mothers, or in the case of the farmhouses, by a farmer and his wife. For ten months in the year the boys attend school, just like other boys; during the remaining two months they work the land.

The educational course up to the age of fourteen is the usual one; then the boy has to decide whether to take up a commercial, industrial or academic course. There are many practical courses for the boys, which will be helpful to them in later life. When they reach the age of eighteen they are sent out into the world with one hundred dollars, which is perhaps more than many other boys get not so situated. The school finds a job for them, too. Some, of course, stay in Hershey and go to work in the chocolate factory.

The boys have no distinctive uniform as they do in institutions, but wear clothes just like other boys. Living in such quarters is healthy and the boys are enabled to go out into the world well equipped for the future.

The school will continue, even after the kindly donor of it has gone. It is endowed with 500,000 shares of the 729,000 shares of Hershey common stock. The school also owns the $30,000,000 sugar development in Cuba. Altogether the endowment totals something like $65,000,000.

It is a rare thing when a man can make a fortune by pleasing millions of people—which is just what Mr. Hershey has done with his delectable chocolate bars. A simple thing but a delightful one. Nobody knows how many hungry and exhausted boys found it a veritable godsend "over there" when any other food was very scarce. And nobody can measure what great good the money received will do for those other boys who needed a father, and found such a good one in Milton S. Hershey.

JOHN DANIEL HERTZ

BUILDER OF CABS, BUSSES AND TRANS-PORTATION LINES

(Blank-Stoller Inc.)

JOHN DANIEL HERTZ

JOHN DANIEL HERTZ

BUILDER OF CABS, BUSSES AND TRANS-
PORTATION LINES

A S you grow older you will hear much talk about
a most speculative subject—the Great American
Novel. Who has written it? Who will write it?
Will it ever be written? But to boys of the early 1900's
there was no such question at all. They knew definitely
who had written it. As far as they were concerned the
Great American Novel was written (in about fifty volumes) by one Horatio Alger, Junior. He was the master
of the success story for boys—and retains his laurels to
this day.

Mr. Alger's theme was simple. He took for his hero
a poor but honest boy, loaded him to the breaking point
with adversities, and brought him home to splendid success through the power of grit, acumen and, if not luck,
at least the ability to see good fortune when it arrived.

If Mr. Alger had met the subject of this sketch, John
Daniel Hertz, he could have written a splendid specimen
of his famous works by no more than just setting down
facts. It was all there (with perhaps the absence of one
arch-villain)—adversity, grit, alertness, push and the
ability to see a lucky break when it arrived. It is an
inspiring story and, though minus Mr. Alger's fine talent,
we'll try to tell it.

John Hertz was born in Ruttka, a little village in Austria (now Czechoslovakia) on April 10, 1879. At the age of five he was brought by his parents to America; the family settled in Chicago. The great immigration to the land of golden opportunity was at its height and this little family, like thousands of others, entered the contest, picking out one of the liveliest cities in this liveliest of countries. A great adventure, one of the greatest.

However, the promised land did not turn out so happily as was hoped. John's father got work, and perhaps they were better off in the new country than they would have been in the old. At least there were free schools, no military juggernaut to roll over one and, while it was a hectic scramble, there seemed to be a chance to get somewhere.

Young John entered the public schools of Chicago when he was old enough. There he stayed until he was eleven—and that completed his academic education. At the age when most lads are just getting to know what school is all about, he did as adventurous a thing as a boy ever did.

One day his father gave him a licking for some minor misdemeanor. It hurt. And moreover, it was the first time such a thing had ever happened. Now John had a temper and he didn't relish punishment. So—whether it was right or wrong—he just left the scene of his humiliation. He ran away!

Eleven years old and on his own. You know, perhaps, how most runaways end up. Twenty-four hours or so and the adventure seems frightfully tame, and one gets hungry and lonesome—and why did one do such a silly thing in the first place? But this runaway was different. He made plans. Two things he knew he had to do— get some money for a stake and get a job. The first he managed by selling his school books. They brought not quite two dollars, the biggest amount of hard cash the boy had ever had. With two dollars one could eat for a while and the lodging part of it did not worry him.

He got room and board at the Waifs' Home for two dollars a week. That solved that problem—for a week. He wasted no time in looking for a job. He landed one almost at once on the old Morning News as copy boy at the salary of $2.50 per week. The adventure now had a sound foundation. Two dollars for shelter and board—fifty cents for clothes and so on. Pretty fine sailing it would be, but he felt he could manage.

A copy boy was a most useful part of a newspaper in those days. The reporter covering a big story, took along two or three of these boys with him. Why? There were few telephones then and the news, often piecemeal, had to be relayed to the city editor hot off the bat. The reporter could not leave the scene, hence the agile boys who knew all the arts of legging it and hopping what rapid transportation they could find.

It was an intensely busy life and an interesting one. Young Hertz met the keenest men, some who were to rise to journalistic fame in the succeeding years. He himself, soon developed a nose for news, a thing that was to help him in the near future. This life was not so bad; he was learning something and earning something.

However, two dollars and a half isn't a great lot. He

needed more. So after his strenuous day of copy-carrying was over, he sold newspapers on the street. What a life! Eleven years old and fighting a battle like that. Yet who shall say that young Hertz was not getting a valuable education? At least he was on the fringe of a profession, journalism. And let nobody tell you that selling newspapers on the streets is not a course in business administration!

This lad must have been made of steel. He stuck at this thing for a year, fighting his own battles and supporting himself. Then one day the blow fell. His father found him and made him come home. There was no getting away from it. Back to school he went, into a life which now seemed tame and tasteless. He had seen the outside world, business men doing all sorts of vital things—and staring at a book meant next to nothing to him.

The whole thing was wrong in his estimation. Education was all right for some, but his own case was different. The father earned only ten dollars a week, running a freight elevator. The mother had to work hard, too, in taking care of the family; out of six children four were home, too young to work. And so John Hertz who knew his way about, decided to leave home again, this time for good. There was no other way out of the problem. After six months of schooling he told his family of his decision. He would not run away. He just gave up school, at the tender age of twelve—and went.

There was only one job he knew and that was making himself useful in the peculiar atmosphere of the city room of a big newspaper. By now he knew his way around and this time he was put to work running errands of various kinds for the night editor. It was no work for a young growing boy, spending so many waking hours in the dark and missing the needed sunshine. But he stuck to it for three years. The pay was small, $4.50 per week.

He became pale and ill looking. His boss urged him to see a doctor and sent him to his own physician. The prescription was a blow: to quit night work, get outside in the fresh air and join a gym. He told the story to his kind-hearted boss, who promptly fired him—to save his life.

He was now fifteen years old, already a man of the world in many ways. He soon got a job driving a delivery wagon for a firm of two brothers. The hours were long but the work did give him the much needed open air and sunshine. He got six dollars a week.

To build himself up he joined a gym and went to work at that. This particular gym was frequented by several prize-fighters, who trained there for their bouts. Young Hertz thought it would be a grand thing to be able to defend himself the way these athletes did, and he laid out a precious ten dollars for a course of lessons. He was quick and courageous—two qualities needed for a boxer. It was not long before they put him on in an exhibition bout at the Chicago Athletic Association. Before many years he would appear before that Association in a far different capacity—but of that later.

The association with athletes and his former connection with newspapers now developed into a curious but welcome merger. While he knew nothing about writing, he did recognize a piece of news when he saw it. He was given a chance at supplying stray bits of sporting news by the sporting editor of the old Chicago Record, Ed Sheridan. The little squibs, contributed orally, were paid for at the rate of twenty-five cents an inch. Such bits built up his income by a dollar or two a week.

But the busy editor was doing the actual writing. He told the embryonic sports reporter that he would have to do his own composing, or else there would be no pay. Here was a bad break in fortune. With so meagre an education, how could he be expected to cast his little stories into good newspaper English? Still it had to be done; he needed that extra money. Young Hertz began, grinding out his sentences with what trouble and pains only he knew. But do it he did. And the kindly editor snapped it into the required smoothness. Practice does make perfect, and it was not long before Hertz could set down in readable English the bits of sports gossip that came his way.

It was fortunate for him that he went to the trouble of doing all this. Because his connection with the delivery firm was due to come to an end. He hurt himself in handling some heavy crates one day and protested. He was told he would not have to perform such labor again, but the promise was broken. He was ordered to do the work and he refused. One of the partners fired him. Once again he was out of a job.

However, this proved good fortune rather than otherwise. The delivery business had served its purpose. Hertz was now strong and healthy from the long hours outdoors.

It was only a step from sending in squibs to the newspaper to handing in longer and more important stories. He got paid space rates which appealed to him more than a salary. In those days the sports writers were poorly paid and the high-speed Hertz found he could beat the highest salary two or three times over on his pay by the column.

This connection ran along for several years and he did very well with it. All in all, he had done well and he had all the reason in the world to feel proud of himself. He might have gone on in this field but for an unforeseen occurrence. His paper merged with the Herald and all the Record men were fired. His newspaper days were over.

Naturally he was familiar with the sporting situation in Chicago, especially with the boxing world. He soon became a manager for a couple of fighters. For a year he did this, and it turned out to be a very profitable venture. One of the fighters was a top-notch performer and began mowing down everything in his class. Within the year the modest boxing enterprise cleaned up around $40,000. As manager Hertz got $10,000, a sum both welcome and creditable.

But this had to be given up. Young Hertz had become acquainted with a girl and she frowned on his connection with fighters. It was a question of giving up one or the other, so he gave up the boxing game. There were other methods of making a living and he had no doubt of his ability to find them.

So many times we hear of the big opportunity arriving and being almost lost through inability to recognize it.

It was so now with young Hertz. He had become acquainted with an old chap who was a demonstrator for
an automobile firm—or perhaps it would be better to
call them horseless-carriages as they were then. At the
turn of the century automobiles occupied anything but
a dignified position in the world of industry. They were
a rich man's toy; and generally a rich man who liked
roughing it. Automobiles in those days were most undependable.

Young Hertz could see nothing in automobiles then.
He would not listen to the urging of his acquaintance,
who wanted him to get into the game. But one morning
he looked out of his window and there was the old chap,
seated in the "benzine-buggy." It resulted in a ride
and an interview with the man for whom the acquaintance worked. The result of the interview: Hertz made
his entry into the automotive world as a salesman on a
straight commission basis. No salary, no drawing account. But if he could persuade any decent number of
Chicagoans to risk their lives in his wares, maybe there
would be something in it. At any rate, he would try it.

Then followed a most discouraging interlude. Nobody
wanted any part of the snorting, erratic creatures that
were neither carriages or locomotives, but something
part way between. Hertz kept plugging, mainly because
it was a challenge to his ability, rather than any faith
in the product. He went about for weeks, seeking prospects, arguing, demonstrating, urging. Yet to no avail.

But finally, when he was almost convinced nobody
would ever buy a car from him, somebody signed on the
dotted line. He sold a car. Commission, eighty-five

dollars. And Mr. John Daniel Hertz was definitely in the automobile business.

At the end of his first year in this business he found he had made less than he had as a sports writer—and considerably less than he had reaped as a fight-manager. Yet the thing seemed to have possibilities. There were indications that the product would soon snort and rattle less, and purr and glide more. Also people and horses were becoming less scared of them. He decided to cast his lot in with the new industry and see where it went.

There came a vacancy. The manager of the agency for which Hertz worked was fired. Hertz got on a train and went to the factory to see the big boss. He asked for the position and was laughed at. What did he know about managing an agency?

They both made a mistake. The big boss didn't know a good manager when he saw one—and Hertz didn't know what a good salesman he really was. The agency manager's salary was $2,500 per year. And that second year Hertz made $12,000 in commissions, with no managerial headache! The following year he increased that figure by another thousand.

Now Mr. Hertz had a policy as a salesman, one which he had developed himself. The usual plan was to sell a car and trust to Providence that it would function all right. Mr. Hertz decided to augment the power of Providence by some of his own. To be sure, he was no auto-mechanic but he did know how to adjust a carbureter (and how they needed adjusting in those days!), fix a magneto and so on. The average buyer was utterly helpless in such matters at the period.

Mr. Hertz's plan was no more or less than the now frequently advertised (and sometimes lived up to) plan of service. But he meant what he told his customers. He told them if anything went wrong with the cars he sold them, to call him up and he would come to help them, at any hour, day or night. He did, too. He kept a car in his backyard, ready for emergency. He made such a reputation for honesty and extra service that his customers sold cars *for* him! Of course his plan was just sound common-sense but how many of us would want to go out on a cold, rainy night to minister to a sick car?

Mr. Hertz did not remain long with that company. It was having financial difficulties and he decided to get out. At the time he had more than one opportunity in the new industry. He was becoming known. He finally went in with a wealthy young man who owned the agency for a fine French car. In those early days the foreign cars were superior to ours, and this car was a good one. But in spite of that the agency had run behind some $45,000 during its first year in business. The young man offered Mr. Hertz a one-quarter interest in the business for $2000 and it was promptly accepted. He was now a partner in an automobile agency.

Mr. Hertz turned on full steam. In that first year the agency did a business of half a million dollars, Mr. Hertz bringing in about four-fifths of that. The partners cleaned up $90,000 in profits.

The bugaboo in the automobile business was (and still is), turned in cars. Fast changing styles and improvements caused many good cars to be taken off the road. They accumulated and Mr. Hertz cast about in his mind for some solution to the used car problem.

The taxi-cab had come by then, but it was not the sturdy little performer with which we are familiar. In fact, it was any car made over—or even left as is, even touring cars. There was no uniformity, either in cabs or in the business. It was, in a sense, simply motorizing the old livery stable business.

Mr. Hertz was never at a loss for ideas. Why not put a few good closed models on the road as cabs and see what happened? He did. And carefully watched the results. Chicago was a big and busy place, full of people in a hurry; naturally the taxi-cab was built to order for such a city.

In 1910 Mr. Hertz got a chance to make a bid for taxi service on a more extensive scale. The Chicago Athletic Association wanted some concern to operate a private cab service for their members. They required a fleet of at least ten cabs, and Mr. Hertz had but two equipped for that special service. The thing looked worthwhile, so he hustled off to another city and borrowed eight more cabs. Then he paraded them up and down the street in front of the Association headquarters. He got the contract.

The taxi business had different angles than the automobile agency business. One of the chief problems was human—the drivers. The Hertz outfit suffered from a strike, almost at the outset. Mr. Hertz had left the handling of the men to a paid manager, whose methods were wrong. Mr. Hertz investigated and saw what the trouble was. The men were not treated well and he knew that this would have to be changed if the service was to be good. He figured out a plan of profit-sharing, by which the drivers were given one-fifth of the profits before dividends were paid. The undesirable drivers were weeded out, and only dependable ones hired. The Hertz drivers were trained in the business of driving before they were allowed to take a cab out on the streets.

In 1915 Mr. Hertz went to Europe to see how the taxi-cab business was run there. The French especially were past masters in the art. He found an entirely different situation abroad. The cabs were smaller, thus more economical. Luxuries were cut to the bone (our cabs at the time were big limousines with many niceties.) And people simply stepped to the curb and signaled to the cruising cabs. It was very simple. In the United States nearly all cabs were called on the telephone. There were other economies abroad, too, as in the matter of concessions. In the United States large sums were paid to hotels for the exclusive right for a taxi stand. That was not the situation abroad.

The reason people telephoned for cabs in the United States instead of hailing them was because of their lack of uniformity. They were all different. A big car might be a cab and it might not. There were countless amusing (and otherwise) instances of people piling into private cars, thinking they were cabs. Mr. Hertz thought it over on the way back to the United States. He knew what he wanted. A sturdy, dependable car, small enough to maneuver in the crowded streets and yet comfortable. And he wanted it distinctive, so it could be seen a mile away and immediately known.

He hit on the idea of painting them all in one bright color. And yellow was the color selected. Laboratory tests showed this bright color the most easily recognized day or night.

The first fleet of yellow cabs, thirty in number, appeared on the streets of Chicago August 2, 1915. They had been advertised and a good patronage was expected. But the public held off for a week or so. Then they suddenly found they were good—and the Yellow Cab Company was on its way.

Up to that time there had been little uniformity in taxis. There were all sorts of cars masquerading under the name of cab. They might be able to stand the battering of taxi service for 35,000 miles or so, when they had to be scrapped.

The Yellow Cab Company started to build cabs, at first for themselves. They evolved a short, sturdy and comfortable cab that could maneuver in a crowded street much better than the bulky limousines. Out on the road it could hold its own in speed, too. It was a taxi-cab and looked like nothing else. And it had, in its staunch construction, something like a reservoir of 300,-000 miles!

The Yellow Cab Manufacturing Company could not keep up with their orders. Other cities wanted them. The factory worked night and day. Improvements were incorporated. The Yellow was probably the first to install receipt meters, as well as heaters, inside lights and robes. The growth of the business was phenomenal. The Yellow cabs sprang up like mushrooms in big cities all over the country.

Transportation had been undergoing many changes. When John Hertz came to America as a lad of five the horse-drawn street car was the only means of city transportation. Then in the early nineties came that great innovation, the trolley-car. For a score of years this reigned supreme. But after a War a new conveyance began to appear on the city thoroughfares. The motorized bus. It was generally a box-like body (with trolley-car motif!) mounted on a truck chassis. Some of these weird juggernauts still remain, ungainly and noisy.

New York City's Fifth Avenue bus line was famous all over the country. Everybody who came to New York had to take at least one ride on one of these things, preferably on the top deck. O. Henry wrote one of his famous stories around the upper deck of one of these old green busses.

For all their noise (they operated in second speed most of the time) people liked them. It was a motor car and many people had no chance to motor except in one of these.

Mr. Hertz was interested in transportation. He could see that the days of the trolley car would soon be over, once these busses became what they should in mechanics and management. He now proceeded to do with the bus what he had done with the taxi-cab. Glorify it.

In 1922 he began his operations. He hired men well versed in engineering and in the operation of bus lines. He bought the engine works of the R & V Motor Company which made the Knight sleeve-valve engines used on the better busses. At about the same time he organized the great Chicago Motor Coach Company out of a

bankrupt bus line. Then came the acquisition of the
Fifth Avenue Coach Company of New York City, and
the People's Motorbus of St. Louis. Out of all these
acquisitions came the Omnibus Corporation of America,
with John D. Hertz as Chairman.

The Yellow Coach Manufacturing Company was
started to build the coach Mr. Hertz had in mind. No
more clanking, grinding juggernauts. Soon the new
busses appeared on the streets of Chicago and St. Louis
and New York. Trim affairs, with huge tires, smooth
running motors and gears, and seats more comfortable
than those of motor cars. Business boomed. Over the
next few years the Company sold 420 of these giant con-
veyances to the Chicago Motor Coach Company, 90 to
the St. Louis line and 80 to the Fifth Avenue line. In
1924 and 1925 they began selling outside. Two big orders
were to the Public Service Corporation of New Jersey
($5,000,000 worth) and the Philadelphia Rapid Transit
Company ($6,500,000 worth.)

In 1926 the Yellow Cab Manufacturing Company was
absorbed by General Motors Corporation, Mr. Hertz
selling out at a handsome profit. Still later, 1933, he
became a partner in the New York firm of Lehman
Brothers, investment bankers.

That, in brief, is the story of John Daniel Hertz, the
poor boy who started as copy-boy on a Chicago newspaper and kept going until he had acquired taxi-cab
and bus manufacturing companies, as well as operating
companies, and a partnership in a great banking firm.
Such a career would be possible in no other country
but America. There is wizardry in it.

JESSE HOLMAN JONES

BUILDER AND BANKER

(Photo by Bachrach)

JESSE HOLMAN JONES

JESSE HOLMAN JONES

BUILDER AND BANKER

WE wish that this man (as well as all the others in this book) had kept a diary from the time he was able to write descriptive sentences. Then we could know the interesting things he did as a boy, and above all, what he thought about. Afterwards, when a man is very successful or famous, everybody wants to know what he looked like and what he did as a boy. If you were a biographer you would know how seldom this happens! It's a good habit to write about yourself in a diary; and even if you don't turn out famous it will be mighty interesting reading in later years.

Jesse Holman Jones was born in Robertson County, Tennessee, April 5, 1874. A boy born in that locality at that particular time could not be considered to have come into a land of opportunity. The Civil War had been over but a few years. Tennessee had had more battles fought in its territory than any other state except Virginia. Crops were ruined, the troops had fought up and down, and back and forth across the State.

The plantation operated by his father, William Hasque Jones, grew tobacco, and as soon as Jesse was able to handle farming implements he was out in the fields, tending to the delicate green plants. He was a husky lad and he liked to work. He also liked a good time, especially travel of any sort. And travel where he lived meant one thing—a horse.

One day, when he thought he was big enough to do a bit of cantering on his own account, he asked his dad for a horse. His father knew he loved animals and thought some other creature would answer the bill. So he offered him a small pig!

Jesse. said nothing. But he did a lot of thinking. He took his little pig, put him in a pen and started a little intensive fattening. The little pig eventually became a fine hog. He swapped the hog one day for a calf. Then he kept the calf until it was a cow. And finally he traded the cow for a horse. That showed two things: that when he wanted a thing he found a way to get it, and that he was a born trader. It's easy to trade *down* the scale, but much more difficult to trade *up*. From a mere piglet to a horse is mighty good trading.

School days were not too many and neither were the schools fitted to do any more than teach the barest fundamentals. But there were other ways than through books to acquire an education. The boy, working in the quiet of the tobacco fields had his dreams. He wanted to see what was beyond those sleepy purple hills of the Cumberland—cities, people, railroads, business—the whole fascinating picture out there. And in 1893 something happened that brought his longings to a head. The World's Fair at Chicago. He, like so many other boys of the period, felt he just had to see that great exposition. But it would cost money. How to get it?

So the boy who would later lend more money than anybody who ever lived, placed a mortgage for $60 on his tobacco crop (still in the ground). He got a cut-rate round trip ticket for $10. And a ten dollar bill he had sewed in the lining of his suit; the city slickers might get his roll but they'd have to tear his clothes apart to get that ten! The balance, $40, would enable him to stay a week or more and see all the sights. He arranged with some of the colored boys on the farm to take care of his tobacco plants, promising as their pay a faithful and complete description of everything he saw at the Fair!

He enjoyed a healthy appetite but he had no idea of spending that $40 for food, not when Tennessee had so much food. So he packed a telescope suitcase (pulled out to the last strap-hole) with food from home. A whole ham, three roasted chickens, several dozen biscuits, a lot of bread, homemade pickles and preserves.

He stayed two weeks at the Fair, saw everything and never spent a cent for food. The sewed-in ten dollar bill came home intact. He lived royally from his own commissary. It got dry towards the end of his stay and even a little mouldy, but he pared away the damaged parts with his jack-knife. That Fair was a great event in his life and it left a vivid and lasting impression. The buildings, especially took his fancy. He had never seen anything like them, never imagined anything could be so tall and so wonderful.

When he was twenty years old his father died. He could have stayed on the farm and become a tobacco grower. But he wanted something else than a life of sticking tiny green plants in the ground in the spring and cutting them down in the fall. Like so many country boys, the city called and nothing could have made him stay. He had two sisters and he turned over to them his share of the estate.

There was an uncle over in Dallas, Texas, who owned a lumber business, and one day Jesse set out for that place. He had written and had received a letter stating that he could have a job. Dallas in 1894 wasn't such a big city, but it was a veritable metropolis compared with the village he had come from.

Lumber. It was heavy work, but Jesse Jones was a strapping big fellow and tireless. He liked the business, and apparently the business liked him, for inside of a year he was made manager of the yard.

His first venture in business was a queer one for a young man. He had kept his eyes open to everything that went on around him, and he had come to the conclusion that to succeed one either had to have a big sum of cash on hand or an equal amount of credit. The reason: opportunities were always turning up and they wouldn't wait; the fellow who could slap down on them would win.

So he set out to cultivate a banker and to build up a line of credit. The banker's name was Ferris. The first thing young Jones did was to apply for a loan of $100— which he got and for which he had no use. When the note came due he paid it promptly, with interest from his wages. Next he did the same thing with a $200 loan. Then he borrowed $500, paying it promptly when it came due. After a little waiting he applied for a loan of $2000 from the banker, paid back $1300 when the note was due and renewed $700 of it, then paid back the $700 with-

out ever having used a cent of the money. He had simply
been building up his borrowing capacity.

Then the day came when he could use this carefully
manufactured ammunition. He learned of some timberland that could be bought for $10,000. He went to his
banker friend and asked for a loan of that amount. The
banker laughed. That was too much money to lend any
young fellow on a note.

But young Jones had no idea of being put off. That
timberland project was good; it would turn over a nice
profit and he meant to have it. He hung around the
bank all day, sticking his head in the banker's office so
often that that man became exasperated. In fact, to get
rid of the pestiferous young lumber plunger, he took a
train out of town to one of the bank's branch offices.

But the next morning young Mr. Jones was there at
the branch, still going strong and still thinking he was
good for $10,000. Finally the banker wilted under such
persistence. He granted the loan. And it turned out just
as young Jones had known it would. He made money and
bought an interest in the lumber business.

He could see possibilities in a deal that were overlooked
by others. One day a man came into the lumber yard
office and asked somewhat irritably if Jones would rent
him some lumber. Rent lumber? That was a new one,
but he quickly turned it over in his mind before refusing.

"Why, yes," he drawled. "I think we could. How much
do you want and what do you want to rent it for?"

"That's good," replied the man, relieved. "You know,
I've been to every lumber yard in this town, but they all

want to *sell* lumber. I only want to rent it for a short time. I want to build a big platform to hold a tent. You see, I've got a show, displaying buggies and carriages. Got to have the platform to hold them."

Jones supplied the lumber and had a carpenter friend do the laying. After the show was over, the buggy demonstrator went on to another town, leaving the rent lumber to the astute Mr. Jones, who had charged the same price for rental as he would have for a sale!

From local manager young Jones became general manager of the concern in 1898 and went to Houston the seat of the main office. And now began a remarkable career in several lines, lumber, real estate, building and banking. He operated several large yellow pine sawmills and many retail lumber yards in Texas and Oklahoma.

His original idea of getting credit and keeping his credit good helped in this rapid progress. Once he had credit practically thrust upon him. Along in 1900, when he was just getting a good start, he had occasion to go abroad to visit a relative. He took with him a rather eulogistic letter from a Houston bank. In New York he went to a banker to arrange for a letter of credit and drew a check on the Houston bank.

The New York banker asked if he had an account in New York but Jones replied that he had not—and not much of one in Houston. He went to Europe and on his return called again on the banker in New York. While talking Mr. Jones mentioned that he was quite an active borrower and that he had made money borrowing.

"That so?" nodded the banker. "Well, we are lenders."

Jones smiled. "How much will you lend me?" he asked, just to see what the New Yorker would say.

"How much do you want?" came the instant retort.

Mr. Jones thought rapidly. He owed then around $25,000. A loan of $40,000 would pay up all his debts and give him a comfortable operating margin. He mentioned this sum, stating that he had no security other than his name and record.

The banker's reply was to hand him a blank note and a fountain pen. The name of Jesse Jones was good for $40,000 in a New York bank—and before he was thirty years old. Of course the New York banker had made inquiries and found the young Texan was good for whatever he signed. This impressed him strongly. He realized then that he might suffer losses in business, but never could he afford to lose his credit standing. He never did.

The city of Houston was on the way up. Seventeen railroads entered it, tieing it with Mexico, the West and the Mississippi Valley. It grew rapidly and Jesse Jones was as much responsible for its amazing growth as any other man, perhaps more so. He went into real estate. And finally he began a remarkable career in building.

From the days of the Chicago World's Fair he had thought of buildings. It seemed to him the most wonderful thing a man could do, to take stone, steel and concrete and build something beautiful and enduring. It was his method of self-expression, the desire to create something.

One building after another went up under his wizardry in financing and planning. He always knew what he wanted. Once he requested his architects to make him a detachable model of a big building which he proposed to erect. They gave it to him, and for three weeks he monkeyed with the various sections and set-offs and wings. He had had doubts in the first place of its efficiency, and when he got through with the model he felt he had it so it would produce the greatest possible revenue. He called in his architects, showed them how he thought it ought to go. They were amazed at his ability in planning—and the building was put up the way he had worked it out on his office table.

He had seen the sky-line of New York City and had been thrilled by it, like everyone else. He proceeded to make a sky-scraper city out of Houston. One of his buildings rose 37 stories into the air, in a spot which forty years before had been as flat as the proverbial pancake. He built a hotel, the Rice, with 1000 rooms, one of the swankiest hostelries in the Southwest. As Chairman of the Houston Harbor Board he was responsible for making his city a great port. A channel many miles long was dug through the Bayou, allowing ocean-going ships to dock in the city of Houston.

One after another, these buildings of various kinds rose in the air—a hotel, a theatre, office buildings. Meanwhile Mr. Jones had gone into banking. He built the banking house of Jesse H. Jones & Company, was president of the Texas Trust Company which later was consolidated into the Bankers' Trust Company. He became president of several banks in Houston. His building operations were not confined to his home town; he put up splendid structures in Dallas and Fort Worth.

During the World War he was appointed Director General of the Department of Military Relief of the American Red Cross, and spent eighteen months in France. Here he utilized his genius for building things by taking charge of the erecting of canteens and recreation buildings in all the American Army camps. It was a big job and he was as successful at it as he had been in his private business career. His work was so well done that in 1919 he was sent over with Henry P. Davison to help organize the World League of Red Cross Societies.

While on this job Mr. Jones had an adventure which got into the newspapers and caused a lot of amusement. He had been cold all the way over on the ship, and his hotel in London around Christmas time seemed damp and chilly compared to his own warm home in sunny Texas. One day he was to confer with President Wilson on a Red Cross matter, and he went to look for him at Buckingham Palace. Lackeys guided him into the big reception room of the famous building. It was a raw, foggy day and the first thing Mr. Jones saw was a roaring log fire at one end of the room.

There was nobody around. He sat down in front of the welcome blaze and took off his shoes. That fire was grand—and soon he was dozing with his stockinged-feet thrust out towards the fire.

Then, before he could do anything about it, two men entered the room—King George and President Wilson! There was nothing in the book of Court Etiquette to cover that situation! So Mr. Jones of Texas stood right up in his stockinged-feet and met the two rulers, unperturbed. Nobody said anything about the strange court costume affected by Mr. Jones, and finally the King left. President Wilson smiled and said, "Perhaps you'd better put your shoes on, Jesse. We're going out."

After the war Mr. Jones went back to his old game of putting up buildings and organizing banks and such. New York City itself offered a challenge. Why shouldn't he run up a few buildings in that place? He did. He built cooperative apartment houses on Park Avenue and Fifth Avenue, an apartment hotel in the Sixties, a theatre, a professional building. Then he went back to Houston, bought a newspaper and took a hand in the game of politics.

One of his greatest achievements was getting the Democratic Convention to Houston in 1928. Other cities were clamoring for the honor—Kansas City, Chicago and San Francisco. The committee tried to pick the one that seemed most suitable.

Mr. Jones rose up and spoke eloquently of his city, which had never been honored by such attentions. "Try Houston," he suggested. "Houston has everything."

"No," said the committee.

"No?" echoed Mr. Jones, suavely. "Well, take a look at this." And he laid down his personal check, certified, for $200,000. The Democratic Convention, as everybody knows, was held in Houston. If there was anybody in the country who didn't know Jesse Jones before, they certainly did now. At the Convention his own State placed his name in nomination, with the pledge of its own 43 votes, and Alabama gave him 3 of its votes. Mr. Jones was the host to the big Convention, the only time one man has acted in that capacity. It was a big job, nothing for a little man to do, but this big Texan did it successfully without fuss or feathers.

Before the depression Mr. Jones's personal fortune was estimated at somewhere between $75,000,000 and $100,-000,000. Naturally so much of it being in real estate, it depreciated some. But his foundations were so secure that he was not blown over like so many heavy property holders.

And now we come to the biggest job of all. When the Reconstruction Finance Corporation was first organized, President Hoover asked John N. Garner, then Democratic leader in the House, for a list of Democrats from which to select a director of the RFC. Mr. Garner obliged and presented a paper on which was written, "Jesse H. Jones, Houston, Texas."

"But I want a *list* of names," said Mr. Hoover.

"Mr. President, that *is* the list," replied Mr. Garner.

It was a huge job. Nobody at that time knew just how large it would be. Roughly speaking the RFC was to act as a great lending bureau, the biggest pawnshop in the world's history. By its help all sorts of industries, big and little, were to be put on their feet, to function again after having come to various kinds of grief during the first years of the depression. It was created by an Act of Congress early in 1932. Its capital stock was $500,000,000 paid in by the Secretary of the Treasury.

Mr. Jones came to Washington and took up his duties. He threw himself wholly into the job, working long hours, much harder than he ever worked in his own interests.

The salary was $8500 a year, peanut-money to a man of his earning powers. But here was a big job to be done, and personal gain had nothing to do with it.

When President Hoover went out of office and President Roosevelt came in, it was thought that the latter would let the RFC die. It had not been a conspicuous success. But he surprised everybody by giving it more scope and power. The original chairman resigned in March, 1933, leaving Mr. Jones acting chairman, and two months later the President appointed him Chairman.

Jesse Jones was eminently fitted for such a job. He was no theorist, no fledgling out to test a lot of wonderful ideas at the taxpayers' expense. In the big game of business he knew all the questions and answers. He was nearly sixty years of age and he had had both feet on the ground all that time. Uncle Sam, sorely beset and puzzled, couldn't have picked a better man to sit on the cash register of the biggest banking institution in history.

The RFC had 32 branches. It aimed to do what banks would not do—lend money to sound business men without getting 100 per cent collateral. The big institution was willing to look at the borrower's character and brains as well as what he had to pledge.

It loaned to all sorts and sizes of borrowers. Railroads, banks, factories, stores—anything that was a sound going concern that could not get help from a bank. Once it loaned a fisherman $200 on his boat. Why not? He was a worker, he knew where to get fish and how to sell it. Mr. Jones felt that such a man should have assistance just as much as a million dollar concern in the doldrums.

Perhaps he remembered his own first two hundred dollar loan in those long ago days in Dallas.

The doings of the RFC are incomprehensible to most people, owing to their size. Up to the end of 1935 it had loaned $5,700,000,000—and of this vast amount over $3,000,000,000 had been repaid. The funds were borrowed by the RFC from the Treasury at two and three-quarter per cent and loaned out at three and one-half and four per cent, thus it actually made money. As a matter of fact, by the first of 1936 it had shown a proft of $115,-000,000. It had made over 20,000 loans, of many sizes and kinds.

As this book is written, Mr. Jones, or the Dough Doctor as he is called, is still sitting in his office in Washington, listening to tales from his fellow citizens, and helping them with either money or advice. Often the latter is more valuable than money.

He is six feet two and as muscular as in the days when he wore out mules on his father's tobacco plantation. He never gets excited and never raises his voice. He works twelve or fourteen hours a day and, as you might suppose from his peculiar job, is pestered during all those hours. Unfortunate indeed is the man who holds the money bags for any institution, let alone for a nation as big as ours. He must know when to say no and when to say yes. President Roosevelt is reported to have said that, "Jesse Jones was the only man in Washington who could say yes or no intelligently twenty-fours hours a day."

It is a remarkable story, this one of Jesse Jones. It

rivals anything read in the Arabian Nights when viewed in panels. The poor boy driving mules on a Tennessee tobacco farm, the country lad gazing in awe at the weird buildings of the old World's Fair, the lumberyard apprentice, the shrewd young dealer in lumber and land, the builder of many buildings, and finally the biggest banker in the world. Nothing more remarkable ever happened in the tales of Sinbad or Aladdin. Indeed, he went Aladdin one better. Aladdin was given a lamp. But Jesse Jones made his wonderful palaces and buildings rise from the ground through no other magic than the power of his own keen brain.

CHARLES FRANKLIN KETTERING

INVENTOR OF THINGS AUTOMOTIVE

(Photo by Blank-Stoller, Inc.)

CHARLES FRANKLIN KETTERING

CHARLES FRANKLIN KETTERING

INVENTOR OF THINGS AUTOMOTIVE

CHARLES FRANKLIN KETTERING has risen from an Ohio farm boy to the topmost rung of American research engineering. Eight colleges and universities have conferred honorary degrees of Doctor of Science and Doctor of Engineering upon him. He has received the Washington Award, Franklin Institute Medal, John Scott Memorial Reward, and the Sullivant Medal for his pre-eminent contributions in science and engineering to promote the comfort, happiness, and well being of humanity. He is a member of eighteen of the leading technical and scientific societies and is on the board of directors of half as many companies. His main position is Vice-President and Director of the General Motors Corporation, and the General Director of the Research Laboratories Section.

With the dozens of activities in which he is interested, he could use titles by the yard—President Kettering, Vice-President, Banker, Doctor, Trustee. But he is usually thought of by the men within his organization and by many friends outside as "Boss Ket" or just plain "the Boss."

You would recognize "the Boss" anywhere. His lanky six-foot-three stature; his dark, searching, deep-set eyes; and his broad sloping forehead gives him a distinct Lincolnesque appearance that makes him stand out in a crowd anywhere. But the most recognizable characteristic of "Boss Ket" is his way of probing down to the fundamentals of a problem. A motto hanging on the walls of his research laboratories expresses this characteristic. It is, "A problem understood is always fairly simple." Mr. Kettering has an uncanny ability to go to the bottom of a problem and dig out the simple fundamentals, so it can be understood and solved. He is continually telling his boys, as he calls the technical men in the laboratories, that a simple solution is always the easiest solution. It is only when you try to make a problem complicated that it becomes hard.

Charles Kettering was born in 1876, on a farm near Loudonville, Ohio. His father was both a farmer and carpenter, and Charles Kettering learned to do most everything with his hands. But of all the mechanical jobs connected with farming, blacksmithing was, to him, the most interesting. It was his intense interest in blacksmithing which later led him to engineering.

In his elementary schooling he was a good student and a hard worker. His former principal, Mr. Budd, said, "I suppose he was what we'd call an A student today." But even though he was an unusual student in high school, no one recognized the abilities he was developing and which were to make him one of our foremost engineers.

When he was twenty-one, he was recommended for the job of teaching school at Bunker Hill, a small Ohio village. He almost lost his job when he took his class to a nearby town to see an X-ray machine which was on exhibit. The students walked five miles each way to see this new discovery of the German scientist, Roentgen. He was defended by a farmer who said his three children learned more from Kettering than any other teacher they ever had.

But Kettering was interested in going to college. He wanted to enter Wooster, a classical school nearby. To obtain the Latin required for entrance, he went to summer school. At this time he was having trouble with his eyes, even though he wore heavy glasses. He was constantly troubled with terrific headaches.

It was at his boarding house that he ran across a catalogue from Ohio State University. Here was a school which taught the courses which he was really interested in. They even had a professor of blacksmithing and metal working. So he figured that instead of fooling around with Latin, he'd go over to Ohio State and take that course in blacksmithing. Of course when he got there, he found dozens of other things he wanted to take.

But it was in the fall of 1898, when he was 22 years old, before he went to Ohio State to take that course in blacksmithing. When he arrived at Columbus he had $35.00 and a desire to probe into the mysteries of chemistry, physics, electricity, and the many other subjects which would lead him to a degree in mechanical engineering. By the spring of his first year, his eyes were so bad he could do very little studying. His roommate had to read the lessons over to him. His memory soon developed so he could remember an entire assignment when it was read through once. To this day, he has a remarkable memory for anything he has seen or read.

It was just after he had started the second year when

his eyes again failed. Disappointed, he went home almost blind, believing that his school work was over. By the next spring his eyes were much better, but not well enough for study.

For the next year and a half, he worked near Ashland, Ohio, installing telephone service to the rural community. Starting as a common laborer digging post holes, he was a foreman of the gang by late summer. That fall, the Star Telephone people asked Boss Ket if he could install the central exchange. Although he knew nothing of the work, he took the job.

Hurriedly ordering "American Telephone Practice" by Kempster B. Miller, he studied day and night to learn the fundamentals of telephone practice of that day. Here was a book to his liking with simple diagrams and plain experiments which explained the most complicated telephone circuit in its most elementary form. The job was completed, not by a brilliant spurt of effort, but by patiently following a few fundamentals throughout the work. He was the first man to accurately measure telephone currents and he accomplished this before he was through school.

In the fall of 1901, Kettering went back to Ohio State University. This time his eyes allowed him to finish his course in engineering. To augment his meager resources he continued to do telephone trouble shooting.

A job which he did while in school, well illustrates how Mr. Kettering combines science and common sense. A small factory near Columbus had trouble keeping up steam in a boiler. The engineer was stumped. Mr. Kettering got the job of fixing what was wrong.

As he came into the boiler room, he noticed the door was hard to open and that it slammed shut behind him. Propping the door and windows open, he started to shovel coal on the fire. The pressure gage immediately started upward. The boiler room was just too tight to obtain enough draft. But the owners thought his solution was too simple and didn't want to pay him for his trip.

Just before he graduated, he was asked to go to Dayton to see the National Cash Register people. Here he got a job as electrical inventor with a salary of $50.00 a week. He was then 28 years old. His job was to electrify the cash register which up to that time was operated with a hand crank.

Electrical engineers said it would take a motor as large as the cash register itself to operate it. The motor would have to develop more than one horsepower. A smaller motor, they said, would get hot and burn out. That would get the insurance people down on them.

But Kettering argued that it only took a fraction of a second to operate a cash register. A small motor wouldn't have time to get hot. All it would take was a lot of turning effort for a short time. In several months time, the first of the electric cash registers was installed in a customer's store. After much more work to make it usable on all kinds of current, it became the standard product of the National Cash Register Company.

For seven years "Boss Ket" worked for the National Cash Register Company. After the electric cash register, he developed a telephonic credit system for large stores which is used even today. Things did not always go along smooth and easily. Problems, many not of an engineering nature, had to be solved. There was the time when the president became impatient for the development of a new model. After looking over an experimental model, he said, "This looks good. When can we go into production? When can we have the drawings?"

"I can't be certain, but it looks like it will be about a year," inventor Kettering replied.

"That will never do. How many men have you in your department, Kettering?"

"There are ten machinists and six draftsmen."

"We'll fix that up. We'll double your space and give you ten more machinists and six more draftsmen."

"What good will that do, Mr. Patterson?"

"Well, you know if you have ten men to dig 100 rods of ditch, twice as many men will dig it in half the time, won't they? Do you mean to tell me double the number of men can't do double the work on your development?"

Kettering looked at President Patterson and drawled, "I'll answer your question by asking another. If one hen can hatch a setting of eggs in three weeks, could two hens hatch it in half the time?"

To this day, Boss Ket believes that you can't rush development work. It takes time to change people's minds to accept the new and different. All along the line from the research worker, production men, sales departments, dealers and finally the customer must be sold on the idea. A new idea or product must be presented again and again before it will be accepted.

Boss Kettering's next venture was to develop a more satisfactory ignition system for automobiles than the magnetos then in use. This work, he did after he was through for the day at the National Cash Register Company. Cadillac, then owned by the Lelands, became interested and installed the system on the 1910 model.

About this same time, a personal friend of Mr. Leland's had his jaw broken by a kick-back when he tried to crank a car. This later caused his death. One day when "Boss Ket" was in Mr. Leland's office he mentioned that he thought a car could be cranked electrically. Mr. Leland told Mr. Kettering of his friend's accident and assured him he was interested. That started him on his second and biggest research project on the automobile.

Back at Dayton, the problem was immediately attacked. An engine was set up and an electric motor with a good many sprocket wheels and chains purchased. A barn housed the equipment. With this material, the power and gear ratio necessary to crank an engine was determined.

Next came the design of a storage battery starter. The experts said the same things they had about the electric cash register. It would take a motor as large as the engine. You couldn't possibly get enough power out of a small storage battery to crank an automobile engine.

But within two years, the electric self-starter was standard equipment on the 1912 Cadillacs and other manufacturers were becoming interested. The story of all the troubles, problems and disappointments is too long to relate here. It was not all smooth sailing. The Boss and his men worked day and night. The experts said it couldn't be done. The battery companies refused to have anything to do with the work. When one experimental car was completed and ready for a demonstration, the garage burned and with it the only completed model. Boss Ket broke his leg the day before and the doctor ordered him to stay on his back for six weeks. The next day he traveled from Dayton to Detroit, climbed under the car with his leg in a cast, and fixed the starter. But the starter was such a great improvement over anything then available, that it was a success from the beginning.

It has been said that the self-starter is one of the greatest developments in transportation. It at once doubled the usefulness of the automobile, since now every woman was a potential driver.

He now had a plant of his own with orders pouring in. To many men, this would have been success enough. But to "Boss Ket" it was only the beginning. He soon developed farm lighting, known as Delco-light, and made it possible for farmers and others in outlying districts to have the advantage of electric power and light.

During the great war, Mr. Kettering was connected with the development of aircraft engines, and other technical activities of the government. The ignition system on the Liberty engines was his invention.

In 1920, Delco was taken over by General Motors and "Boss Ket" was retained to head the Research Laboratories. In 1925 the Laboratories moved from Dayton to Detroit, where it is now housed in an eleven-story building in the center of the motor car district.

Since his research activities were taken over by General Motors, he and his men have continued to contribute to the improvement of the automobile and other products of the Corporation. Ethyl gasoline, Duco finishes, crankcase ventilation, balancing machines, harmonic balancers, to mention only a few, came out of his research organization.

In the past few years, the two-cycle Diesel engines, which power the streamlined trains, were developed by his research laboratories. This type of engine has possibilities of entirely revolutionizing railroad equipment and operation. From a high of over 200 pounds per horsepower, the weight has been cut to only 16 pounds. Fuel and operating costs are lowered and speeds increased to over 120 miles an hour.

"Boss Ket's" widespread interests have led him into many other fields. He is the inventor of the fever machine which gives promise of curing man of many ills which were heretofore incurable. These machines are now in daily use in many of the leading hospitals of the country. The work on this problem is just beginning. Dr. Kettering says the next great advance in science will have to do with the nature of man and the world. Discoveries in biological chemistry and medicine will help to make man's stay on earth much more happy and with much fewer ills.

His philanthropic and educational activities are widespread, although little known. He supports several research projects in colleges, one on why grass can change the raw elements of the earth into useful products by the action of the sun. As he puts it, "Why is grass green?"

"Boss Ket" is a vigorous preacher for industrial preparedness. The world isn't finished. We don't even have a good foundation laid. We know very little about anything factually. What we need is more research aimed at finding new products to put our unemployed men and

capital back to work. We have in no way exhausted our
ability to progress. New industries, developed by industrial research, will go a long way to solve our economic
problems. Research means progress.

COLONEL FRANK KNOX

VETERAN OF WARS, CAMPAIGNS, NEWSPAPERS

COLONEL FRANK KNOX

COLONEL FRANK KNOX

VETERAN OF WARS, CAMPAIGNS, NEWSPAPERS

IF you think success in life comes from accepting only the easy assignments, this chapter in the book is not for you. Or perhaps it most particularly is! It tells the story of a man who from boyhood deliberately picked out the hard ones, stayed with them, and usually came out on top. If he was afraid at times (and no doubt he was) nobody ever found it out. Speaking of assignments in the larger sense, Frank Knox selected three, all of them full of grief: newspaper work, soldiering and politics. Success in any one of them would be enough, but this man made a good mark in all of them.

Frank Knox, christened William Franklin Knox, was born in the Dorchester section of Boston, on New Year's Day, 1874. His father, William Edwin Knox was born in St. Johns, New Brunswick, but the family had come to Boston when he was very young. Frank's father had originally been engaged in the plumbing business but had given it up for marketing. Vicissitudes overcame the family, however, and Knox Senior decided to move his family out West. When Frank was about seven years old they left for Grand Rapids, Michigan, a place which seemed to be a coming municipality.

But the family fortunes were little bettered in the newer land. Times were hard and it was difficult to throw

235

off the jinx which seemed to dog their progress. There were seven in the family, the parents and four sisters younger than Frank.

The boy felt he had to do something to better the family fortunes, so he took that usual job which boys have called their own for generations; he delivered newspapers. He was only eleven at this time but he was strong and healthy. He had to be, because he had to get up long before the roosters did to deliver all his papers. It was hard work but it gave him some money, enough to buy his clothes and the little things that boys just have to have. All this hard work did not spoil his work in school. He always got satisfactory marks, and he was especially good in English composition, receiving several prizes in this subject.

When he was fifteen he left high school with one year to go. He felt he must begin to earn his living in earnest, and dreams of a higher education had to be abandoned. He got a job with a wholesale book and stationery concern, beginning in the shipping room at a small salary. Promotions followed rapidly for the alert, hard working young fellow, and soon he was the proud possessor of a traveling salesman's job. This was higher education and first-class higher education, even if not academic. The man who puts in a few years "on the road" learns something extremely valuable, something not to be had from books.

But in 1893 there came a panic. It was quick and decisive, and all over the land men were thrown out of work. Factories shut down, stocks tumbled and business was paralyzed for months. Young Knox, though a competent salesman, was let go, as he was the last one to be hired. It was a dark time for an ambitious young man; schooling over, job gone and no prospects.

But what seemed like misfortune was really a blessing, not only to young Knox but to many other young men. Thrown out of what they were doing, they were forced to look for something else, and in many instances immeasurably bettered themselves. So what looked like black misfortune turned out to be something far different.

A friend urged him to continue his education, pointing out the advantages a college degree would give him. Knox had come to realize that, but he had been unable to save very much of his not too big salary. And, too, he had not finished high school.

However, the seed was planted. He turned his eyes in the right direction and went ahead to find ways and means. At Alma College, Alma, Michigan, he was admitted to the preparatory department, to finish what he had not taken in high school. It meant hard work, picking up the threads again, but hard work was nothing fearsome to young Knox. All he wanted was an opportunity; the steam he would supply himself, in adequate quantities.

And supply it he did. He worked like a Trojan all through his college career, paying for everything himself. He waited on table in the college dining hall. He spaded gardens in the town. He did all sorts of odd jobs to earn a dollar.

In his old shipping-room days with the stationery concern he had learned to letter packing cases and now he "enlarged" the technique to cope with such things as country barns and fences. With another fellow he traveled around the countryside in his spare time, painting advertising signs on whatever virgin space he could wangle from the farmers.

All these extra duties did not interfere with his studies, nor did they keep him off the athletic field. He made the baseball team and was captain and half-back on the football team. In his junior year he managed to get appointed to the position of physical director of the college, and the pay for this helped a lot.

His senior year in peaceful Alma College was rudely interrupted. One day young Knox was just an ordinary, hard working student—and the next he was listening to a siren call which made all things collegiate seem very tame indeed. That call was the summons to War.

Now in those days young men had little real knowledge of what war meant, nothing of the utter horror later days found it to be. Then it was something rather gay; blue uniforms and rifles flashing in the sun, bands playing, songs in the air, like "Good-bye Nellie, I Must Leave You" and "There'll be a Hot Time In The Old Town To-night." It was serious, of course, but nothing of the drab horror connected with those later days of 1917. To any young man of adventurous disposition, war looked pretty interesting.

It did to young Knox. He rode his bicycle 120 miles in one day to a nearby camp of Michigan Militia he went, on a sort of scouting expedition. The result was his departure not long after that, for Tampa where troops were being gathered for service in Cuba. There had been many small assignments before in his life; now had come this walloping big one—the job of fighting for his country.

Young Knox, however, was not destined to stay with the militia company with which he had started out. At Tampa he saw something which took his fancy—something that was also fancied by a great many other eyes, near and far. It was the First Volunteer United States Cavalry, nicknamed the Rough Riders. Never was there an outfit like it before or since. Its ranks held cowboys, policemen, social registerites, polo players, football players, both Eastern and Western he-men; all sorts of men, in fact. But as widely assorted as they were in regard to professions, they were as like as one pea to another in one thing—they wanted to fight. To fight early and often.

There was something else about the Rough Riders that made them interesting. Its second-in-command was the most colorful figure of his time, and destined to become one of the greatest figures in American History, Lieutenant-Colonel Theodore Roosevelt, knowing next to nothing about professional warfare, but a whole lot about men and their doings.

This dauntless figure is now gone and to the present generation he is just a name in the history books. But while he lived he was ever the man on horseback, the man who had but to wave a hand and a million men would gladly follow. There was never anybody like him before or since. He was Teddy, with thick eyeglasses, flashing teeth and pugnacious jaw: Teddy the Strenuous and greatly beloved. You either frankly worshipped him or hated him; he inspired no half-way feelings. But most red-blooded men, young or old, were glad, even hysterical, to acknowledge him leader. No man since Lincoln has been such an inspiration to others as this supremely indomitable Teddy. And as Teddy he will always be remembered by those of his time.

To young Knox such a man in such an outfit was irresistible. Through a friend, who was a member of the Rough Riders, he managed to get an audience with Colonel Roosevelt. As luck would have it, Knox had not been sworn into service and he was free to join any unit that would take him. T. R. looked him over, snapped a few questions at him, and, with his usual bullet-like decisiveness, took him on. There was room for a few more, and young athletic looking fellows who were still game after getting away down in Florida, could be accommodated. And so the ex-collegian from Alma became a khaki-clad trooper of the boisterous, swaggering Rough Riders.

The Spanish-American War was a short affair and, in the light of what came after, is sometimes looked upon as a sort of mild adventure in the Tropics. Actually it was an experience of great suffering and danger, and no unit was more exposed than the Rough Riders. There were fever, intolerable heat, terrible insects and bad food to contend with. And, in spite of some opinions, the Spaniards were not the comic-opera soldiers many supposed them to be. They were well armed, knew the country and could and did fight.

Trooper Knox had from choice enlisted in the fightingest unit he could find—and fighting he soon got. He was in that first short battle of Las Guasimas. The engagement was soon over, but it was vicious enough while it lasted; several Rough Riders were killed and many were wounded. The Spanish sharp-shooters were concealed in thick trees and other vantage points and they proved intensely bothersome until routed out.

Not long afterwards came the famous battle of El Caney where the volunteer regiment under the strenuous Lieutenant-Colonel covered itself with glory. They fought on foot as infantry and were in the thick of it. Knox went through the whole battle uninjured although a Mauser bullet went through his hat.

After El Caney his fighting career was cut short by an attack of sunstroke, followed by yellow fever and dysentery. The stricken trooper was sent to the hospital. Later, in spite of his protests, he was placed on board a ship sailing for Hampton Roads. By the time he had recovered some of his strength and was anxious to rejoin his regiment, the war was over. He was mustered out at Montauk, Long Island and shortly afterwards returned to his home.

Now he was an ex-soldier and out of a job. However, he found that things had been breaking for him while he was away. He had written a good many letters home, telling about his experiences. They were interesting, breezily written pieces, and had been printed in the Grand Rapids Herald, for whom one of his sisters worked. The editor sent for the ex-soldier and offered him a job, a reporter's job. Ten dollars a week, in the most fascinating business in the world. This appealed to him far more than selling stationery and greeting cards.

Here was something lively, ever-changing. No mere exchange of commodities for dollars, but something to engage one's best wits and courage. Next to war it was life's most thrilling adventure.

From the start he was a good reporter. He had plenty of push, could size up a story accurately and put it into snappy, common-sense English, once he had the facts. The work was the most fascinating thing he had met; in fact, it didn't seem like work. Within a year he had made such a record for excellence in his chosen craft that he was appointed city editor. The salary was not much but that would be taken care of later. He was building up a wide and important acquaintance and, still more valuable, building up a reputation for honesty, hard work and ability.

From the first he evinced a keen interest in politics. However, his interest lay more in a desire to work for the good of government generally, rather than any wish to get himself a job. He hated evil in public life and bent all his energies to drive it out. Like his famous old Rough Rider Colonel, he enjoyed going after the evil-doers and putting them in their places—which was out!

He had held his job of city editor but a short time when he was asked to become circulation manager. He knew nothing about this exacting and specialized job but he took it on and doubled the paper's circulation in one year.

During all this time he had become well known to the prominent men in his part of the State. They recognized him for a hard worker and as a young man due to go up.

Life was pleasant and reasonably exciting in Grand Rapids but Frank Knox wanted a newspaper of his own.

There were things he wanted to do and he realized that with his own paper he could be free to pursue his own course. He had met a man in Grand Rapids named John Muehling, who ran a printing business. He also was looking for a partner and an opportunity, so the two teamed up.

One day Knox learned that there was a newspaper for sale, a weekly called the Lake Superior Journal, published in Sault Ste. Marie. It wasn't much of a paper but the locality showed promise; Sault Ste. Marie was thought to be headed for a great boom, owing to its position in the State.

A paper of his own! That stirred young Knox to the center of his being. What if the presses and type and everything else were poor and out of date? A paper of a sort, could be printed. And they could turn the sleepy old weekly into a humming daily. He told the story to his partner and he, too, saw the possibilities. The result: the two men pooled their scanty resources, borrowed the rest that was needed and bought the paper.

They renamed it the Evening Journal and from its first issue the people of Sault Ste. Marie realized that they had a real newspaper in the town. Its equipment might be run down but it now had spirit and plenty of initiative. The town in those days could be called tough. It was full of lumberjacks, workers on the big hydro-electric project besides all sorts of riffraff that invariably follow a boom town. The place was overfull of cheap saloons, dives of all sorts and nothing much was done about it.

The young Evening Journal decided to do plenty about it. The one-time soldier who had faced Mauser bullets and yellow fever was not intimidated by the threats aimed at him, once he started his crusade for a better town. He kept it up, demanding a cleaner municipal government and a more moral town to live in. It was not a short fight nor an easy one. Once he was attacked by a saloon keeper in his office and Knox hit him so hard, he knocked him downstairs. On another occasion some enemy took a shot at him in his office, the bullet going through the window but missing the editor.

Slowly, as is generally the case, the better element of the town, spurred on by the hammering young editor, made itself felt. The town did become a better place in which to live and do business.

The new paper gamely struggled on, in spite of a scarcity of ready cash. There was a rival paper in town and at the end of a year it had to give up. It could not beat the aggressive and brilliant Knox. It was purchased by the partners and that left a free field for the Journal. The paper was renamed the News.

As a newspaper man, Knox's chief interest had always been politics and government. His interest grew and so did his prestige. In 1910 he was appointed State Chairman of the Republican party and his efforts were greatly instrumental in electing his candidate, Chase Osborn, to the Governorship of Michigan. By then he was one of the best known citizens of the State.

A year later Knox was asked by President Taft to manage the campaign for him in Michigan. There had been murmurings that Roosevelt might be prevailed upon to run again, and Knox, before agreeing to become the Taft manager in his State, stated to the President that in case his one-time commander ran he would have to support him. Mr. Taft assured him that Roosevelt would not run, so Knox agreed.

However, nobody imagined the terrific political upset that was to come in 1912. There were many people in the country who did not want Taft and who did want Roosevelt. Through great pressure (a lot of it applied by Mr. Knox of Michigan) Colonel Roosevelt agreed that he would be a candidate if the people really wanted him. But he wanted to be sure.

The Republican convention of that year is history. The Taft machine rode rough-shod over the Roosevelt men. The latter felt they had a genuine grievance and much more than that. They held a convention of their own, one of the wildest ever held anywhere at any time, and the Progressive or Bull Moose Party was born, with Theodore Roosevelt its candidate for President.

Mr. Knox had done a lot of hard work for Roosevelt up to that time. But soon there came a misunderstanding between Chairman Joseph M. Dixon and Mr. Knox over the Progressive ticket in Michigan. Knox felt that pledges made to him by Col. Roosevelt himself had been broken. He withdrew from his position in the party ranks and did little active work in the campaign. Roosevelt and Taft both went down to defeat and Woodrow Wilson became President.

In 1912 Frank Knox and his partner said good-bye to the Soo. They had built a good newspaper but the town was not growing as it had seemed to promise. Through the efforts of the young Governor of New Hampshire, Robert Bass, Mr. Knox had become interested in the city of Manchester, the State's largest city. There were already two newspapers in Manchester but neither rated as a first-class publication. Mr. Knox and his partner sold the news for $50,000, and left for the Granite State late in 1912.

They were unsuccessful in buying either of the established newspapers in Manchester, so started one of their own, calling it the Leader. Fifty thousand dollars was a very small stake with which to start a newspaper in a city the size of Manchester, where the people were familiar with the big Boston newspapers and expected a paper which would make them proud. But Mr. Knox and his partner were past masters in the art of newspaper building. Knox applied all his talent and aggressiveness, and soon the Leader passed the other two papers, his circulation going over double his nearest rival's in nine months. The people of the big mill city liked the new Leader and speedily got aboard the circulation bandwagon. The venture often struck snags but the rivals never knew it. Somehow all obstacles were overcome.

In nine months the ex-Michiganers were able to buy out the rival Union with borrowed capital from a local bank. However, such assistance would not have been forthcoming if the bankers had not had great faith in the newcomers and their enterprise. The loan was $200,-000—and any time a Yankee bank lends that much, you may be sure it has plenty of faith in the project. Now Mr. Knox had two papers in Manchester, the Union (morning) and the Leader (evening), both under the same roof. Still later he acquired the other paper, the Mirror—and that was that. On paper that sounds easy but to anybody versed in the newspaper business the accomplishment of Mr. Knox and his partner was little short of marvellous. It took courage, genius and hope—in large measure.

Nineteen years after Rough Rider Knox hung up his khaki campaign outfit he got into uniform again. At the time he was over twice the age of the usual soldier enlisting for service in Uncle Sam's greatest army.

When the World War started it was supposed to be the thing to keep neutral; let the foreigners pursue their own squabble. But as the squabble grew, outspoken Americans refused to stay neutral. Frank Knox and his newspapers were not in accord with the watchful waiting policy of the Administration. He knew what war was like and yet he knew that something else was worse—being stepped on and not doing anything about it.

When we finally did get into the fight, Mr. Knox was not going to stay here if he could help it, either in uniform or out of it. There was only one place he wanted to go and that was overseas.

He enlisted in the First New Hampshire Infantry as a private, and not long afterwards he was picked as one of the candidates to attend the officers' training camp at Madison Barracks, New York. The training was especially rigorous but he was successful and was appointed captain, and assigned to the division staff on personnel. This was not overseas service and Captain Knox was restive. He was soon obliged by being promoted to major in command of the horse-drawn section of the ammunition train of the 78th Division. With this outfit he went overseas in the early part of 1918. His outfit saw severe service at St. Mihiel, the Argonne and other engagements. He was promoted to a lieutenant-colonelcy in the fall of 1918.

Back home from the War he took up the threads again. He organized the American Legion in New Hampshire and was its first commander. He was chairman of the Resolutions Committee at St. Louis when the American Legion became a national organization. As an adopted son of New England he had early applied some of his Western aggressiveness to the problems of business. Industries had for some time been in the habit of leaving New England for some seemingly fairer clime—fairer as to taxes and other matters. Colonel Knox saw this, thought something could be done about it, and went at the job. He was a prime mover in the organization of the New England Council, a body devoted to the building up of New England business and institutions.

In 1924 he ran for Governor of New Hampshire. He was not an apathetic candidate but it was his opinion that no candidate should spend more than a thousand dollars for his election. He stuck to his decision—and lost by some 2500 votes.

All this time, however, he was pursuing his main business, that of running his newspapers. While Manchester is not a large city and therefore could not be expected to have a newspaper comparable with cities ten times its size, the work of Colonel Knox was attracting a lot of interest. In Boston, for example, where a couple of newspapers had been "killed", the exploit of starting a new one and making good with it was something noteworthy.

One of those who watched was the owner of the greatest

newspaper chain in the world, William Randolph Hearst. In 1927, after having made several overtures to the New Hampshire publisher, Mr. Hearst succeeded in getting him for his Boston American and Advertiser, which had been losing money. Colonel Knox's salary was said to be over $50,000 a year. He left for Boston with the knowledge that his New Hampshire newspapers would roll along all right in his absence.

Colonel Knox was well versed in the art of running a newspaper, if not on a shoe-string, at least on a limited budget. Having been on two small newspapers he was expert in all the details of the business from the front door to the back door. He was just the man for the job he now took, where strict economy had never been the rule. Within a year he had taken the Boston American out of the red and put it on a paying basis, a remarkable achievement in so short a time.

In 1928 Mr. Hearst put him in complete charge of all his newspapers at a salary three times as large as the one he had been getting. He had a free hand, subordinate only to Mr. Hearst himself. Again he applied his policy of sound common sense, which had always been so successful. If a tried and true policy with a little and a medium size newspaper, why not with a whole chain of big ones?

There was no doubt about his success in running the huge chain. He cut out waste, straightened out the lost motion and put the system on a sound, economic basis. When the depression settled down on a flush world, Colonel Knox did some cutting. There came a disagreement in policy with Mr. Hearst over economies. And finally, at the end of four years service, Colonel Knox announced his resignation. He had done a good job and had made enough money to retire—granted he wanted to quit.

But the newspaper business is fascinating and few men who really love it ever retire until they have to. Colonel Knox was as strong and competent as ever, and after a few months rest he was ready to take on something else. The something else proved to be the biggest proposition yet—the purchase of one of the country's largest and finest newspapers, the Chicago Daily News.

The News was no ordinary chattel which anybody with a lot of money could buy. There was far more to it than that. It was a newspaper with a splendid reputation, the family paper of Chicagoans for generations. A great editor and publisher, Victor F. Lawson, had built it; during his administration the News had made many innovations. It was one of the first papers to publish truthful statements of its circulation, and to sell advertising on a fixed schedule of rates. It was a pioneer in having its reporters do detective work in solving crimes. It was also one of the very first newspapers to install linotype machines. All in all it was a great newspaper, an institution which people really believed in.

Mr. Lawson died in 1925. Its next publisher was Walter Strong, who enlarged its plant and continued its splendid traditions. Mr. Strong died in 1931. And the great newspaper was again in the market for a publisher.

The executors and directors began the search for the right man. Under the provisions of the will of Mr. Strong the employees had the first chance to purchase the paper

and were given three months in which to do so. After
that, in case they failed to buy it, the trustees could sell
it to an outsider. The employees were unable to do it.

Over a score of applicants offered to buy the paper.
The trustees examined the list carefully. Among them
was the name of Colonel Frank Knox. General Charles
G. Dawes, one of the best known Chicago business men,
knew Colonel Knox and enthusiastically recommended
him as the proper man to be the publisher of the News.
Still the search went on; there should be no hurry.
Finally one of the directors of the company, Sewell
Avery, went to New York City to investigate further. At
every place of inquiry the name of Colonel Knox was
suggested as the right man. Mr. Avery went back to
Chicago and reported. Then followed another investigation, by another director. He sought information from
erstwhile competitors of Colonel Knox and again the answer was the same. It appeared that this publisher of
the two newspapers in the comparatively small New
Hampshire city was the one candidate who satisfied
everybody.

And so the one-time ten dollar a week Grand Rapids
reporter acquired one of our greatest newspapers. With a
business associate, Theodore T. Ellis of Worcester,
Massachusetts, Colonel Knox bought the News.

The newspaper had been operating with a reduced
revenue since the depression. It had never paid a dividend on the common stock, and its gross revenue had
dropped from fifteen and one-quarter millions to twelve
and one-third millions. Colonel Knox went to work. He

cut the unnecessary appendages everywhere, as two branch pressrooms, a radio station and other things that could be eliminated without hurting the News.

While the revenues have run smaller during the hard years of the depression, Colonel Knox's better management has enabled the News to make a profit. Bank loans were paid off, a good reduction in the funded debt was made, and a portion of the preferred stock was retired. A little over a year after Colonel Knox took over, the preferred dividends were brought up to date and the first common dividend paid. Chicagoans now realize that they picked the right man, one who could run their great newspaper in a business like way and also keep up its traditions.

In 1936 public life again claimed Colonel Knox. In the Republican convention of that year he was nominated as candidate for Vice-President of the United States. As this is written the election is some weeks away. Whatever the result, Colonel Knox has taken up his assignment in his usual forthright, aggressive way. Win or lose, he will have enjoyed the fight for its own sake, as he has in all his activities.

CLARENCE HUNGERFORD MACKAY

COMMUNICATIONS ENGINEER

CLARENCE HUNGERFORD MACKAY

CLARENCE HUNGERFORD MACKAY

COMMUNICATIONS ENGINEER

THE year 1849 is a romantic one in the history of the United States. In that year thousands of adventurous young men left whatever they were doing and journeyed to California, there to dig out of the earth one of the richest treasures ever buried. Some were successful; many more were not. One of them, the father of the subject of this sketch, was among those who did not strike pay dirt. He might well have joined the other unlucky ones and gone back to the East, the possessor of a thrilling adventure to contemplate and little else. However, he was not done pioneering. The West had impressed him and he felt there was more to it than that initial rush to California's El Dorado.

John W. Mackay was born in 1831 in Dublin, Ireland, of Scotch-Irish descent. He came to America when a mere boy and settled in New York City. For a time he worked with a ship-building concern. But he had scarcely got a start in this business when the news of California's rich find struck the East. Young Mackay determined to go and soon got together a party of twenty-five other adventurers who had the same ambition.

He was not entirely unsuccessful in his quest for gold in California. At one time he did have a small fortune, but this he lost. In 1860 he left California and went to

Nevada, where it was reported, silver had been found. By then he was an expert in mining engineering.

What happened during the next few years sounds like a story of Aladdin, although there was considerably more work involved than the simple rubbing of a magic lamp. Mr. Mackay, with a couple of partners, acquired some mines in the Sierra Nevadas under what is now Virginia City. There was silver there in quantities and also gold. Finally, in 1873, after much hard work and disappointment, they opened the Comstock Lode, the richest vein of silver ever discovered up to that time. John W. Mackay owned two-fifths of the mine. From it he and one partner took out $150,000,000 in silver and gold within a few years. During the active yield of these mines, he personally superintended them, working sometimes as an ordinary miner. He opened a bank in Nevada and became a leader in the state.

In the early eighties he turned his face towards the East, having made an immense fortune. A pioneer by instinct, he sought out ventures which took daring and courage. At that time the business of transmitting words by cable was new in the world, as far as commercial use went. This seemed to offer a big opportunity, and Mr. Mackay, with James Gordon Bennett, formed the Commercial Cable Company. It was not an unoccupied field, however; the new concern had to battle the telegraph and cable company built up by Jay Gould, a formidable opponent. Against the universal opinion that the new venture would never succeed, Mr. Mackay and his partner went ahead, and in 1884 laid two submarine cables to Europe. Then followed a bitter struggle for a year and a half, but finally the Commercial Cable Company succeeded. A short time later Mr. Mackay organized the Postal Telegraph Cable Company and commenced the construction of telegraph lines on land. He was successful again. Later he planned another great step in his system by laying a cable across the Pacific to Shanghai, and he was engaged in this project when he died. There was also another cable laid between the United States and Cuba.

There were other interests, too, in real estate and building. In fact, the Mackay fortune was a vast affair, of many projects and widely scattered. This remarkably clever business man had built wisely and courageously— and it had all been done within a period of thirty years.

Mr. Mackay had married in the early days of his struggles. Mrs. Mackay was Maria Louisa Hungerford, daughter of Colonel Daniel C. Hungerford of New Orleans. They had two sons born to them, John W. Junior and Clarence H. John W. Junior died in France in 1895.

When John W. Senior died in London in 1902, the second son, Clarence H. became the heir to the huge Mackay interests. The newspapers knew very little about this young man, who was more a European than an American, having lived abroad most of the time since he was a small boy. To the public he was a young man who lived most of the time in France and England, who had a string of racing horses, and who shunned the spotlight. What would he do? And particularly, what would he do about the vast business empire built up by his father?

Clarence H. Mackay was twenty-eight years old when he became the ruler of the Mackay millions. His youth

had been spent abroad. When very young he was taken
to France and his boyhood days were spent at Villebon,
near Paris, the beautiful estate later occupied by W. K.
Vanderbilt. While at Villebon, Clarence Mackay attended Vaugirard College. Later he was a student at
Beaumont College, Windsor, England, from which he was
graduated in 1892. He showed a remarkable aptitude for
languages, speaking French, German and Italian fluently.
His studies were selected with a view to the demands of
the business which he would later inherit.

In 1892, after graduating from the English college he
returned to the United States and soon entered his father's
offices. One of his first connections was with the American
Forcite Powder Company, of which he later became president.

It is related that one day he walked into his father's
office with the air of having something on his mind.
Looking up, his father asked, "Well, son, what's the matter now?"

"Nothing, governor. I'm satisfied. As long as you live
you are the boss, and that's right. But when you get
tired and want to quit, I want to know enough to be ready
to get into harness. I want a job, that's what's the matter
today, and the sooner the better."

As a result of this interview the young man was made
a director in his father's cable and telegraph companies,
and shortly after that he became vice-president of these
interests. He soon took his place in the world of business with the same spirit he had shown in sport, with
enthusiasm and energy.

As an athlete, young Mackay had shown more than average ability. Although only of medium height, he was powerfully built and had a quick eye. At trap-shooting he was an expert. Polo, a game demanding great stamina and speed, was a favorite pastime with him and he had a splendid string of polo ponies. He was also good at golf and tennis. And one year he got his name on the sporting records for all time; in 1903 he won the amateur championship at racquets. That his athletic ability was outstanding is shown by the collection of silver cups he has won in various branches of sport; there are over sixty of them.

Perhaps he is best known in the world of sport for his racing stable. He loved horses and early in his career he took more than an ordinary interest in them. When in Paris he imported the American trotting stallion, Sweaza, which he bought in New Jersey for $2500. The horse won the International Stallion Race in Paris in three straight heats. His first important venture on the American turf was with his famous horse Banastar, with which he won the Metropolitan Handicap in 1901. At that time he was making extensive plans as a patron of the turf, but soon after his father died he sold his racing stable. His splendid horses all went, that he might devote all his time to his business.

One of the great tasks that fell to him was the laying of the cable from the Pacific Coast to China. With his associate, George Gray Ward, he put this gigantic project over. The great cable line was 10,000 nautical miles in length, touching Honolulu, Midway Island, Guam, Manila and ending at Shanghai. At that time it was more than three times as long as any Atlantic cable. The cost was $9,000,000.

In 1900 Mr. Mackay built "Harbor Hill," his great estate near Roslyn, Long Island, one of the finest homes in America. The ground comprised about seven hundred acres, a parcel almost as large as Central Park. Some of it was in small farms which had been operated for generations, and part of it was land just as nature made it. The site was just west of Wheatley Hills, the highest point of land on Long Island. While miles of road were put in, great care was taken to leave the natural beauty as it was. Trees were preserved, as were any other natural specimens of beauty. More than three hundred thousand dollars was spent on improving the land.

Stanford White, the famous architect, designed the big house, which is of the French chateau type, of the style of Mansard, and the period of 1649. Its lines are strong and dignified. Inside the chief feature of the manor house is its Gothic Renaissance hall. Banners hang in this room— war, processional and guild flags of the sixteenth century. One, perhaps the most interesting, is a banner of St. Sebastian which belonged in ancient days to the city of Liege. Here also is the display of medieval armor, one of the greatest private collections in the world. There are priceless hangings, some tapestries of Louis XII and Anne de Bretagne, one of them a famous old cathedral piece from Avila.

One of the suits of armor is a superb piece made by the famous "Jacob, the Armorer," the most celebrated ar-

morer of the Middle Ages, for Henry, second Earl of
Pembroke. The suit is the finest specimen known and
of the best period of decorated armor produced by the
great school of English arms craftsmen, which was opened
in 1511.

During the World War Mr. Mackay was a heavy con-
tributor to causes to forward America's success. He made
the first important contribution from a private source,
the gift being a completely equipped hospital base of five
hundred beds. The hospital was known as the Mackay
Unit and was accepted through the National Red Cross.
Provision was made for a staff of twenty-two surgeons,
seventy-five nurses, one hundred and fifty orderlies and
other things necessary to operate such a unit. The gift
was anounced March 28, 1917. The hospital was sent to
the battlefields of Europe through Roosevelt Hospital.
Aside from this fine gift, Mr. Mackay also offered the
use of his magnificent home as a hospital during the war.

Mr. Mackay has increased the business left by his
father. The Mackay System consolidated its position in
the Atlantic by contracts with the German Cable Company, operating between New York and Emden, and by
laying two additional cables, one connecting with the
Azores and serving southern Europe, the other linking
New York and Ireland, serving England and northern
Europe.

In 1928 negotiations between the Mackay System and
the International Telephone & Telegraph Corporation resulted in a merger of the two interests. The Mackay System also acquired operating rights in the Federal Radio

Company, thus becoming the first communications service in the world to operate radio, cable and telegraph lines under one management.

Mr. Mackay has always been keenly interested in music, a trait doubtless acquired from his mother, who was an enthusiastic patron of music and painting. He is a member of the board of directors of the Metropolitan Opera Company and chairman of the board of directors of the Philharmonic Symphony Society of New York. In 1926 he received the gold medal of the National Institute of Social Sciences in recognition of his services to the public in connection with the development of music and the maintenance of high musical standards. New York University conferred on him the honorary degree of Doctor of Music in 1926.

WILLIAM SAMUEL PALEY

A YOUTHFUL BUILDER OF A GREAT
RADIO NETWORK

WILLIAM SAMUEL PALEY

WILLIAM SAMUEL PALEY

A YOUTHFUL BUILDER OF A GREAT
RADIO NETWORK

WHEN William Samuel Paley was born his future profession did not exist. To be sure, an Italian by the name of Marconi had taken out a patent on wireless telegraphy five years before, but at the time of the advent of young Mr. Paley into this already noisy world, radio was unknown and undreamed of. In fact, his parents figured the infant was destined for the father's business, the manufacturing of cigars.

William Paley was born in Chicago, September 28, 1901, a lucky period in which to start life. The first twenty-five years of the twentieth century could be called the "Crowded Age;" more big things were crowded into that period than in any other equal space in history; the greatest of inventions and discoveries, the most marvellous of opportunities, the biggest war. Even if this magic twenty-five year period was capped by the world's worst headache, at least the young men born in it could truly say that the show had been worth seeing. It was a privilege to live in it.

William Paley attended the public elementary schools where he was a good scholar. Lessons had no terrors for him. After this first schooling, he entered Western Military Academy in Alton, Illinois. These were the war years and the military part of the education was more emphasized than usual. No man could guess when the great conflict would end, and boys in military school in 1917 and 1918 considered themselves as already on the steps that would soon take them over the top. But the War, seemingly so interminable, finally did end and the young man's dream of a soldier's career was over. However, later he served as lieutenant brevet in the Illinois National Guard. He was graduated from the military academy in 1918.

Then came a year at the University of Chicago. From there he transferred to the University of Pennsylvania, where he spent three years. He managed the swimming team during his last year. He received his B. S. degree in economics in 1922.

The cigar business loomed ahead. It was a good business. Young Paley had known since boyhood that he would enter the business and had planned his education accordingly. He had no notion of engaging in anything else—but the cards were stacked against him. It is significant to realize that in the very year of his graduation from U. of P. one of the major events in radio history occurred. For the first time wire lines were used as an adjunct to broadcasting, the major event being the transmission of the Chicago-Princeton football game in Chicago by wire to a New York broadcasting studio.

Commercial broadcasting was only two years old at this time. KDKA had sent out the returns of the national election in 1920, and the following year saw the early programs go on the air. Programs were crude affairs in those days, and so were the sets. The usual receiving set was one which operated with a sensitive crystal. One had to clamp a pair of head-phones on his ears and sit for hours, paging the air for any intelligible sounds. It was an event when you got something, but those little crystal sets had one thing; as sweet and pure a tone as any set ever made.

However, progress in radio, regardless of its swift and magical changes, meant nothing to young Mr. William Paley. He entered the business of his father, the Congress Cigar Company. It was no plunge into icy water for him. Already he knew a lot about cigar manufacture. As a boy he had watched the girls (those picturesque creatures, like Carmen!) on high stools, deftly rolling the damp, fragile looking Java wrappers and Havana fillers into perfectos, londres, panetellas and all the other favorite shapes and sizes. It was a fascinating atmosphere and one of which he never tired.

As a matter of fact, he had worked in the factory when he was eighteen, long before graduating from college. During the summers he had studied the tobacco industry, not only at the Paley factory, but in Havana and in Holland. He had gone with his father to Philadelphia to open a branch factory there when labor troubles threatened the Chicago plant. His father hastened back to Chicago, leaving the new Philadelphia factory in charge of William and his Uncle Jacob. Then *they* got a strike on their hands to make it interesting. It has been said that young Paley solved the troubles by taking the girls out to lunch and talking them out of it. He was tall, handsome and of an intensive personality, so perhaps he did. At any rate, the labor troubles were settled and the girls went

back to their high stools, to begin turning out the millions
of La Palina cigars again.

During his first year in actual full time employment
with his father's company he traveled all over the United
States and Europe, with his La Palina cigars. He was a
persuasive salesman and sent many a luscious order back
to his admiring and appreciative father. After a year or
so of this he was made vice-president in charge of production and advertising.

Young Mr. Paley liked his job. It was a job you could
do something about. Cigars were a staple and, if you
made a good one, hustle and salesmanship would put it
over. However, there were certain signs in the "smoking"
industry that were none too reassuring to cigar manufacturers. It had nothing to do with La Palina or any
other particular brand of cigar. But young men were
taking to cigarettes and pipe smoking more than to cigars.
The War may have had something to do with the change;
short intervals for a smoke when a cigar would have to
be thrown away only one-quarter smoked. At any rate,
cigar production in the La Palina plant had dropped from
600,000 per day to 400,000. And something had to be
done about that.

It would be nice to follow the pattern of true-story-
success and say that the young advertising genius sat
down at his desk and thought up a revolutionary campaign that put La Palina into the best seller list. But the
facts are far from this. In the summer of 1927 Mr. Paley
went abroad for a long business trip. While he was gone
fate stepped in and altered the whole course of his business life. The advertising had to be attended to in the

advertising manager's absence, and in this instance it was done by Mr. Paley's father and his Uncle Jacob. And, of all things, they fell for the new medium, radio. They signed a contract with the still newer Columbia Broadcasting Company for thirteen weeks, at $50,000. It is said that Uncle Jacob muttered in melancholy tones, even as the ink on the dotted line was drying, "This is the biggest mistake we ever made."

Young Mr. Paley returned to the United States sometime later and found what had been done in his absence. It looked as if there had been poaching on his own pet preserves and he was inclined to resent it. But the thing had been done, the program was under way, and there wasn't much that could be done about it.

And now for a moment, let us look at what the present CBS was at that time. Perhaps Mr. Paley could be forgiven for casting some doubt as to the wisdom of hooking up with what then was more like a spider's web than a network. This was in September 1928. And at that time Columbia was only an infant in years, having been born in January 1927. It had been founded by several gentlemen, among them Mr. George A. Coats, Mr. Arthur Judson and Major J. Andrew White, the latter one of the pioneers of broadcasting. These men had a few new ideas and they launched a company called the United Independent Broadcasters, Inc. Later the Columbia Phonograph Company came in—and shortly went out again, leaving the name Columbia behind.

Later a Mr. Jerome H. Louchheim of Philadelphia, a wealthy contractor, became interested in the company, as well as a Doctor Leon Levy, who was related to Mr.

Paley. At the time Mr. Paley's cigar company bought their first time on the air, Columbia had twenty-two stations. The contracts with those stations had not been too carefully drawn up, and the company was in a dangerous position owing to certain phases in the agreements.

However, the new broadcasting company was on the air and ambitiously reaching out for new business. Mr. Paley sat down to watch developments. He knew all about putting advertisements in newspapers and magazines, about posters in drug store windows and so on. These could be keyed and checked up. But this new thing was a lot too ephemeral—all except the $6500 per week which La Palina paid for reaching millions of listeners for a few—oh so few—fleeting minutes once a week. Suppose millions did listen. Was there any certainty that they smoked cigars—or if they did, would the music and fun, coupled with a few spot-talks about La Palina make any difference in sales? It all seemed frightfully "up in the air," and young Mr. Paley watched the thing with some misgivings.

But the wonder of wonders began to happen. With one warm eye on the sparkling programs and the other cold one on the figures at the factory, Mr. Paley discovered that the mistake hadn't been a mistake at all. In six months the daily sales of La Palina cigars rose from 400,000 to a million! This was very illuminating—not only in regard to the concern wishing to sell its wares, but to the medium by which it was done. Here was something brand new, a field into which anybody with nerve and a pioneering instinct could find considerable employment.

Mr. Paley became more interested in broadcasting as the days went on. He learned that Mr. Louchheim's interests were for sale. And, having quite a lot of money, Mr. Paley decided he would buy a controlling interest in this young outfit. It would be an added interest in his life; running his part of the cigar business did not take all his time, and he could easily devote two or three days a week to the broadcasting business. It was a fascinating business, a mixture of technical, theatrical, advertising and, most of all, uncertainty. Anything could happen. Mr. Paley thought it would be very interesting.

He was correct about everything except one thing. That was the amount of time he had decided to give to it. He had hardly taken on his new business when it suddenly began to grow. New contracts with stations were drawn and sent out. The twenty-two stations then comprising the outfit grew to forty-seven—more than double the number—almost over night. In short, instead of Mr. Paley taking the little broadcasting system, it took him. He was in over his head and completely mixed up in a venture which had all the interest and speed of a three-ring circus. The spider web had cast aside its fragility and emerged as a network.

Consider the situation of this young man, who might be compared with a legendary youth about to enter into combat with a giant, the giant being the already well established NBC. He had a lot of money in the venture, and it would be all too easy to dissipate it in a business which was too new to have any rules and recipes. He might go thundering up to success—or make an equally loud noise going down.

Mr. Paley says of those early days: "My imagination went wild over the possibilities of radio, but wild as it went, it didn't go wild enough to keep up with the realities."

The new contracts with the affiliates were more satisfactory; they gave an option on certain hours of its affiliates. In addition to cash, Columbia gave its stations sustaining programs free. (NBC made a charge for this service.)

Mr. Paley's original idea of devoting a couple of days each week to the broadcasting business suffered a change. Instead, it became necessary to turn his attention on getting sufficient time to sleep. Radio stations work about two-thirds of the time—and lots of things can happen during such a generous slice of time. He ate and slept with radio. It was exhausting but exhilarating.

Best of all there was the opportunity to do bigger and better things all the time. A cigar is a cigar, and there is nothing much you can do with it. But in this new business there was no limit to the possibilities. What would seem like a wild and absurd dream in an ordinary business, could turn out to be a positive hit in radio. There were so many things in it—humor, education, art, drama —all these and more could be used in it. And the thrill of finding and introducing some new star to the air.

The business grew at a fabulous pace. Larger quarters were inevitable, and ten floors were contracted for in the building at 485 Madison Avenue before it was built. Into these sumptuous quarters moved the fast growing CBS, but a scant two or three years after the birth of the organization.

Motion picture interests began to look with some apprehension on this upstart industry, headed by such youthful generals (Mr. Paley's associates were in their twenties or early thirties.) Paramount Publix Corporation offered to buy a half-interest, suggesting something like a million and a half for it. Mr. Paley smiled and told them they could have a half-interest for five million dollars. He took this in the form of Paramount stock, which was selling at that time for sixty-five dollars per share. This was in 1929. The motion picture company agreed to buy it back at eighty-five dollars a share in the spring of 1932—*if* CBS earned two million dollars in that time. CBS succeeded in doing this, with a margin, to the surprise of many. They made a fine profit on this deal, and Mr. Paley showed his amazing business genius in accepting such a proposition and in pushing it through to a successful finish.

There were many things to learn about this newest and most amazing of industries—and next to no precedent. Most of it had never been done before. It was pioneering and, with the stake involved, the pioneering had to be right. It was a case of being general—with no military books of tactics to guide one. Yet Mr. Paley, not yet thirty years old, negotiated the perilous course with nothing but victories.

From the start he intended to have the name CBS mean the best in radio programs. He turned down any doubtful program, even if the amount of money involved did seem tempting. The cost of the talent on the CBS hours has more than doubled in the short time of Mr. Paley's ownership, showing his desire to give only the best. Aside from that, Mr. Paley has been generous with free programs which have become famous for their excellence, and this on time which could have been sold. These programs are well known all over the country and they have entertained millions of listeners for several years: the Sunday Philharmonic concerts, the Church of the Air, School of the Air and other special programs such as international broadcasts.

One of Mr. Paley's brilliant moves was the building of the Columbia Artists' Bureau, which is a sort of clearing house and training school for applicants for radio honors. It has discovered many artists, trained them in microphone technique and set them on the road to fame.

Another of Mr. Paley's organizations is the Columbia Concerts Corporation, which handles a large proportion of the concert artists who tour the United States. Some of these attractions appear on CBS programs.

The growth of Columbia can be shown in many ways. Of course the affiliate stations show an indication of progress. In 1928 there were forty-seven stations. A year or so later this was increased to sixty. In 1931 there were seventy-six and in 1933 there were ninety-one. In 1935 the number had risen to the total of ninety-seven, covering the entire country and constituting the world's largest commercial network. All in seven years. Progress is a faint word; this is a sprint!

In 1929 CBS did a little more than $5,000,000 worth of business. Next year it did $8,700,000, and the following year the figures rose to $14,500,000. In 1934 it did over $19,000,000 worth of business.

It has been a remarkable success. One can say that it

all started because Mr. Paley's father signed a radio-advertising contract while his son was abroad, but that is only one of those "maybe" statements. Chance does play a most important part in the lives of men. Every man experiences such things. But few men recognize them, appraise them correctly and, once seen, have sense enough to follow the indications.

Mr. William S. Paley recognized his chance when he saw it. Call it a star if you like. In which case he hitched his wagon to it and proceeded to dazzle the heavens.

Successes in this newest of industries are pleasant to contemplate. We remember what the world was like before 1920. When time was heavy, it positively sagged. But since then nobody can truthfully say that there is nothing to do, nothing to interest him. The air fairly reeks with good things and there is something for every taste.

The tall, brown-eyed young man who sits in his magnificent office at 485 Madison Avenue, New York City, did not do all this. We cannot give him a medal or put him in the Hall of Fame for being the Father of Radio. There isn't any such man. But when we tabulate the doings of the various persons who gave us our present excellence in air entertainment we can say that William Paley did something about it. And that something was— Plenty!

JOHN D. ROCKEFELLER, JUNIOR

HE DID WELL IN A JOB HE DID NOT CHOOSE

JOHN D. ROCKEFELLER, JUNIOR

JOHN D. ROCKEFELLER, JUNIOR

HE DID WELL IN A JOB HE DID NOT CHOOSE

STRANGE as it may seem, the story of successful men is not so liberally sprinkled with the names of those who were born to riches. We find, on examining the careers of those who reached the top, that nearly all of them started with next to nothing or at least only enough to inspire them into trying their wings. Whatever truth there may be in it, there is the popular opinion that the sons of rich men rarely amount to much.

There is at least one shining example to the contrary. The father of this particular man represents to us the richest of the rich; he is the symbol of vast wealth.

To say that John D. Rockefeller, Junior, started life with a handicap would not be believed by many. But in many ways he did have a fight on his hands to reach a really successful position; not one fight, but a lot of them.

Before we begin the story of this man, let us look at what he had to step into. When we say Rockefeller we think of three things—great wealth, Standard Oil and philanthropy. John D. Junior's father made Standard Oil from nothing more than an idea into one of the biggest business organizations the world has ever known. From the bedlam rising from the discovery of oil in Pennsylvania, the elder Rockefeller made his great business. While other men fought and scrambled for individual and quick success, he alone seemed to see what could be done with that nasty looking stuff that so thoughtfully shot itself up out of the earth for man's use. They all had the same chance, hundreds of them; but he alone had the vision and ability to make the truly remarkable concern.

Rivals sought to knock it down; politicians tried their various arts on it; the Government, led by that great trust-buster, President Theodore Roosevelt, turned the mightiest of guns against it; yet so well had it been planned and built, that even after all the battering, it was still there. No one business ever got the pummeling that one did, and after each giant attack, the beseigers would draw off to one side and wonder what was keeping it up.

That is a great story, having no place in these pages, but it has to be considered as a background for this one. When young John D. Junior was born it was already a lusty business. It was not the Standard Oil as we know it, with the white and red filling stations and all its modern appurtenances. The business was that of marketing kerosene; it lighted the world after sunset. It was worth millions even in 1874, the date this story really begins.

John Davison Rockefeller, Junior, was born that year in the Rockefeller home in Cleveland, Ohio. It was a fine big house, yet not as imposing as some others in Cleveland. Four girls (one of whom had died) had already been born to the Rockefellers and the advent of a boy was most welcome.

Young John, destined to rule an organization greater than that of many a royal potentate, had little idea of any such thing as he grew up. Life was a good deal like that of any other well to do family. There was a winter home in Cleveland, and a summer home at Forest Hill on the outskirts of that city. There was no attempt made at ostentatious living. To the children no stress was laid on the fact that their father was a millionaire; indeed, they had but a hazy idea of the real extent of the senior Rockefeller's importance and wealth.

Naturally the great estate at Forest Hill charmed the boy. There was a pond, big enough to swim in in the summer and to skate on in the winter. In both these sports John D. Senior engaged with his children. He taught them how to swim, being a very good swimmer himself. He also taught them how to skate. These play hours were very happy for the great oil man, already harassed by many enemies. Here he could relax and play. As a matter of fact, he liked the simple outdoor sports of the children and regretted that business curtailed his time with them.

Like most boys John D. Junior liked a little pin money, but there was no golden fountain into which he could dip his little fingers. That was not his father's idea at all. He had to earn any sums that he wanted by some sort of toil.

When he was eight years old he was paid nine cents an hour for raking and sweeping paths around his home. A year later he got a raise, fifteen cents an hour, and he sawed wood, broke stones and split hard wood logs for the open fire. There were miles of fence around and across the vast stretches of the big summer estate at Forest Hill. Fence posts got knocked over or became rotten. For all the wrecked posts found young John D.

Junior got one penny; for repairing them he received fifteen cents. When he accumulated a sum by saving small amounts his father would duplicate it.

Another source of revenue was payment for performing his violin lessons—five cents an hour. Such little things as these taught him what money was, that you had to trade something in labor or service for it. When in his turn he came to be a father, he gave thirty cents pocket money to each of his boys—ten cents to be saved, ten cents to be given away, and ten cents to be spent.

Once when John D. Junior and his sisters were quite young, their father suggested getting each one a tricycle but their mother said no, to buy only one for them all. "But tricycles don't cost much," said Mr. Rockefeller. "I know," replied she, "but if they have one between them, it will teach them to give up to one another."

When John D. Junior was a little older the family moved to New York City, there to take a permanent winter address. The house was at Number 4 West Fifty-Fourth Street and is still owned by the family.

Now young John was a New Yorker and he entered a preparatory school, located a few blocks from his home. He walked to and from school every day. The Rockefellers had carriages and coachmen, but the parents had no intention of pampering the children. Walking was good for them. Other children of wealthy parents rode to school in the more or less ornate vehicles of the day, but the young Rockefellers, wealthy as any, walked.

John D. Junior was a thorough if not outstanding scholar. Any lesson was a definite assignment, something to master to the best of his ability; this habit of thorough and deliberate study became a fixed principle which he has pursued all his life. His father never insisted on brilliant marks in scholarship if these were not to be had, but he did insist on an honest effort being made. This he got from his son; little John learned not to shirk early in his life.

As he grew older his eyes opened at the scene which began to be known to him. The name of his father was invariably in the newspapers and magazines. What an education that was for a boy! Cartoons, articles, stories —always written in the same uncomplimentary vein. Why was this? Young John could not understand why this father of his, so kind and gentle, should be pictured always as a frightful ogre, the blackest sort of villain.

Through with preparatory school, young Rockefeller considered the question of college. Yale University had been in his mind but as the time drew near he changed his plans, deciding that a smaller college would suit him better. He selected Brown University and passed his entrance examinations in 1893, entering that institution in the autumn.

While in college he took no business courses and did not specialize. He pursued his even way, which was now the customary way with him. Already he realized that the Rockefeller name and Standard Oil were looked upon with disfavor by many. Unkind things were often said, but this extraordinary young man had his father's ability to keep his temper and poise. It has been said that the Senior Rockefeller was the best waiter in the world—and his son knew how to wait, too. There would come a time when the world would know a different story, a story which he knew to be the true one.

In college he was a good student, if not a brilliant one. He was elected to Phi Beta Kappa, honorary scholastic fraternity, in his junior year. He did not go out for any sport, but he did become treasurer of the football team and conducted his office so successfully that a deficit of former years was turned into a profit during his administration. During his college life he received the modest allowance of one hundred dollars per month from which he had to buy his clothes. As a matter of fact, he saved something from the allowance. Indeed, he wore one coat for so long a time that it became shiny, and this provoked some amused comment from the other students. A millionaire's son wearing a coat until it had a gloss was too good a morsel to pass unnoticed by the wags. But young Rockefeller continued to wear it, not from stubbornness or a pose, but just because he liked it. It was a comfortable, faithful garment and he saw no reason to throw it away.

He was graduated and now school days and playtime were over. His father offered him a trip around the world, which would have been of practical value, seeing the S. O. signs were already up in most places in the civilized world, and there was something worthwhile to learn in such travel. But young John had something to face—and he was anxious to face it. No need of being afraid of it; no use in putting it off. He was going into his father's office (John D. Senior had retired the year previous), sit at that rather terrifying desk, and take over!

This may seem, at first sight, not anything to be frightened of. But for more careful examination, let us look at the layout at Number 26 Broadway. To begin with there was a choice collection of generals, all occupying offices in that famous stronghold in lower Manhattan. These men were the pick of big business. There was the personable Henry H. Rogers, who could terrify the stoutest opponent by merely glaring at him, the bold and resourceful Henry M. Flagler, the shrewd John D. Archbold and several others. All these men had won success through their brains and ability.

To make it more difficult John D. Senior had given no instructions as to the duties or position given to his son. Apparently it was the father's intention that the young man should make his own way. The business was there; it would show the calibre of the boy to see just how he would conduct himself. In short, it was a sort of sink or swim test.

To begin with, young John D. studied the books of accounts, acquainting himself with the affairs of the office generally. He had had no formal law school training, and, realizing the importance of it, studied a book of common law. There were conferences and business meetings, and he attended these, listening much and saying little. He spent a good deal of time sitting in on interviews with one of his father's associates, Frederick T. Gates, who was very helpful in familiarizing the young man with the various affairs of the huge business.

Day by day, added one responsibility to another. While his father had retired he kept in touch with the business. As young John D. established a closer touch with affairs, he signed various agreements and important papers for his father, notwithstanding that he had no power of attorney. Somebody had to sign those papers and the young man felt that he could do so and act in accord with his father's wishes. He felt that his father trusted him and so he took the chance of acting without orders. It was a unique method of initiating a son into his father's business, but evidently it was John D. Senior's idea that the young man should learn what he could, and make a place for himself if he had the ability.

Gradually, as the years went on, John D. Senior shifted the load to the shoulders of his son, with the result that it was not long before the younger man was carrying the burden of looking after the huge Rockefeller interests.

It would have been possible and easy for any young man in such a position to make mistakes, even disastrous ones. No doubt there were some who would have liked to trip young Rockefeller, something they never could do to his redoubtable father. But the young man kept his head and successfully dodged the pitfalls.

Once he did venture into speculation and came out of it with burnt fingers. This was early in his life at 26 Broadway. He went into a stock venture with another man who proved to be untrustworthy. One day, after young Rockefeller had paid out quite a large sum, he came to the sad conclusion that he was "holding the bag." But it was good medicine. Young John D. swallowed it with as pleasant a face as possible. He went to his father with the story. The older man offered no criticism, never chided him. In fact, he said he would see him through on the transaction if he needed help.

Like his father John D. Junior early became active in

church work. The Rockefellers' religion was no surface
affair; they believed in it deeply. For many years young
John was teacher of the Men's Bible Class in what is now
the Riverside Church in New York City.

Young Rockefeller had done well with the great load
which had been laid upon him, a load which once prompt-
ed him to say, "I did not choose this job." To be sure he
had not set the world afire with spectacular actions; that
was not his way, but he was successful in conducting the
big job he had taken over.

But in 1914 came an event which might be called the
fork in the road for him. He may not have realized it but
now came a chance to become an insurgent or to stand
pat. In the previous autumn a strike had broken out in
the Colorado Coal and Iron Company, a property in
which the Rockefellers held a large interest. It had nothing to do with Standard Oil and the Rockefellers considered it simply an investment. There was no doubt but
what the miners had plenty of grievances; the conditions,
both living and working, were bad. Worse still, those in
actual charge proceeded to quell the disturbance with a
most intolerant hand. The news filled the newspapers
for weeks.

John D. Junior determined to find the facts for himself. Before many hours had passed, once having made
the decision, he was on his way west to see things with
his own eyes. First hand information was what he wanted
and nothing else.

At the company store on the mining property he got a
suit of overalls, put them on and went down into the
mines. He stumbled along the way, knocking his head

against the rough roof and getting wet and dirty. Soon he came upon a group of three men, at work with their picks. Just three common, dirty laborers, toiling in the feeble light many feet underground. And these three laborers were just what he had come to see and talk with. They held the secret he wanted to know.

He told them who he was. Then he grabbed a pick and tried his hand at the job, to get the feel of it, to see just what these men had to do day after day. The black lumps loosened and fell on his legs and feet. So this was what these men had to do. It was illuminating, a better way of getting information than any other.

He spoke to the men. "If I had all the money in the world I couldn't run these mines without you workmen, and you with all your brawn and muscle could not earn a living digging coal out of the ground unless there was capital to buy these mules and lay tracks and provide a market for coal. We are partners—and I want to do business with you on that principle."

He turned to leave. "You are not as bad as you are painted," said one of the men, and the three went back to their work.

He did his job of investigating thoroughly. He went everywhere, to a steel mill where he had to dodge red-hot ingots and flying metal. He visited the miners' cottages, talked with anybody he happened to meet. Once he attended a miners' dance and danced with great enjoyment. He ate wherever he happened to be, and enjoyed even a simple dish of baked beans. He mixed with everybody and made a fine impression on the people who had associated him with all their troubles. Once they had met him, they liked him.

From all this came good. An expert was called in to devise a plan for better working and living conditions. The new plan was quite drastic and aimed to correct the evils that had existed. Young John D. looked it over and approved; it corrected the bad things he had seen with his own eyes. The elder Rockefeller did not approve, yet he did not object; of course he had not had the young man's opportunity to see things for himself. But it was the young man's show and he went through with it. It was the wise thing to do and the young man's decision was correct. He had come to that "fork in the road," taken time to look it over, and then gone boldly along the way he thought was right. Afterwards his father approved heartily. The elder Rockefeller had always been a considerate employer with his Standard Oil people; he had never had a strike and conditions were good. There was no doubt but what John D. Junior would do the right thing, once he knew the facts. Months later at the industrial conference at Washington he declared a policy so liberal that the trade union group were delighted, yelling at him "to come over here; you belong to us!"

In the early days the name of Rockefeller meant acquisition. Later it came to mean giving. The wisest sort of giving. Indeed, it is almost safe to say that a hundred years from now people will think of them as Rockefellers the Givers rather than Rockefellers the Money-Makers. No other wealthy family in America has been so generous.

The story of these gifts would fill a book; indeed, they would make several books. We can note them but briefly.

National Parks and Historic Sites.

Benefactions have been in excess of $30,000,000 for the preservation of historic sites and parks in the United States. More than $10,000,000 has been spent for the restoration of Williamsburg, the old capital of Virginia. The complete restoration will present an accurate view of American urban architecture of the Eighteenth Century and is already becoming a center of interest for tourists and scholars.

In addition, gifts have been made for the acquisition of land, construction of roads, and erection of buildings in such national parks as Yosemite, Yellowstone, Shenandoah, Great Smoky Mountains and Acadia. Other donations have been made to preserve the historic redwood trees in California and to preserve wild bird and game life in the Grand Chenier Tract in Louisiana.

The Rockefeller Institute for Medical Research.

This institution was founded in 1901 by the Senior Rockefeller and today has an endowment fund of $60,-000,000. It has three departments: 1. Department of the Laboratories. 2. Department of the Hospital. 3. Department of Animal and Plant Pathology. In general the Department of the Laboratories deals with the problems of diseases in their physiological, pathological, bacteriological, chemical and physical aspects; the Department of the Hospital studies disease as it actually appears in human beings; the Department of Animal and Plant

Pathology deals with all aspects of the diseases of animals and plants. The Institute has taken a leading place among the world's laboratories. There is hardly a field of medical research in which it has not fruitfully labored. Medical experts were drawn from every part of the world to join its staff. One of the outstanding achievements of the Institute was in ridding America of yellow fever. Two of the experts who succeeded in this immensely valuable study lost their lives in the work, Doctor Noguchi and Doctor Stokes. The colonial administration of West Africa adopted similar methods in its colonies and stated that the Rockefeller plan was Civilization's greatest gift to mankind.

The Rockefeller Foundation.

The Rockefeller Foundation, incorporated in 1913, has capital funds of about $200,000,000. Its purpose broadly is to "promote the well-being of mankind throughout the world." It was designed to provide an agency which should deal with the problem of philanthropy, objectively and efficiently. Under its auspices the International Health Division has assisted in training public health personnel, in creating and improving governmental health agencies throughout the world, and, cooperating with them, has gone far in eradicating malaria, hook worm and yellow fever.

The General Education Board was founded in 1902 and its funds today approximate $50,000,000. Its principal function is the promotion of education within the United States without discrimination of race, sex or creed. The Board has already contributed over $250,-

000,000 for the improvement of education in all parts of the country.

The Foundation has made many gifts to medical schools in carrying on important work. Some of its largest donations have been to the Peking Union Medical College and other institutions in China, public health education, relief work during the World War, studies to eradicate hook worm, yellow fever, malaria and other subjects. Its benefactions have been granted in many parts of the world. The work of the Foundation is well-nigh universal; it operates in such widely scattered countries as Bulgaria, Italy, Holland, India, Palestine, Philippines, Java, Borneo, the Celebes and the Straits Settlements.

Rockefeller Center.

Probably the most talked about group of buildings in the world is that known as Rockefeller Center, a remarkable collection of buildings being erected in the heart of New York City. Late in the 1920's John D. Rockefeller, Junior became interested in this large plot of land, of about twelve acres, which was once the site of a botanical garden established by Doctor David Hosack for medical students.

Mr. Rockefeller and his associates decided to build along new lines, to build for New York tomorrow, to create a group of buildings so related and equipped that they would set a new standard for service, so staggered that they would be exposed on all sides to the maximum amount of sunlight and air, so beautiful and simple that they would originate new esthetic criteria for commercial construction.

Despite the world-wide depression, Mr. Rockefeller proceeded with his plans and today the area which is bounded roughly by 48th and 51st Streets and Fifth and Sixth Avenues is occupied by two theatres, the Center Theatre and the Radio City Music Hall, the latter the largest theatre in the world, seating over 6,000 people; the 70-story R. C. A. Building; the 31-story R. K. O. Building; The British Empire Building; La Maison Francaise; the Palazzo d'Italia; and a 41-story International office building. In all, twelve beautiful buildings have been erected or are planned.

Actual work on Rockefeller Center began on May 17, 1930, and the building is still under way. The development includes offices, shops, restaurants, libraries, theatres, clubs, permanent exhibitions of art and industry, and may truly be called a city within a city. The various buildings are connected by underground passages and eventually they will house a daily population of 100,000 persons. One of the noteworthy activities is the studios of the National Broadcasting Company from which daily radio programs are broadcast over two nation-wide networks of radio stations.

International Houses and Gifts For International Understanding.

Shortly after the World War Mr. Rockefeller Junior contributed several millions of dollars for repairs to and reconstruction of the Palaces of Versailles and Fontainebleau and Rheims Cathedral. As a further means to increase international friendship he has given four international houses, the first being opened in September 1924, adjacent to Columbia University in New York City. Two others are located at the University of California in Berkeley, California, and at the University of Chicago, at Chicago, Illinois, and the fourth in Paris, France.

The International Houses provide meeting and recreational quarters for the large numbers of students of various nationalities attending educational institutions in the four cities in which they are located. These Houses afford an opportunity for thousands of students from all parts of the world to meet, discuss problems and become better acquainted, and to know the history, customs and culture of other lands.

Parks In New York City and Environs.

Several years ago Mr. Rockefeller Junior gave to the Palisades Interstate Park Commission a strip of land extending along the crest of the Palisades from near the George Washington Bridge northward for thirteen miles, for the creation of a parkway which will preserve this beautiful site forever for the enjoyment of the people of New York City and nearby communities. In October 1935 he formally presented to the City of New York a large tract of land known as Fort Tryon Park. Fort Tryon Park in addition to park areas will contain the Cloisters, which is a branch of the Metropolitan Museum of Art and which is now under construction. The old Cloisters, which the new building will replace, began in 1906 as a private collection. The new museum will incorporate a cloister from Cuxa, the chapter room from the ancient Abbey of Pontaut, near Pau; tombs, pillars, altar carvings, tapestries and other works of art which are being assembled into a composite whole so that excellent examples of Gothic beauty may be studied by Americans at home.

These gifts form a total that is more staggering to realize in physical properties than it is in money, great as that latter is. The total amount of benefactions given by the Rockefellers long since passed the $600,000,000 mark. The figures and details are too intricate, too far reaching for us to appreciate. But this much we know; that this great amount of money has already accomplished an amount of good not to be appraised. Even the Rockefellers and their officials can never know all the good their work and benefactions have done and will continue to do. We see the figures, we see the buildings, we read of the works done by the experts employed. But nobody can know the amount of human suffering relieved, the amount of value done to young people in need of proper education, the great satisfaction given to the people everywhere in the matter of parks, museums and restorations. It was wise giving. It has been Mr. John D. Rockefeller's great job to oversee and direct this work. He has done wisely.

John D. Junior has always had the courage of his convictions. Once upon a time we had Prohibition and that is a story that everybody knows. But in 1932 there was a mere handful of prominent men who dared to come out openly and tell the truth about it. To do so meant political death.

John D. Junior was never a politician but he was a prominent man, undoubtedly the great pillar in the Dry Edifice. He and his father had contributed $350,000 to the Anti-Saloon League over a period of years. Both were teetotalers.

Yet in June 1932 the younger Rockefeller fired a shot that certainly was heard part way around the world—3500 miles of it anyway. He wrote a letter to Doctor Nicholas Murray Butler, who was a delegate to the Republican convention to nominate a President, advocating the repeal of Prohibition.

He gave his ideas in clear-cut sentences, with no pussyfooting. It was a brave letter by a brave man. He knew what it would mean, that thousands of well meaning drys would turn against him. But as in other tests he showed the stuff he was made of and gave the reasons for his stand.

He said that he was convinced that Prohibition had failed, that drinking had increased, that the speakeasy had replaced the saloon and increased in numbers over the saloon, that many of the best citizens had openly flaunted the amendment because they thought their rights had been infringed and that respect for the law had become lessened on account of the amendment, and that the law had bred an organized band of gangsters constantly growing more powerful. He had come to these conclusions, he explained, not all at once, but over a period of years. He had spent a good deal of money on a survey of vast proportions, conducted in various parts of the country. All this thought and investigation pointed definitely at one conclusion—and that conclusion he had stated.

In 1901 John D. Junior married Abby Green Aldrich, daughter of Senator Nelson W. Aldrich of Rhode Island. The wedding was a great social event, owing to the prominence of the two families. After some years John D. Junior built his own town house next door to his father's residence on West 54th Street in New York City. It is a magnificent white edifice, larger than the one next door in which he spent his boyhood. His was a larger family to house.

John D. Junior has raised his own family, five boys and one girl, in the same simplicity that marked his own youth. His children walked to and from school as he did. And he spent many hours with them in their play as his own father had done with his family, skating, boating and swimming. There are many tales illustrating the simplicity in which the young Rockefeller's children were raised. Once, when two of the boys were very young, they pooled their allowance for a few weeks to buy a baseball bat—as many boys have done. And later, when they were operating a rather dilapidated row-boat somebody suggested that they ask their father for an outboard motor to push it around. They are reported to have shouted in reply, "Who do you think we are, Vanderbilts?"

Not quite forty years have passed since young John D. sat down at the big desk for the first time on that day in 1897. His father still lives, the last of the great business generals of the nineteenth century. A great

amount of work has been done by the young man during
these four decades.

Did he really want to do it? When he said, "I did not
choose this job——" did he have some knowledge that he
kept to himself? Perhaps. We know plenty of examples
of men who have succeeded in a job already laid out
for them, who have heroically stifled the urge they had
to try something else. He has never said that this was
so. But we do know that there couldn't have been a
better man to do the big job he had to do.

Mr. Rockefeller considers himself a trustee with the
responsibility of administering to the best of his ability
the wealth that has come to him and the benefactions
established by his father. He explained this once in an
interview. "We are each custodians of the gifts with
which we are blessed, and are obligated to use them for
world betterment."

He has lived what he has preached. He has worked
long and diligently in his stewardship. Just that part of
it which entailed the successful giving away of over half
a billion dollars is life work enough for any man. There
aren't any text books or college courses on this most
difficult of courses. John D. Rockefeller Junior had to
be his own college, professors and pupil in this exacting
study. He has been graduated with honors.

ROBERT PAINE SCRIPPS

EDITOR OF A GREAT NEWSPAPER CHAIN

ROBERT PAINE SCRIPPS

ROBERT PAINE SCRIPPS

EDITOR OF A GREAT NEWSPAPER CHAIN

A S has been said in another chapter of this book, there are two things next to impossible to escape, once one has been inoculated with them. These two things are actor's grease paint and printer's ink. When either of those things gets into the system, the result is invariably the same; you carry on.

Robert Paine Scripps was well endowed with printer's ink. His great-grandfather, William Armiger Scripps, was a successful editor and publisher in London. Other descendants of his great-great grandfather, William Scripps, who came to America in 1791, engaged in the newspaper business. His own father, the famous Edward W. Scripps, was one of the greatest figures in American journalism. Another Scripps, James E., half-brother of E. W. Scripps, became owner of the Detroit News.

From the time of his earliest consciousness Robert Scripps realized that his orbit revolved around the newspaper business. It was the thing talked about, the thing which ever assailed his youthful ears. Unconsciously he absorbed this talk which went on all around him. The consequence was that a newspaper plant was never a novelty to him, any more than horses and cows would be to a boy born and brought up on a farm.

A boy's first hero is his father. The father of Robert

Scripps was a great figure, one that would have captured the fancy of any boy. He was big and dynamic. And the things he did seemed wonderful to the boy, Robert, as he heard about them: a newspaper started in some new city, a great campaign in journalism, celebrities and heroes intimately mentioned in a never ending stream. In some way, this tall, bearded man, his father, seemed connected with the doings of the entire world.

The story of E. W. Scripps is a remarkable one. He was born on an Illinois farm and grew up in the country atmosphere. But he had no taste for the life of a farmer. When he was little more than a lad he left the farm in Rushville and went to Detroit, where his half-brother, James E., was manager and part owner of the Detroit Tribune. After working at a few jobs, he went to work for this half-brother. James E. in the meantime, had started a paper for himself, the News. E. W. got a job with him as collector.

But he wanted to be a writer and finally he managed to get into the editorial end, first as reporter, and later as city editor. He worked on the News for several years. But he wanted to have a paper of his own. He succeeded in borrowing ten thousand dollars from his brother and in 1878 started the Cleveland Penny Press with a cousin, John Scripps Sweeney. The idea of a penny newspaper was new at the time, the usual price being two or three cents.

The little paper grew fast from the very start. E. W. Scripps had definite ideas about what a paper should be. Briefly, the cause of the under-dog evoked his sympathy, and the little paper was designed for him, the common working man. The paper was small, only four pages, was set in large, easily read type, and aimed to tell the truth without fear or favor.

From that simple beginning grew a great chain of newspapers. E. W. Scripps would pick out a city that looked good, hire an old building on some back street, buy some second-hand presses and go to work. The venture generally succeeded. In a period of thirty years a chain of some thirty newspapers was started, most of them being successful.

Of course he did not do it all himself. He would select a couple of young men with brains and ambition, and start them off on their own as partners with him. His only instructions other than to get the news, were to tell the truth and take the side of the working man. One of the young men would be the editor and the other the business manager. Contrary to the plan in most newspaper organizations, the editor was supreme. He dictated what went into the news columns, and also had the final word about the advertising columns as well.

When E. W. Scripps died in 1926 his fortune was said to be the largest ever made by any man entirely out of newspapers. It was a great empire, spread out over the country, in the east, west, central and southern parts.

E. W. Scripps had three sons to succeed to this immense business, James G., who later was to take charge in 1908, John Paul, who became editor, and Robert Paine. The two former sons died, James G. in 1921 and John P. in 1914.

Robert Paine Scripps was born October 27, 1895. He was educated by private tutors and later at Pomona College, California. His father had definite ideas on education. A good deal of academic education he held to be a detriment. Some things, he admitted, had to be learned, facts contained in the multiplication table and spelling books—the fundamentals. One had to submit to having those crowded into one's brain. But too much academic education he felt tended to stereotype boys. He believed that information without the capacity for making decisions is useless, so he loaded his sons with responsibility as soon as he felt they could stand up to it.

As a youth Robert was so lanky and thin that his family worried about him. A gymnasium instructor was called in to take charge of the youthful six-footer and build him up. The two went on interminable hikes over hills and fields surrounding the country estate, Miramar, near San Diego in California. They boxed, wrestled, played ball and tennis. Young Bob took it all without complaint. The tall body took on no fat but plenty of steely muscles. And one day in a boxing match he hung a haymaker on his instructor. The family ceased to worry; anybody who could knock his athletic teacher spinning was apparently all right. That ended the athletic coaching.

The two-thousand acre ranch in Southern California was an ideal place for a boy to grow on. E. W. wanted to supervise the education of his sons; he intended they should succeed him in the management of his newspapers and meant they should get the proper sort of education for such a goal.

They were all treated alike. As soon as they were old enough to understand such things he required them to

read the correspondence between him and his many lieutenants, both in the editorial and business side. There was
a great deal of this correspondence and it was an illuminating education, certainly one not to be obtained in any
school. When Bob was twelve, he was compelled to read
history three hours daily; his examiner in this was generally his father.

It was not all study. The big ranch was a perfect
Paradise for all kinds of play and sport. There was a
small artificial lake big enough for the sailing of boats.
The boys had guns and dogs, and there was good quail
shooting. There were horses to ride and automobiles and
motorcycles. The days were not long enough to get in
all they wanted to do.

When he was fifteen years old Bob was appointed manager of the big ranch with all its many employees. This
was a lot more serious than it sounds. It was an actual
assignment and the responsibility of the conduct of the
ranch fell on his shoulders. E. W. believed in figuratively
throwing his sons into the water and seeing whether they
were sinkers or swimmers. It was a rather stiff test for
a youngster but, of course, if successfully engineered, it
was very valuable—and greatly appreciated by the
father.

All the sons had gone through this test. But Bob's
brother decided to make this particular one both sudden
and definite. On the first day of the young brother's
regime, James went around among the help and secretly
engineered an insurrection. He told them to strike for
more wages. Of course he meant no harm; he thought it
would be good medicine for the younger brother. Bob

was left alone with his trouble and had to settle things the best he could. He did not get panic-stricken; neither did he lose the help.

The growing lad had his dreams. There was a big job waiting for him. He knew that. There were Scripps newspapers spread out over the country, and to one of them he would have to go.

But there was an independence of spirit in him. One of his early ambitions was to be a writer, and more particularly a poet. His father watched this phase of his son's life with more sympathy and understanding than many fathers would have shown. As a matter of fact, E. W. had been particularly fond of poetry himself, and as a boy had committed to memory whole volumes of poetry. It was not unnatural that Bob should like poetry, and, having writer's blood in him, want to do something more than just read it.

At any rate he wrote a lot of it. In his case there was more to it than to the usual bursts of poetry put out by many young men. He really went over. In the volume of Poetry Magazine for July, 1918 appears a poem "Island Song," and the author is Robert Paine Scripps. Anybody who can actually make a professional magazine with a bit of verse is a lot more than a mere verse-scribbler; he takes his professional status thereby, even if he never writes again.

At one time he wrote a book, too. This was at his father's orders. He wanted to see what he could do with such a task and he gave him six weeks in which to do the job. E. W. wanted to find out just what particular talent his son had. He knew that all the newspapers in the world couldn't stop a real poet from being one; neither could all the poetry in the world stop a good newspaperman from being one. One must wait.

In 1912, before he was seventeen, young Scripps went to work on one of the Scripps-McRae newspapers, the Philadelphia News-Post. His first assignment was that of circulation-solicitor, a job that had started his father on his journalistic career. There was no writing to do on this job. He just had to go around and see people, and get as many as possible to take the News-Post. It was a fine elementary course for any writer; not all newspapermen think of meeting their audience first before trying to write for them.

He spent only a year with the News-Post. During part of this year he tried his hand at reporting. He was pretty young to venture into the hard-boiled business of gathering news, but his father thought it was the thing to do.

In 1913 he spent several months in Europe with a group of prominent Americans. On this tour he had a fine chance to learn about business and government in other countries. He saw for himself and also had the advantage of the opinions of his older associates.

A year later he went to work in the Western Central office of his father's newspapers at San Diego, California, this time in the editorial department. During this short connection he initiated and organized the Scripps editorial bureau.

He stayed in no one place very long. It was really a post-graduate course to his academic schooling. All the various posts he filled were particular subjects in the larger education of newspaper study. After a short stay in San Diego he worked on several California papers, investigating business conditions. In this period of acquiring knowledge and experience he did not confine himself to newspapers. There was a stretch as a day laborer, where he learned some most illuminating things. Rubbing shoulders with the proletariat taught him a lot.

Again he was a hotel clerk for a brief interval. Then an insurance salesman. Note this widely assorted list of roles he played before he was old enough to vote; circulation-solicitor, reporter, foreign observer, editorial worker, day laborer, hotel clerk, insurance salesman. It was a most valuable training, one that would give him a truly sympathetic and understanding outlook on the people, who were representative of the millions he would have to serve later. His father watched all this jumping about, approved of it. He knew that a newspaper man would be pretty hopeless if he did not *know* the people for whom he must supply news.

This was all very well, necessary perhaps as a grooming for a future job. But he had seen much in his various assignments, had observed all sorts of men. One day he came to the conclusion that it would be very pleasant to be—his own man! As free as one of those laborers in the street or the insurance salesmen or hotel clerks. They had their own courses to chart; if they steered on the rocks that wasn't so good, but at least they'd had the fun of running their own show.

He decided to get away from home and, like any other ordinary boy, strike out for himself. If he did not, then he would never be quite contented in his mind about what he might have been if left to himself. A rather bold adventure, but a creditable one.

His first stop was at Bakersfield, California, in the oil field district. He applied for a job with the local newspaper and got one—hustling for subscribers. It wasn't much of a job, but it was something resulting from his own engineering.

Consider him. The son of a millionaire, who might conceivably be spending his time in social pursuits or in some dignified spot in the industrial world. Well, he was in the industrial world all right, but the dignified part was sadly lacking. He went around every day to interview the busy housewives—with a *washboard* under his arm. That washboard was a premium with which to lure subscribers into the fold of his particular newspaper. And that wasn't all. There were others out, like himself, sporting glistening electric flatirons with which *they* hoped to lure those same subscribers into the fold of rival newspapers!

This took a lot of spunk. It would have been so very much easier to work for Dad in the office of one of the Scripps newspapers. Carrying around an unsympathetic corrugated washboard under his arm was not the happiest way to spend a long day in the hot sun. Neither were the interviews with housewives with anti-washboard and pro-flatiron complexes. But he stuck it out; his feet stayed on the first step until he got something better to rest them on.

He felt he would rather meet men than argue about washboards with women. Journalism was fine but the

washboard side of it was too far away from the part he
was interested in.

So he wangled a job in the oil fields. Into the land of
derricks and pumps he went, determined to learn something about that queer business. He started contracting,
building foundations for gas engines, and finally loading
iron pipe. It was hard work but interesting for a time.

However, the new environment lacked one important
thing for him. Those in it didn't speak the language and
he missed it; the language of ink. Oil, derricks, pumps,
barrels, gushers and whatnot. No human drama to thrust
his nose into, nothing to put down on paper after he had
learned what it was.

So he left the oil fields and got a job on a newspaper
in Eureka, Humboldt County. The pay was one dollar
a day. The dollar wouldn't buy much fancy provender,
but the situation did offer considerable interest. He was
put on a certain routine reporting, his chief job being
to report marine arrivals and clearances.

Apparently he was not expected to rise to those occa-
sions, so often met with in journalistic fiction, because
one day he saw a good story in the wind and went for it,
leaving his regular duties to their own fate.

News came to the sheriff that a fight had broken out in
a town forty miles distant, between a gang of lumberjacks and a group of circus performers. Young Scripps
heard of it, too, and got aboard the sheriff's car without
telling his boss where he was going or anything about it.
He saw the end of the fight, got all the facts, rushed back
and wrote it up, as any good reporter should. His boss

didn't like this rugged individualistic performance however, and said so. Then he proceeded to spread the story all over the front page!

During all this time when he was away from home, he wrote regularly to his father, detailing his experiences and progress.

He held this job only a short time, and early in 1916 he made a trip to Honolulu. Here he enjoyed himself, and continued his habit of observing what he saw and setting it down on paper. It was on this trip that he met a man whose writing had charmed him, Jack London. Young Scripps had seen and talked with many writers, but now he had come upon one who had lived more exciting adventures than he had written in fiction. Naturally the boy was interested in this most pictureque of writers. He and London cruised about in the latter's little yacht and it was a thrilling experience for the youngster.

There was more of this roving education to come before he settled down. Later in that same year he went to Australia. There he worked on newspapers and studied political, social and business conditions. He found time to do some writing for several American magazines and newspapers. Not the least of his writing assignments were his detailed letters to his father.

Late in that year he came back to the United States. He continued writing. One of his assignments was the writing of a book in six weeks, which has already been mentioned.

Then came that cataclysmic year, 1917. In every chapter in this book you have seen how that greatest of wars altered the lives of men. It reached out and claimed everybody, in this country as well as in all the others.

In this particular family E. W. Scripps himself answered the call like the old war-horse he was. On the United States' entry into the war he left his ranch, where he had been in retirement for nine years, and came to Washington. There he took a suite of rooms in a hotel and gathered a corps of editorial assistants around him. He threw the whole weight of his great organization into supporting the cause of the Government.

Bob waived exemption of his status as a married man with family responsibilities (he had married Margaret Culbertson early in 1917), and was assigned to Headquarters Company at Camp Sherman.

In the meantime there had developed a difference of opinion regarding the editorial policy of the Scripps newspapers between E. W. and his son, James, who had had control since the elder Scripps' retirement. It was decided to appoint Robert to be editor-in-chief of the papers. His exemption was asked of the War Department on business reasons and it was granted. Robert Scripps left the service and assumed editorial charge of all the Scripps newspapers.

His father was sixty-three and the work he had thrown himself into with such ardor proved too much. His health broke down late in the year and he was ordered into strict retirement. It was now up to Robert Scripps, only twenty-two years old. At the age when the average boy comes out of college, he was editor-in-chief of some twenty-five papers, with a big syndicate and a news gathering association. One of his tasks was to organize the editorial and news war activities of all the Scripps papers, telegraph and features organizations, both domestic and foreign.

E. W. Scripps recovered and after the war lived his life on the yacht he had built for himself. From that time on he spent most of his life on the water. He wanted five years more to live, he said, that he might complete the journalistic education of his son Robert.

In 1920 E. W. Scripps retired from editorial direction of the newspapers and delegated full authority to Robert and to Roy Howard, who had had charge of the business end of the big organization. In 1922 all the Scripps newspapers and other property were deeded to Robert Scripps in trust. Then followed a six months' cruise on a new one hundred and eighty foot yacht, the Ohio. During this trip around the world, E. W. gave the final tutoring to his son, Robert, who went along. It was a valuable training, away from the hustle and bedlam where a more deliberate study could be given to the intricate subject. E. W. Scripps died in 1926 and at his wish was buried at sea.

In 1920 the name Scripps-Howard was adopted for the organization. Robert P. Scripps is now president, controlling stockholder and editorial director of the Scripps-Howard newspapers and affiliated companies. Since he assumed full charge of the management of the organization in 1920, the following newspapers have been purchased, reorganized or established:

Birmingham (Alabama) Post, Fort Worth (Texas)

Press, Washington (D. C.) Daily News, Knoxville (Tennessee) News and Knoxville Sentinel, now combined as Knoxville News-Sentinel; Youngstown (Ohio) Telegram, Indianapolis (Indiana) Times, El Paso (Texas) Post and El Paso Herald, now combined as El Paso Herald-Post; New Mexico State Tribune, Pittsburgh Press, Akron (Ohio) Times, now known as Akron Times-Press; Memphis Scimitar, now known as Memphis Press-Scimitar; Rocky Mountain News, Denver, Colorado; New York Telegram and New York World, now published as New York World-Telegram; Buffalo (New York) Times.

In addition to the acquisition of newspaper properties there have been purchased or organized the following affiliates:

Allied Newspapers, Inc., United Features Syndicate, Acme Newspictures, Metropolitan Features Service, Newspaper Information Service, Ocean Press, City News Service of Los Angeles, United News Service, United Press Wireless, United Radio Features, Continental Radio Company.

Mr. Scripps is a trustee of Science Service, Inc., of Washington, D. C., a scientific service organization, founded and endowed by his father in 1919; trustee of Miami University, Ohio, where the Scripps Foundation for Population Research is located; and a director of the Scripps Institution of Oceanography at La Jolla, California, founded by his father and his aunt, Miss Ellen Browning Scripps. In 1935 he organized and endowed the Ellen Browning Scripps Foundation, a philanthropic corporation. He is a writer and speaker of note on economics and journalism, and was awarded a medal of honor by the school of journalism of the University of Missouri in 1931 for his achievements in the field of journalism.

AUGUSTUS EUGENE STALEY

MANUFACTURER OF CORN PRODUCTS

AUGUSTUS EUGENE STALEY

AUGUSTUS EUGENE STALEY

MANUFACTURER OF CORN PRODUCTS

ONE of the figurative medals we like to pin on a person we admire is in the form of the catch-phrase "He can take it." By it we really mean that he can weather the fight without cringing or crying. But it is only a half-way success, "to take it." The man we most admire is the one who can take it *and* keep on fighting.

The man who is the subject of this sketch is one of this latter class. If we had a graph of his business life we would see a line starting at the very bottom (his boyhood) and ending at a most satisfactory pinnacle at the other. But along this rise to fortune were four major—the best word to use is—wallops! Four times in his life he was down, emphatically down—and four times through his grit and will to succeed he came up again. We are familiar with lowly starts and steady climbs to success, but quadruple ones are not so common.

To say that Eugene Staley was born and raised in abject poverty would not be true. The scene of his starting point was on a farm in North Carolina, and nobody starves on a farm in a section of the country which has two hundred and fifty growing days in the year. But actual cash was a rarity. The whole South was trying to get on its feet after the Civil War; it was a time of discouragement. The Staley farm, of some 250 acres, raised tobacco as the main crop. That product was its business; but it could raise plenty of foodstuffs for the family to live on.

Young Gene had the valuable asset of a good line of ancestors. Originally they had come over from Staleybridge, near Manchester, England, settling in the seventeenth century near Harper's Ferry, Maryland. Here the Staleys lived for many years, but early in the eighteenth century they moved down into North Carolina, taking up a promising section of land in Randolph County. They prospered during the succeeding generations until the dark years of the Civil War. Then came uncertainty and a much reduced living.

Eugene was born at Julian, N. C., February 25, 1867, the first child of William and Mary Jane Ledbetter Staley. The home was a weather-boarded log cabin, set in the beautiful, mellow country of rolling hills and wooded stretches. As a setting it was as lovely a place as one could wish; it had everything but—Opportunity.

Gene, the boy, grew up in the atmosphere of farming. Tobacco, cotton, vegetables. All these things he learned to care for. At the age when most boys are spending five hours a day in school and five more in play, this lad was toiling on hands and knees between the rows of tobacco plants, the hot sun burning his neck and back, patiently hunting and destroying tobacco worms. Patiently? Nobody but a dolt could do such a job, day after day in patience. He wanted something else. As he grew older he heard of the life which was all around him, but tantalizingly distant—cities, people, stores, railroad trains. All these were beyond the hills which encircled the farm.

Until he was sixteen Gene had little contact with the outside world. To be sure there was the church, to which the entire family went every Sunday; this was an event of great social interest, as well as an opportunity to worship. All the farmers drove in from the outlying districts on the Sabbath; it was about the only thing open to them to break the monotony of their lives.

Perhaps the major event of the year was the big camp meeting, usually held in August. The Staley family never missed this. They hitched up the rig and stowed a quantity of provisions in the back—hams, roasted chickens, pies, cakes, bread and jellies. Then off they would go, to be gone for a week or ten days. It was a real camp meeting, for all the families camped in the grove near the church. There were sermons preached every day, and much singing of good old Methodist hymns. And, of course, between services the welcome meeting of old friends. Gene loved these camp meetings. He liked to meet people, older folks as well as those of his own age. And it seemed an awfully long time from one August to the next!

Life on the farm was an endless round of work. Gene's mother spun her own yarn of cotton raised on the farm, and before he was old enough to work on the crops, he helped her spin and weave. Later he assisted in mixing the dyes, which were made from roots and berries gathered in the woods. These primitive dyes gave wonderfully soft, rich shades of browns and reds.

Gene's father wanted him to become a minister, or if

not that, a farmer. But neither of these callings seemed to strike a warm note in the boy's heart. Had he shown a liking for the ministry, ways might have been found for an education. As it was, however, he got a very meagre schooling, perhaps two or three months in the year. His only school book was a copy of Webster's old blue-backed speller. From that he was taught to read, spell and write.

One day, when he was fourteen, his father called him in from the tobacco field and told him he could load the truck with vegetables and try his hand at selling them in the village of Randelmann, some nine miles away. Randelmann wasn't much of a town and the vegetables did not sell for much in a vicinity where so much was grown. But Gene leaped at this chance. Here was what he wanted to do, to sell goods to people. He could knock on doors, tell the folks what marvellous cabbages and potatoes he had, and what remarkably low prices. What an adventure! A wagon heaped with vegetables going in to town; an empty wagon coming back, with money jingling in his pocket—and perhaps a simple gift or two for his mother.

Selling goods was what he wanted to do. Vegetables would do for a start. But some day——!

When he was sixteen years old, Gene's father died. The burden of running the farm now fell on him. Any dreams that he may have had about a life outside would have to wait, and perhaps for a long time. The paramount job was to keep that tobacco crop going, to keep the eatable produce growing, and to keep the roof over the heads of his mother and younger brother and two smaller sisters. He was the man of the house.

It was a hard job but he carried it on successfully. In time he might have made something of it, with his undeniable gifts in business. But at that age he was untried and inexperienced. And he wanted to leave the farm and try some business where there was selling to do.

After some persuasion his mother agreed to his going to Greensboro, some fifteen miles distant. Greensboro was a delightful town, with some 2500 people and quite a number of stores. It seemed that in such a place a young fellow could certainly "get his toes in and get hold of something."

It was a wonderful adventure, this getting a job, to the tall, husky lad clad in a home-made suit of home-spun. He was not dismayed at the first refusal of his services, nor the second. He plugged on. And finally he managed to make his first sale—of himself—to the Odell Hardware Company. He had a job!

Not many yards away worked another young fellow, who would some day be famous wherever English is read. He was filling prescriptions in his uncle's drug store, Clark's Pharmacy. Sometimes he drew cartoons, sometimes he wrote "pieces." Some day millions would read his "pieces" signed by the name "O. Henry."

Gene went to work on the first of September in the year he was sixteen. The work assigned to him was a little disappointing; he had to help the colored porter rack up carloads of nails, steel plows, bars of heavy iron and steel and do other hard, dirty work. He did not meet the public at all as a salesman. But that was all right; he understood. One had to learn the goods before he could talk intelligently about them. And hardware probably has more detail than any other business. His pay was fifteen dollars a month, of which ten dollars went for board.

One day just before Christmas time he was called into the office by the manager, Charles H. Ireland. The manager was sorry—but he was fired!

"You'll never make a business man, Staley. You'd better go to Sargent's Foundry and get a job where you can use your brute strength. You'll never be good at anything else."

Young Staley stared at him, dumbfounded. It was inconceivable. He had tried so hard. It was a tough disappointment, when he had hoped for so much from this job, for himself and his family. He swallowed the lump in his throat, and answered quietly.

"Well, sir, you can fire me, but you can't take away my ambition. Some day, if I live, I will be the head of a business as big as this!"

That was an unhappy home-going at Christmastide. No job, hopes dashed and little money to show for all his struggle. It looked like a dead-end; he had let go of farming—and business had let go of him!

But a few days of the home atmosphere saw his spirits up again. He would go back again to Greensboro and he *would not* go into any iron foundry. This time he would sell goods. In his heart he knew he was a salesman and nothing on earth was going to stop him from being one.

He managed, after some high-pressure talk, to land a

job, or rather a chance to sell plug tobacco for a small concern. He knew tobacco; heaven knows he had weeded and de-bugged enough of it! And it was a lively, staple product. Everybody either "chawed" or cut the plug up into pipe smoking tobacco; in those days granulated smoking tobacco was unknown.

He went out on the road, selling the plug tobacco on straight commission. He could sell anybody at all—grocery stores, hotels, general stores; any concern that could pay for the stuff. He made all the calls he could on foot, and when he had to, hired a horse. Now and then he opened new territory by riding a bit on a railroad.

At the end of the first year he knew two things; he was a salesman and he had some money to demonstrate the fact. It was not a lot of money, but it represented a satisfying, worthwhile effort. He went home and this time he had something happier to tell.

His mother listened to his story and looked amazedly at the money he had brought home. Her reaction gave him the surprise of his life.

"Gene," she said, "did you come by this money—honestly?"

It was a staggering thing for him to weather, that she doubted him. But then he understood. She just couldn't believe that anybody could make all that money by just asking people to buy tobacco.

However, the next morning she drove in to Greensboro to find out for herself about the source of this amazing wealth. It was all true. Her boy had honestly earned it, and she went back home satisfied—and proud. Later she **bitterly** regretted this momentary distrust of her son's honesty. He realized that it resulted from the long poverty of the family and their lack of knowledge of the world outside.

Young Staley remained with this concern for two years. He was very young to be a traveling salesman, but he was husky and big. His territory was mostly through the rural mountain districts, and his usual mode of travel on a horse. It was a pleasant, happy life for the young fellow; he had never thought such good luck would be his.

His customers were for the most part small town merchants. The jumps from town to town were often long. Of course roads were mostly pretty bad, especially in rainy weather, and the hotel accommodations left a lot to be desired. But that mattered little to him; it was all a part of the life—and that life he liked exceedingly well. As his ability increased, so did his earnings. Before he was twenty he was doing very well, earning more than he had ever dreamed of while on the farm.

At the end of the two years, young Staley branched out in a new line. He went to work for the Southern Manufacturing Company of Richmond, Virginia, selling teas, coffees, spices and baking powder. Now he got a bigger territory and, of course, had a wider range of goods. His earnings increased, and at the same time, so did his acquaintance with merchants, the one most valuable asset for a salesman.

After a year or two with this concern, he went back to his first business, tobacco. He worked for the Bloch Brothers Tobacco Company of Wheeling, West Virginia, selling, introducing and advertising Mail Pouch Tobacco. Then came a connection with the Price Baking and Flav-

oring Extract Company of Chicago, with a selling territory in the northwest. This part of the country was thinly
settled then. Stage coaches were the usual mode of travel
from place to place. He sold baking powder to the stores
that supplied the isolated ranchers and homesteaders.
He was a member of the little group that rode on the first
train that crawled through that vast country now composed of Montana, Idaho and Wyoming. It was raw,
new country and no Paradise for any salesman who had
to have all the niceties of living. But young Staley loved
it all. Later he was transferred to another territory, and
this time he went from the primitive to the most thickly
settled section in the country, New England. Here was a
salesman's heaven, towns almost sitting in each other's
laps, and stores all over the place. The longest jumps
could almost be made by a lively frog!

Then came a connection with the Royal Baking Powder Company, as salesman working in Illinois and Wisconsin. As the busy years went by his earnings had constantly increased. After twelve years of traveling and
selling he was earning $5000. a year above his expenses.
And that man in Greensboro had said he would never be
any good in business!

Life was pretty good. He had plenty of money, health,
and the roving life of a salesman was just to his liking.
But there was a fork in the road which he was coming to,
one which was to cause him some thinking.

He had become engaged to a young lady who was
studying music in Chicago, Miss Emma Tressler, whose
home was in Bryan, Ohio. But it was an engagement
conditional upon the establishment of a home and the

usual permanent residence in that home of the man of the house! There was a nice problem for a traveling salesman, especially one whose territory consisted of several big states. In fact, it just could not be done.

That fork in the road meant just one thing. He would have to get into some business that would make a stay-at-home out of him. He hated the idea of giving up the colorful, ever-interesting life of the road, but he decided it was the thing to do.

Next step in the problem: what to do? The obvious thing, especially for a man who had done considerable selling on commission, was to go into some business for himself. Inside jobs took long training before a good salary could be commanded. He knew of many successes that had been made by young men who dared to take the risk of starting in for themselves. What they could do, he could do.

There was a fly in the ointment, though. He had always lived well, been generous with his family and consequently his capital was not very imposing. In fact, it totaled only $1500. A little business might be started on that; in those days before the big mergers and trusts came, it was possible to start on a shoe string.

And now for the mind of business. There was tobacco, baking powder, flavoring extracts, all of which he knew something about. For years he had been visiting grocery stores, and there were long waits whenever customers came in. A salesman can never resist watching another sale going on, even if it's only for a box of matches or a couple of candles. One thing had always impressed him. Starch was something every grocer carried and which had a ready sale. There was no arguing about starch and people had to have it. "Give me a package of starch," the customers would say, with no hesitation. It was cheap, it was a staple. In fact, it was something sound and an essential.

He knew he could get all the starch he wanted in bulk. He could put it up in packages with his own name on them, and sell to the army of grocers who knew him. Such a business might grow into almost anything. He thought it over from every angle and at last decided to take the plunge. He arranged with the manufacturer of the starch he considered the best, to supply him starch in bulk.

Mr. Staley now took the plunge. In Baltimore, a city strategically placed in a good territory, he hired an inexpensive little loft room for two hundred dollars a year. He got his starch, his packages, and started to work. Rather a humble beginning for the future largest independent starch concern in the United States, just a room in the top of a small building—and one man comprised the whole working force.

He made his first sale on March 3, 1898. He packed the starch at night and went out the next day, selling it to the grocery stores of Baltimore. It was a very humble beginning, but there was one highly significant thing about it. Heretofore it had been Mr. Staley selling Somebody else's tobacco, baking powder, etc. But now it was Mr. Staley selling Staley's Starch! There was no getting away from that thrill, even if the rest of the venture seemed pretty small for an ex-salesman capable of earning one hundred dollars a week.

There was nothing soft about the creation of that business. It was all hard work. Packaging starch all night, selling it in the daytime, tramping all over the city on foot, waiting for payment, making out bills—and wondering most of the time how it was all coming out.

Once he had lived at the best hotels and spent money freely. Now he hired a hall bedroom; his board and room cost $3.50—and diamond-back terrapin stewed in sherry was very, very seldom on the bill of fare! He walked to and from his work. Sometimes the business seemed to be going ahead, sometimes it seemed to be standing still—and there were times when he wondered if it would live at all.

But somehow it did live. If one day looked bad, the next saw some hope. Soon he found he would have to get help; the packaging, selling and book-keeping needed the services of more than one head and pair of hands. In one of the stores he frequently called on he had noticed a boy who was always cheerful, willing and courteous. He offered him a job at $3.50 a week. This lad could handle the starch and leave Mr. Staley free to devote his attention to more important things. The boy came, Billy Pritchard was his name, and before he died he was vice-president of the big concern.

In those early Baltimore days financing was a problem. Sometimes Mr. Staley had to pawn his watch to pay his help, small as the help was. But somehow the little concern kept going. And at the end of the first year Mr. Staley found he had sold $1700 worth of Cream Corn Starch, which was what he called it. He had lost money —but the grocery stores had bought $1700 worth of

Staley Starch, and that was something to go on. Very encouraging.

The next year he sold $5000. And again there was a loss, though not so great a one. The jump in sales was a good sign. It would pay to keep on and find out. The third year would tell the story.

The story was good. He sold $9000. worth of starch and made a profit. The product was taking hold and it could be developed. The fourth year the figures were $17,000, just *ten times* bigger than those of the first year. And the fifth year in business the sales rose to $33,000. The sixth year saw the figure go to $49,000. Staley Starch was on its way up.

But in 1904 came a blow. A great fire wiped out many buildings in the city of Baltimore, and Mr. Staley's modest plant was one of them. He was insured but the company he was insured in had such heavy losses that the fire ruined them, too. His business was gone, and the future looked dark indeed.

He had done quite a little business with one of the banks, and had come to know the president of it quite well. He was a Quaker and his name was William T. Dixon. One day, shortly after the big fire, Mr. Staley went in to see him, explaining that he was wiped out, and that there was some doubt about any insurance being paid.

"Never mind that," said the banker, "This is no time to worry over little things. Get out and find a good place before they are all taken; others are hunting places, too. We can't allow a fine growing business like yours to be ruined by an accident not likely to happen more than once in a lifetime. We'll let you have the money to start again."

This was welcome news, both to know he could start again and that his name and credit were so good. He hustled around and got a location. Within a short time the plant was going again and that year turned out to be a very profitable one. What had seemed like another of those defeats had been turned into victory.

Cream Corn Starch was now known to a much larger territory. It had been introduced into New England, New York State as well as Maryland and adjoining states. As time went on starch manufacturing got more and more into the hands of a few big companies, and they were not so eager to sell starch to Mr. Staley's company; his business interferred somewhat with profits they wanted to keep for themselves.

He thought it over and the more he thought, the more certain he became that the proper thing to do was to manufacture the product himself. Certainly this would make for a more uniform quality, and he would be dependent on nothing but the corn crop itself.

A factory and equipment suitable for turning out enough to supply his fast growing business would cost a good sum of money. It would be necessary to finance the venture by selling stock, as he had nowhere near the necessary amount of cash. He incorporated his company as a start.

He had no influence to gain him a hearing in quarters where big undertakings are financed. He decided to tackle the big job himself; in other words, to tell his own story and sell his stock. He was not without prospects, decided-ly not. He had 2600 grocers who by this time were regular buyers of his Cream Corn Starch. And to these grocers he sold stock in his company. They knew his product and they knew him. The result was most satisfactory; he found himself with sufficient funds to buy a plant and machinery. Naturally such a stock selling campaign had advantages; the grocers, owning stock, were great boosters for the Staley product.

Mr. Staley had traveled all over the country and he felt it would be a good move to be near the supply of corn, of which he needed so much. He found a suitable factory in Decatur, Illinois. With many big grain elevators, in the heart of the corn belt and with several railroads entering it, it was an ideal place. The factory had seen two previous failures in the milling business, so the price was attractively low.

The new plant first operated for a trial run in 1912, but there were imperfections in the process and it was necessary to stop for alterations. These things were smoothed out, a fresh beginning was made, and this time they went ahead. For two years the factory was busy, with a daily grind of 3000 bushels. It looked, at last, as if the concern was really on its way.

But along came the World War and before long the company began to feel the effects of upset business conditions. The starch market, instead of booming like many others, went in the opposite direction. For fifteen months the plant was idle and finally a receivership was threatened. Something had to be done or the thing upon which Mr. Staley had built all his hopes would be lost. It was a dark period for him, and at one time he considered letting go and accepting a salaried executive position with a prominent company.

But that phase passed. He realized that that was not the right answer; it could not be. This thing he had planted, like a seed in the ground, and he could not give up trying to save it until the very last hope was gone.

Of course he did it. A bond issue of $400,000 saved the company. People who knew and who had faith in Mr. Staley bought the bonds. After paying all debts, there remained $70,000 with which a fresh start could be made. And one day the wheels began to turn again, the cheerful noises of activity permeated the Staley plant again. They kept right on turning.

The end of the story can best be told by a visit to the great plant as it has grown to be. The thing that started in a single loft room in Baltimore is now housed in 56 buildings. There is a 15,000 horse-power power plant, grain elevators, garages and mechanical shops, as well as the big factory itself. It has a daily grind capacity of 50,000 bushels of corn. It operates the largest soybean plant in the United States. Fifteen hundred persons work in this huge plant, and 200 salesmen are out every day, telling the world about the Staley products. Some of these products are corn starch, glucose, table syrups, corn sugar, corn oil and so on. Its customers are found in many basic industries such as textiles, confections, tanneries, paper and various food products.

Altogether it is quite an outfit for anybody to have built, especially anybody who was told he would never succeed in business. It was lucky for Eugene Staley that he did not believe what his first employer told him, otherwise he would not have believed in himself. He did believe in himself, and his monument is there in Decatur to prove it. The monument—the very best one a business man can have—is the plant he has built with his unceasing industry and confidence in himself.

JUAN TERRY TRIPPE

WHO BUILT THE LARGEST AIR TRANSPORT
SYSTEM IN THE WORLD

JUAN TERRE TRIPPE

JUAN TERRY TRIPPE

WHO BUILT THE LARGEST AIR TRANSPORT SYSTEM IN THE WORLD

I F Juan Terry Trippe had been born four centuries ago there is little doubt as to what he would have been doing. He would have had a fleet of ships somewhat better than anybody else's. He would have known as well as anybody else just what those ships were likely to find on their trips into the Great Unknown Sea to the West. And, by the time he was fully grown up he would have had a continent or two tucked away in his belt.

Unfortunately all the continents had been discovered before Juan Trippe was born. For anybody inclined to want to do something about continents, it was most discouraging. Everything was discovered; everything beflagged and named. The betting would have been 100 to 1 against anybody doing anything about continents. And yet this young man did do something about them, something both amazing and important. He linked them by means of air transportation.

The foregoing sounds somewhat fanciful, perhaps. But after learning about Mr. Trippe and his remarkable doings, we must come to the conclusion that he is as much an explorer and frontier-buster as anybody from Columbus down. As this is written the work has only begun. But there is enough of it finished for us to know that oversea air transport, after giving everybody in the aviation business grey hair, is a fact. Mr. Trippe did not do it all, but there was a mighty big gap in the biggest transportation problem ever known—and he is the man who filled that gap. We do not have to stretch our imagination at all to place him in that select company containing such big names as Columbus, Magellan, Henry the Navigator and his own contemporary, Colonel Lindbergh.

Juan Trippe was born at a most auspicious time. When he was four years old an airplane got off the ground for the first time in history at Kitty Hawk, North Carolina. By the time he was ten years old "flying machine meets" were being held in New York and Boston and other cities; these air circuses captivated him.

As a boy at Hill School, where he was called Mummy on account of his habit of silence, he was reading and dreaming about the exploits of those immortals of the air, Guynemer, Baron von Richthofen, Fonck and other early World War aces. And before that war was over he had managed to spend a few months himself as lieutenant in the U. S. Naval Air Force. This interlude had interrupted his college career at Yale. He went back and graduated in 1920.

There were prominent sea faring men among Juan's ancestors. One of them, John Trippe, was third in command of the U. S. S. Vixen in 1804 on its expedition against the Barbary Pirates. This Trippe was a valiant fighter and during this expedition he had a hand-to-hand encounter with a giant Tripolitan pirate leader. Lieutenant Trippe had led a small party and managed to get aboard the pirate ship. He was a small man and the leader of the Tripolitans was a huge fellow. They fought with swords and after a terrific battle all over the heaving deck of the pirate ship, the young American officer killed his foe. For his exploits Lieutenant Trippe received the thanks of Congress and was voted a gold sword. The U. S. S. John Trippe is named after him. Juan's great-grandfather, also named John Trippe, commanded a sloop of war in the Battle of Lake Erie.

Juan's father married Lucy A. Terry, whose family somewhere along the line had acquired some Spanish blood in Venezuela. Therefore the historic "John" became "Juan," in honor of a Spanish ancestor. This Spanish blood accounts for Juan Trippe's swarthy skin and Latin appearance, a fact which undoubtedly has helped in his success with Central and South Americans.

The year 1920 does not seem so long ago. Yet, speaking in terms of aviation, in some ways it is downright "antique." Commercial aviation, for example, had not begun, at least in the United States. In France and England airplanes, in a way of speaking, simply threw the machine-guns overboard and took on passengers. But for ten years after the Armistice air transport in our country was almost non-existent.

Young men of an adventurous turn looked to the air in the early twenties. There was opportunity. One could be a pilot, one could get into a factory where planes and engines were built. One could join an air circus and go barnstorming. One could sign up in the Army and Navy Air Forces. Or get a thousand-acre field and be an "airport magnate." It was, however, a very infant industry, unstable and temperamental.

Young Mr. Trippe made a few gestures aloft in those early years. He formed the Yale Flying Club for one thing, while in college. On one occasion he flew in an intercollegiate race. Unknown to him a friend, thinking his plane not wholly adequate, salted the tank with ether. He won the race easily, but the engine was ruined.

His father had been a banker and owned a seat on the New York Stock Exchange before his death, when Juan was quite young. Juan was supposed to follow a financial career, and for a time endured Wall Street. While this was not exciting, the training was valuable. Later he had need of all the knowledge of financing he could get. During this time he made some valuable acquaintances, such as Cornelius Vanderbilt Whitney, Percy Rockefeller and William Vanderbilt.

He owned a battered hydroplane with which he amused himself around the Hamptons on Long Island. Its pontoons leaked and frequently he had to land and bail it out.

In 1922 he started an airline, designed to transport passengers from Manhattan to Hampton, Long Island. He was, in fact, president and general manager of the concern, the Long Island Airways System. This was pioneering in an age of pioneers. In those days somebody was always about to "inaugurate" an airline between some place and another. It was a poor week when at least one "inauguration" of an airline was not announced in the newspapers. Most of them never came off at all; and the few that got into the air died from lack of business, or even worse calamities. Planes were not too reliable then. The Long Island Airways ran Jennies, ships that were not exactly suited to passenger comfort. The life of this company was not long, which was nothing re-markable; compared to its contemporaries, it died of old age.

It was not long after this that something more dignified and much more sound came along. The Colonial Air Transport Company was organized late in 1925, as an amalgamation of Eastern Air Transport and Colonial Air Lines. It flew between New York and Boston. Mr. Trippe was made general manager, and operations start-ed in June, 1926. The flying equipment included one Cur-tiss Lark, two Fokker Universals, and two Fokker tri-motor monoplanes.

This line got United States Air Mail Contract No. 1. It carried no passengers in 1926 but began that service the following year. Mr. Trippe left this company early in 1927. In this brief connection he learned a good deal about the new and exciting business of running an airline. It was interesting work, so interesting that he never in-tended doing anything else. In a period of ballyhoo, when people of the air were all heroes in heavy type, young Mr. Trippe showed a marvellous facility for keeping in the background. As in his school days, he said next to nothing at all, and was content to remain practically un-noticed in the scramble for fame all around him.

The year 1927 was certainly a big one in aviation. A whole series of great things happened, topped by the mas-terpiece of all, Colonel Charles Lindbergh's flight from New York to Paris. Soon after that epic the air was full of attempts to conquer oceans and break records.

It did seem, after the Atlantic had been hopped two or three times, that oversea transport was possible. If one man in a small plane could do it, why not several men in a larger plane? But the thing that looked so simple was anything but that. There was only one thing that was really ready—the pilots. But everything else connected with it needed a lot of developing, planes, engines, radio —and other details too numerous to mention. Eight long years were to pass before the dream became a reality.

While air transport lagged in this country for one reason or another, there were keen minds that realized it would be a reality sooner or later. There was one thing that could be done; plot the territory where such airlines would be most profitable. The United States had a well worked out network of railroads; no part of it could be said to be inaccessible. But there was a rich land to the south of us which was not so thoroughly trafficked. As early as 1920 many men saw the logic of air transportation over the inaccessible reaches of the Caribbean Sea and up and down the mountainous coast of South America. Between the United States and the distant trade centers of South America lay barriers of jungle, mountain, open sea and a new thing to bother transportation— weather of various kinds and intensity. Sixteen-thousand foot mountain ranges, 600-mile stretches of open water, and a one thousand-mile barrier of tropical jungle separated North America from Central America. Eight thousand miles of difficult coastal terrain, climaxed by the 20,000 foot Cordillera of the Andes, were some of the geographical problems facing such a service in the air. It was a rosy dream, accompanied by a colossal engineering headache. But there were men who meant to try it. Young Juan Trippe was one of them.

Early in the 1920's there had been an air service plying out of Key West, called the Aeromarine Airways. This company had the right idea; it used flying boats. They were equipped with Liberty engines and were very expensive to run. This line ran for a season or two but finally quit in 1924.

In 1927 a concern called the Pan-American Airways, Inc., managed, after a lot of hard work, to get the air mail contract from Key West to Havana, Cuba. As airlines cannot run at a profit without subsidy from the government, this meant a virtual monopoly. Two other groups were also interested in the venture, one of which was composed of Juan Trippe, Cornelius Vanderbilt Whitney and T. E. Hambleton. This latter group was called the Aviation Corporation of America. The three groups merged—and the Aviation Corporation of America became a holding company of the future great Pan-American Airways System, which then had nothing but an air mail contract, an idea and some money with which to buy equipment. Mr. Trippe, twenty-seven years old, was made president and manager. His part in the affair had been considerable; he had sold stock to all his friends and worked like a Trojan.

The new company began operations October 19, 1927. It had a ninety-mile route between Key West and Havana. The equipment consisted of two tri-motored Fokker land planes, powered with Wright J5C engines. After a few weeks of carrying nothing but mail, the company announced a passenger carrying service. The service was extended to Miami late in 1928. During the first year the line carried more than 18,000,000 letters and 1200 passengers.

Mr. Trippe took the burden of performing miracles upon his own sturdy shoulders from the start. Selling stock had been only a beginning. Now came a whole procession of "things-that-cannot-be-done." One by one, Mr. Trippe quietly ironed them out. For example, when the Florida to Cuba service was first started, it took more than two hours for notice of the plane's departure to be cabled from Key West to Havana. The plane made the trip in fifty minutes. The need for an airplane radio was immediately apparent. Radio engineers called in on the problem said it was impossible to build a short-wave radio under 1400 pounds with a broadcasting range of thirty miles. Planes at that time could carry a load of only 700 pounds. But a practical radio was a necessity. Mr. Trippe listened politely, said little, then set a few young radio engineers to work on the job that couldn't be done. The result: an airplane radio weighing 85 pounds with a broadcasting range of 150 miles. Later, when the 600-mile oversea flight came, they had to get busy again—and they built a short-wave radio weighing but 65 pounds with a broadcasting range of 4,000 miles.

Another primary obstacle in the early days of airways operation over the Caribbean was the long stretch of open sea. The thing needed was the amphibian, which could land on either land or water. The only amphibian at the time was the military-type Loenings. Pan-American had to have an amphibian that could carry freight and passengers. Mr. Trippe went to Igor Sikorsky, Russian aviation expert, and the result was the Sikorsky S-38, a sturdy, substantial bi-engined, eight-passenger and freight amphibian. Three of these ships were put in service early in 1929; they were the forerunners of the big Clippers to come a few years later.

Juan Trippe had a dream of a great air service that would encompass the southern part of America. He went to work. He got a small line which operated out of Porto Rico to San Juan and San Domingo. Then he acquired the Compania Mexicana de Aviacion which headed south from Brownsville, Texas. Next came the question of the big hop into Central America, the mail contract to Panama. This was put over by a new sale of stock. In 1929 the Pan-American formed an alliance with the Grace Airways, and that resulted in a great airline operating from Panama to Chili.

In 1929 Pan-American operated Foreign Air Mail Contracts 4, 5, 6, 7, 8, 9. It had a fleet of 58 planes, 72 pilots and 330 mechanics. During 1929 and 1930 Pan-American lines were increased rapidly. In September, 1930, the system acquired the N.Y.R.B.A. (New York, Rio and Buenos Aires) giving Pan-American a total of over 19,000 miles of airlines.

Mr. Trippe had difficulties of many kinds to overcome. One of the great tasks was the lining up of thirty-three different countries in Central and South America. There were jealousies between some of these countries, and naturally, some antipathy at times against the North Americans coming in to their land on big business. But the suave and persistent Mr. Trippe had his way everywhere. He flew all over the South American map, doing a Herculean job.

He capped it all with a door-to-door pickup service with 147 trade centers in these thirty-three countries by an arrangement with 23,000 Railway Express Company agencies in the United States. This last meant that it was now possible for the shipper anywhere in the United States to consign express by rail and air direct from his warehouse to its point of destination by means of a single waybill.

It took an immense amount of money to build up such a big system, and quite a slice of this sum went for the radio ground control stations. The United States Government—which spent $630 per mile to build its domestic airways and expends $340 per mile annually to maintain radio communication, weather bureau, beacons and other markings along them—offers no such assistance to extraterritorial airlines. So it was up to Pan-American to establish a chain of 66 radio ground control stations, each of which was also a meteorological bureau. Later this number was increased to 98 stations.

By 1932 Mr. Trippe had started an airline to Alaska. Then he stepped across the Pacific and got China. He went into partnership with the Chinese Government in ownership and operation of the China National Aviation Corporation, holding, with the exception of a single Sino-German line, monopolistic control of all air traffic in China. In that country planes traveled the coast from Peiping 1800 miles to Canton on regular schedule and flew 1200 miles up the Yangtse River almost to the Tibetan border.

Bigger ships were needed, especially flying boats for the run out of Miami over the 7500 mile coastal trunk line to Rio Janeiro and Buenos Aires by way of the West Indies; across the direct trans-Caribbean route to Barranquilla, Colombia and Canal Zone. The Sikorsky Company built them, the S-40, equipped with four Pratt & Whitney Hornet engines. These amphibians were the first of the famous Clippers, the American Clipper and the Caribbean Clipper. They were 24 feet high, with a wing span of 114 feet, length 76 feet 8 inches. The four engines gave 2300 h. p. and a cruising speed of 115 miles per hour. These magnificent flying Pullmans carried 45 to 50 passengers. Travel in them was a revelation. They became famous all over the world and the routes traveled by them were among the most popular with air-travelers. The first one of these splendid ships was flown by Colonel Lindbergh from Miami to Colombia.

But two years later these flying boats were surpassed by two more, the Brazilian Clipper and the Pan-American Clipper; this type was the Sikorsky S-42. The former broke eight records for transport planes on its first flight. It was placed in service on the Miami to Buenos Aires run, reducing the time for this flight from seven to five days. The ships weighed 20 tons. The Pan-American Clipper was transformed into a flying-laboratory, and sent on three epochal flights of exploration and trail-blazing into the Pacific; the first to Hawaii, the second to Midway Islands and the third to Wake Island, 6000 miles by airplane from California. Flying with machine-like regularity the three flights totalled 22,750 miles.

But the Pan-American had even more ambitious plans. Since 1931 Mr. Trippe had been aiming at trans-oceanic air travel. He had called in two advisers, Colonel Lindbergh and Andre Priester, chief engineer of the Pan-American. Together these men made plans, which were no less than the crossing of the Pacific Ocean.

It had been not so long ago that the Pacific was the terror of aviation, a greater antagonist than the tempestuous Atlantic. The first attempts at flying it were most disastrous. The first successful flight from the Pacific Coast to Honolulu was on June 28, 1927, by Lieutenants Maitland and Hegenberger of the United States Army Air Corps. Only once has the still longer flight from Japan to our coast been made.

Juan Trippe, with all the resources of his gigantic airline, determined to make this crossing of the Pacific in transport planes and on scheduled trips. That was the big idea. When he called in his advisers in 1931 there were no seaplanes in existence that could make the long 2600 mile hop to Hawaii with safe fuel reserve, much less with a load. A year was devoted to research and experiment. Only two of the six airplane designers to whom specifications were submitted thought the project possible. These two were Glen L. Martin and Igor Sikorsky. These two designers carried the creative process forward. Early in 1934 the big Sikorskys were ready and later in the year the Martin clipper was ready; it was the largest flying boat ever built in America, able to fly across the Atlantic non-stop with 20 passengers and a ton of mail.

Pan-American had trained special crews for this oversea service, picked from their 200 flyers. They practiced navigation endlessly: by the sun and stars, by drift observations of the ocean's surface, by radio compass. Flight groups of six were drilled, the number needed for trans-oceanic flight: Captain, First Officer, Navigation Officer, Engineering Officer, Junior Flight Officer and Radio Officer.

Bases had to be picked to break the long 8000 mile flight, and equipped with stores. First there was Hawaii. Then the tiny Midway Islands, 1400 miles to the westward. Third, Wake Island, a coral atoll 1200 miles beyond Midway. Fourth, Guam, nicely spaced to break the flight from Wake to Manila. Preparations had to be made on these islands and supplies laid in. A steamer, the North Haven, went ahead to do this work. The preparations cost $2,000,000.

On November 22, 1935 the China Clipper, a Martin 25-ton flying boat, waited off Alameda, California, commanded by Captain Edwin C. Musick, veteran air man and Pan-American's foremost pilot. It would take off for the long flight to Manila with the heaviest pay load ever to rise from an American airport. Nearby, on the placid waters of the Oakland Estuary, lay an old relic, another Clipper which had sailed that same journey many times, the Star of New Zealand.

One hundred thousand letters were aboard the China Clipper. Postmaster-General Farley was on hand to bid Godspeed to the beautiful Clipper. And Juan Trippe stood by his side. The Postmaster-General gave the word, and Mr. Trippe signaled to Captain Musick. The four giant engines hummed, then broke into a roar. Away sped the ship, up off the water and headed west. Juan Trippe gazed out at it until it was a speck, and finally no speck at all.

The China Clipper landed in Pearl Harbor, Honolulu next day after 21 hours of flying. In five daily hops of from 1200 to 2600 miles it made the 8,000 mile flight with ease. Total flying time, sixty hours. At no time was it pushed. And a few days later it made the return trip in 62 hours, 55 minutes. The Pacific had been crossed by a heavily loaded transport plane, and the gallant Clipper had taken it in its stride.

A sister ship, the Philippine Clipper, made the same trip a few days later, and cut the time four and one-half hours.

This longest oversea journey is now made on schedule service. Hotels are being built on the Islands of Midway, Wake and Guam. The materials are being transported by the steamer, and the buildings set up on the islands, one of which was uninhabited until Pan-American came. These little hotels will have 45 rooms and will be completely equipped. The Clippers land in the lagoons and the passengers are taken off in launches. Radio stations, offices and powerhouses are already built and equipped.

Even in our day all this seems like a dream. A generation ago or less it would have been considered the wildest sort of dream, something beyond Jules Verne and possibly taxing Baron Munchausen's fancy.

It seems even more wonderful when we consider the space of time in which it was all accomplished. In 1927 it didn't exist; there was nothing. Eight years later we have an Empire of the Air, consisting of 40,000 miles of airway in three continents, 138 airliners and 3000 employees; airports, radio stations, hotels in mid-ocean. It is one of the most remarkable successes on record.

At the beginning of this chapter no doubt the reader

felt the statements were quite fanciful. They were not. This quiet, unassuming Juan Terry Trippe is quite worthy to take his place with any of the explorers and frontier-smashers of history.

INDEX

355

Selections from
L. C. Page & Company's
Books for Boys

FAMOUS LEADERS SERIES

Each one volume, cloth decorative, 12mo, illustrated by photographs, per volume *$2.00*

BY CHARLES H. L. JOHNSTON
("Uncle Chas.")

"If you see that it's by 'Uncle Chas.' you know that it's historically correct."—Review.

FAMOUS CAVALRY LEADERS

FAMOUS INDIAN CHIEFS

FAMOUS SCOUTS

FAMOUS PRIVATEERSMEN AND ADVENTURERS OF THE SEA

FAMOUS FRONTIERSMEN AND HEROES OF THE BORDER

FAMOUS DISCOVERERS AND EXPLORERS OF AMERICA

FAMOUS GENERALS OF THE GREAT WAR

Who Led the United States and Her Allies to a Glorious Victory.

FAMOUS AMERICAN ATHLETES OF TODAY, First Series.

Cloth 12mo, illustrated from specially autographed photographs *$2.50*

FAMOUS AMERICAN ATHLETES OF TODAY, Second Series.

A companion volume to the above . . . *$2.50*

FAMOUS AMERICAN ATHLETES OF TODAY, Third Series.

By Trentwell M. White *$2.50*

FAMOUS AMERICAN ATHLETES OF TODAY, Fourth Series.

By Charles H. L. Johnston *$2.50*

B-1

FAMOUS LEADERS SERIES (Con.)

FAMOUS AMERICAN ATHLETES OF TODAY,
Fifth Series.

By Leroy Atkinson $2.50
The following except as otherwise noted. . . $2.00

By EDWIN WILDMAN

THE FOUNDERS OF AMERICA (Lives of Great
Americans from the Revolution to the Monroe
Doctrine)

THE BUILDERS OF AMERICA (Lives of Great
Americans from the Monroe Doctrine to the Civil
War)

FAMOUS LEADERS OF CHARACTER (Lives of
Great Americans from the Civil War to Today)

FAMOUS LEADERS OF INDUSTRY.—
First Series

FAMOUS LEADERS OF INDUSTRY.—
Second Series

By TRENTWELL M. WHITE

FAMOUS LEADERS OF INDUSTRY.—
Third Series $2.50

By HARRY IRVING SHUMWAY

FAMOUS LEADERS OF INDUSTRY.—
Fourth Series $2.50

'These biographies drive home the truth that just as
every soldier of Napoleon carried a marshal's baton in his
knapsack, so every American youngster carries potential
success under his hat.'

By CHARLES LEE LEWIS
Professor, United States Naval Academy, Annapolis

FAMOUS AMERICAN NAVAL OFFICERS
With a complete index.

"In connection with the life of John Paul Jones, Stephen
Decatur, and other famous naval officers, he groups the
events of the period in which the officer distinguished himself, and combines the whole into a colorful and stirring
narrative."—*Boston Herald.*

B-2

THE BOYS STORY OF THE RAILROAD SERIES

By Burton E. Stevenson

Each large 12mo, cloth decorative, illustrated . $1.75

THE YOUNG SECTION-HAND;

Or, The Adventures of Allan West
"The whole range of section railroading is covered in the story."—*Chicago Post*.

THE YOUNG TRAIN DISPATCHER

"A vivacious account of the varied and often hazardous nature of railroad life."—*Congregationalist*.

THE YOUNG TRAIN MASTER

"It is a book that can be unreservedly commended to anyone who loves a good, wholesome, thrilling, informing yarn."—*Passaic News*.

THE YOUNG APPRENTICE;

Or, Allan West's Chum.
"The story is intensely interesting."—*Baltimore Sun*.

THE DAYS OF CHIVALRY SERIES

Of Worth While Classics for Boys and Girls
Revised and Edited for the Modern Reader
Each large 12mo, illustrated and with a poster jacket in full color $2.00

THE DAYS OF CHIVALRY

By W. H. Davenport Adams.

THE CHAPLET OF PEARLS

By C. M. Yonge.

ERLING THE BOLD

By R. M. Ballantyne.

WINNING HIS KNIGHTHOOD;

Or, The Adventures of Raoulf de Gyssage.
By H. Turing Bruce.
"Tales which ring to the clanking of armour, tales of marches and counter-marches, tales of wars, but tales which bring peace; a peace and contentment in the knowledge that right, even in the darkest times, has survived and conquered."—*Portland Evening Express*.

B-3

THE YOUNG PIONEER SERIES

By Harrison Adams

Each 12mo, cloth decorative, illustrated, per volume **$1.65**

THE PIONEER BOYS OF THE OHIO;
Or, Clearing the Wilderness.

THE PIONEER BOYS ON THE GREAT LAKES;
Or, On the Trail of the Iroquois.

THE PIONEER BOYS OF THE MISSISSIPPI;
Or, The Homestead in the Wilderness.

THE PIONEER BOYS OF THE MISSOURI;
Or, In the Country of the Sioux.

THE PIONEER BOYS OF THE YELLOWSTONE;
Or, Lost in the Land of Wonders.

THE PIONEER BOYS OF THE COLUMBIA;
Or, In the Wilderness of the Great Northwest.

THE PIONEER BOYS OF THE COLORADO;
Or, Braving the Perils of the Grand Canyon Country.

THE PIONEER BOYS OF KANSAS;
Or, Prairie Home in Buffalo Land.

"Such books as these are an admirable means of stimulating among the young Americans of to-day interest in the story of their pioneer ancestors and the early days of the Republic."—*Boston Globe.*

"Not only interesting, but instructive as well and shows the sterling type of character which these days of self-reliance and trial produced."—*American Tourist, Chicago.*

"The stories are full of spirited action and contain much valuable historical information. Just the sort of reading a boy will enjoy immensely."—*Boston Herald.*

B-4

MINUTE BOY SERIES

By James Otis and Edward Stratemeyer

*Each one volume, cloth decorative, 12mo, fully
illustrated, per volume* *$1.50*

This series of books for boys needs no recommendation.
We venture to say that there are few boys of any age in
this broad land who do not know and love both these
authors and their stirring tales.

These books, as shown by their titles, deal with periods
in the history of the development of our great country
which are of exceeding interest to every patriotic American
boy—and girl. Places and personages of historical interest
are here presented to the young reader in story form, and
a great deal of real information is unconsciously gathered.

THE MINUTE BOYS OF PHILADELPHIA

THE MINUTE BOYS OF BOSTON

THE MINUTE BOYS OF NEW YORK CITY

THE MINUTE BOYS OF LONG ISLAND

THE MINUTE BOYS OF SOUTH CAROLINA

THE MINUTE BOYS OF THE WYOMING
    VALLEY

THE MINUTE BOYS OF THE MOHAWK
    VALLEY

THE MINUTE BOYS OF THE GREEN
    MOUNTAINS

THE MINUTE BOYS OF BUNKER HILL

THE MINUTE BOYS OF LEXINGTON

THE MINUTE BOYS OF YORKTOWN

B-5

BOOKS FOR BOY SCOUTS

(Published with the approval of the "Boy Scouts of America")

THE VAGABOND SCOUTS; Or The Adventures of Duncan Dunn.

By KENNEDY LYON.

Cloth, 12mo, illustrated by Harold Cue, jacket in full color *$1.75*

"The pranks of the boys are amusing and exciting, but never without some useful purpose. Boys in their teens, and especially members of 'Scout' organizations, are bound to enjoy this book, and it is good reading for them in these times."—*Boston Post.*

BY BREWER CORCORAN

Each, 12mo, cloth decorative, illustrated . . *$1.75*

THE BOY SCOUTS OF KENDALLVILLE

Illustrated by Charles E. Meister.

"This is one of the biggest, best and finest Boy Scout books yet published. Every red-blooded American boy who reads this book will give it his hearty endorsement and will be a finer boy for having read the story."—*Book News Monthly.*

THE BOY SCOUTS OF THE WOLF PATROL

Illustrated by John Goss.

"This book is in itself a recommendation. It is the thrilling story of how a Scout Patrol, under the patronage and encouragement of the head of a munition factory, suspected, sleuthed and captured the sky.—*Lousville Times.*

THE BOY SCOUTS AT CAMP LOWELL

Illustrated by Charles Livingston Bull.

"Brewer Corcoran has written a number of Boy Scout stories. His place is secure with thousands of boys who are waiting the announcements of his pen."—*Oakland Tribune.*

WILL BRADFORD'S SCHOOL DAYS;

Or, The Barbarian.

Illustrated by Walter S. Rogers.

"This is a splendid story of friendship, study and sport, winding up with a perfectly corking double play."—*Springfield Union.*

B-6

LAWRENCE: THE ARABIAN KNIGHT

By HARRY IRVING SHUMWAY.
Cloth 12mo, illustrated, full color jacket . . $1.75
No story of courage, endurance, and inspired leadership
will be read by boys with more interest than that of
Thomas Edward Lawrence whose part in the Great War
has made of him a legendary figure.

ALBERT: THE SOLDIER KING: Being the Story
of Belgium's Great Ruler.

By HARRY IRVING SHUMWAY.
*Cloth, 12mo, illustrated from original photographs,
full color jacket* $1.75
"This book for boys emphasizes the democratic ways
and the high ideals of the late King of the Belgians.—
Cincinnati Enquirer.

THE CRUISE OF THE "KINGFISHER," A Tale
of Deep-Sea Adventure.

By H. DeVERE STACPOOLE.
Cloth, 12mo, illustrated $1.75

THE CRUISE OF THE "SALLY"

By EDWARD P. HENDRICK.
Cloth, 12mo, illustrated by Dean Freeman . . $1.75

COPPER COLESON'S GHOST

By EDWARD P. HENDRICK.
Cloth, 12mo, illustrated by Harold Cue . . $1.75
"Baffling encounters with alleged ghosts, a daring under-
water escape from a flooded mine and an exciting ice boat
race are among the adventures experienced by this gallant
crew.

JACK IN THE MOUNTAINS

By JAMES F. CROOK.
*Cloth decorative, 12mo, with a poster jacket in
color and illustrations by Charles Livingston Bull* $1.75

THE INCAS' TREASURE HOUSE

By A. HYATT VERRILL.
*Cloth 12mo, illustrated by Heman Fay, Jr., with
color jacket* $1.75
"This is a book which might well be read by any true-
blue American boy.

MYSTERY CAMP

By M. M. DANCY McCLENDON.
*Cloth decorative, 12mo, illustrated and with a
poster jacket, by P. L. Martin* $1.75

Selections from
L. C. Page & Company's
Books for Girls

THE BLUE BONNET SERIES

*Each large 12mo, cloth decorative, illustrated,
per volume* . . . . $ 2.00
The seven volumes, boxed as a set 14.00

A TEXAS BLUE BONNET
By CAROLINE E. JACOBS.

BLUE BONNET'S RANCH PARTY
By CAROLINE E. JACOBS AND EDYTH ELLERBECK READ.

BLUE BONNET IN BOSTON
By CAROLINE E. JACOBS AND LELA HORN RICHARDS.

BLUE BONNET KEEPS HOUSE
By CAROLINE E. JACOBS AND LELA HORN RICHARDS.

BLUE BONNET—DÉBUTANTE
By LELA HORN RICHARDS.

BLUE BONNET OF THE SEVEN STARS
By LELA HORN RICHARDS.

BLUE BONNET'S FAMILY
By LELA HORN RICHARDS.

"Blue Bonnet has the very finest kind of wholesome, honest, lively girlishness and cannot but make friends with every one who meets her through these books about her."—*Chicago Inter-Ocean.*

"Blue Bonnet and her companions are real girls, the kind that one would like to have in one's home."—*New York Sun.*

THE LITTLE COLONEL BOOKS
(Trade Mark)

By Annie Fellows Johnston

Each large 12mo, cloth, illustrated, per volume $2.00

THE LITTLE COLONEL STORIES
(Trade Mark)

Being three "Little Colonel" stories in the Cosy Corner Series, "The Little Colonel," "Two Little Knights of Kentucky," and "The Giant Scissors," in a single volume.

THE LITTLE COLONEL STORIES:
Second Series   (Trade Mark)

Tales about characters that appear in the Little Colonel Series.—"Ole Mammy's Torment," "The Three Tremonts," and "The Little Colonel in Switzerland."

THE LITTLE COLONEL'S HOUSE PARTY
(Trade Mark)

THE LITTLE COLONEL'S HOLIDAYS
(Trade Mark)

THE LITTLE COLONEL'S HERO
(Trade Mark)

THE LITTLE COLONEL AT BOARDING
SCHOOL   (Trade Mark)

THE LITTLE COLONEL IN ARIZONA
(Trade Mark)

THE LITTLE COLONEL'S CHRISTMAS
VACATION   (Trade Mark)

THE LITTLE COLONEL, MAID OF HONOR
(Trade Mark)

THE LITTLE COLONEL'S KNIGHT COMES
RIDING   (Trade Mark)

THE LITTLE COLONEL'S CHUM, MARY
WARE   (Trade Mark)

MARY WARE IN TEXAS

MARY WARE'S PROMISED LAND

These thirteen volumes, boxed as a set, $26.00

A-2

FOR PIERRE'S SAKE AND OTHER STORIES

Cloth, 12mo, illustrated by Billie Chapman . . $1.75

"'For Pierres Sake,' who works so hard to scrape to-gether the pennies necessary for a wreath for his brother's grave, 'The Rain Maker,' who tries to bring rain to the drought stricken fields—these and many others will take their places in The Children's Hall of Fame, which exists in the heart of childhood."—*Portsmouth* (*N.H.*) *Herald.*

THE ROAD OF THE LOVING HEART

Cloth decorated, with special designs and illus-trations $1.25

This story of a little princess and her faithful pet bear, who finally *do* discover "The Road of the Loving Heart," is a masterpiece of sympathy and understanding and beauti-ful thought.

THE JOHNSTON JEWEL SERIES

Each small 16mo, decorative boards, per volume . $0.75

IN THE DESERT OF WAITING:

THE LEGEND OF CAMELBACK MOUNTAIN.

THE THREE WEAVERS:

A FAIRY TALE FOR FATHERS AND MOTHERS AS WELL AS FOR THEIR DAUGHTERS.

KEEPING TRYST:

A TALE OF KING ARTHUR'S TIME.

THE LEGEND OF THE BLEEDING HEART

THE RESCUE OF PRINCESS WINSOME:

A FAIRY PLAY FOR OLD AND YOUNG.

THE JESTER'S SWORD

THE LITTLE COLONEL'S GOOD TIMES BOOK

Uniform in size with the Little Colonel Series . $2.50
Bound in white kid (morocco) and gold . . 6.00

Cover design and decorations by Peter Verberg.

"A mighty attractive volume in which the owner may record the good times she has on decorated pages, and under the directions as it were of Annie Fellows John-ston."—*Buffalo Express.*

A-3

HILDEGARDE-MARGARET SERIES

By Laura E. Richards

Eleven Volumes

The Hildegarde-Margaret Series, beginning with "Queen Hildegarde" and ending with "The Merryweathers," make one of the best and most popular series of books for girls ever written.

Each large 12mo, cloth decorative, illustrated,
per volume *$1.75*
The eleven volumes boxed as a set . . . *$19.25*

LIST OF TITLES

QUEEN HILDEGARDE

HILDEGARDE'S HOLIDAY

HILDEGARDE'S HOME

HILDEGARDE'S NEIGHBORS

HILDEGARDE'S HARVEST

THREE MARGARETS

MARGARET MONTFORT

PEGGY

RITA

FERNLEY HOUSE

THE MERRYWEATHERS

A-4

HONOR BRIGHT SERIES

BY LAURA E. RICHARDS

Each one volume, cloth decorative, 12mo, illustrated **$1.75**

HONOR BRIGHT

"This is a story that rings as true and honest as the name of the young heroine—Honor—and not only the young girls, but the old ones will find much to admire and to commend in the beautiful character of Honor."—*Constitution, Atlanta, Ga.*

HONOR BRIGHT'S NEW ADVENTURE

"Girls will love the story and it has plot enough to interest the older reader as well."—*St. Louis Daily Globe-Democrat.*

SIX GIRLS

(60th thousand) BY FANNY BELLE IRVING.

Cloth decorative, 12mo, illustrated by A. G. Learned. **$1.65**

No book has enjoyed a steadier and longer popularity than "Six Girls," written by a niece of Washington Irving. It has won its way by the best kind of advertising—personal recommendations among readers.

THREE HUNDRED THINGS A BRIGHT GIRL CAN DO

BY LILLA ELIZABETH KELLEY.

Cloth decorative, 12mo, illustrated by the author . **$2.50**

A complete treasury of suggestions on games, indoor and outdoor sports, handiwork, embroidery, sewing and cooking, scientific experiments, puzzles, candy-making, home decoration, physical culture, etc.

THE SECRET VALLEY

BY MRS. HOBART-HAMPDEN.

Cloth 12mo, illustrated, with color jacket . . **$1.75**

In addition to an excellent action story, young readers will find in this book descriptions of India, land of mystery, which are accurate and interesting.

SECRETS INSIDE

BY M. M. DANCY McCLENDON.

Cloth, 12mo, illustrated by Dean Freeman . . **$1.75**

"This is a story about girls for girls. The author has made a worthwhile contribution to juvenile literature."—*Rochester Sunday American.*

A-5

THE CAPTAIN JANUARY SERIES

600,000 volumes of the "Captain January" Series have already been sold.

"Mrs. Richards has made for herself a little niche apart in the literary world, from her delicate treatment of New England village life."—*Boston Post.*

CAPTAIN JANUARY. *Star Bright Edition.*

Profusely illustrated by Frank T. Merrill . . **$1.75**

STAR BRIGHT. A sequel to "Captain January."

Mrs. Richards' latest book, uniform with above. **$1.75**
Wherein the Captain's little girl reaches the romantic period of her career, and faces the world.

The two volumes attractively boxed as a set. . **$3.50**

The following titles are illustrated by Frank T. Merrill

CAPTAIN JANUARY. *School Edition*

(285th thousand) . . . . . *Net* **$1.00**

MELODY. **$1.00**

The Story of a Child.
Cloth decorative, illustrated by Frank T. Merrill,
each . . . . **$.90**

MARIE.

A companion to "Melody."

ROSIN THE BEAU.

A sequel to "Marie."

SNOW-WHITE;

Or, The House in the Wood.

JIM OF HELLAS;

Or, in Durance Vile, and a companion story, "Bethesda Pool."

"SOME SAY."

And a companion story, "Neighbors in Cyrus."

NAUTILUS.

" 'Nautilus' is by far the best product of the author's powers."—*Boston Globe.*

ISLA HERON.

This interesting story is written in the author's usual charming manner.

A-6

BARBARA WINTHROP SERIES

By Helen Katherine Broughall

Each one volume, cloth decorative, 12mo, illustrated *$2.00*

BARBARA WINTHROP AT BOARDING SCHOOL

BARBARA WINTHROP AT CAMP

BARBARA WINTHROP: GRADUATE

BARBARA WINTHROP ABROAD

"Full of adventure—initiations, joys, picnics, parties, tragedies, vacation and all. Just what girls like, books in which 'dreams come true,' entertaining 'gossipy' books overflowing with conversation."—*Salt Lake City Deseret News.*

High ideals and a real spirit of fun underlie the stories. They will be a decided addition to the bookshelves of the young girl for whom a holiday gift is contemplated.

DOCTOR'S LITTLE GIRL SERIES

By Marion Ames Taggart

Each large 12mo, cloth, illustrated, per volume . *$1.75*

THE DOCTOR'S LITTLE GIRL

"A charming story of the ups and downs of the life of a dear little maid."—*The Churchman.*

SWEET NANCY:

The Further Adventures of the Doctor's Little girl.
"Just the sort of book to amuse, while its influence cannot but be elevating."—*New York Sun.*

NANCY, THE DOCTOR'S LITTLE PARTNER

"The story is sweet and fascinating, such as many girls of wholesome tastes will enjoy."—*Springfield Union.*

NANCY PORTER'S OPPORTUNITY

"Nancy shows throughout that she is a splendid young woman, with plenty of pluck."—*Boston Globe.*

NANCY AND THE COGGS TWINS

"The story is refreshing."—*New York Sun.*

A-7